D1527616

Beyond the Call of Duty

Beyond the Call of Duty

Army Flight Nursing in World War II

Judith Barger

THE KENT STATE UNIVERSITY PRESS
Kent, Ohio

© 2013 by Judith Barger
All rights reserved
Library of Congress Catalog Card Number 2012048161
ISBN 978-1-60635-154-3
Manufactured in the United States of America

Library of Congress Cataloging-in-Publication Data
Barger, Judith, 1948–
  Beyond the call of duty : Army flight nursing in World War II / Judith Barger.
    pages cm
  Includes bibliographical references and index.
  ISBN 978-1-60635-154-3 (hardcover) ∞
1. World War, 1939–1945—Medical care—United States. 2. Aviation nursing—United
States—History—20th century. 3. Transport of sick and wounded—United States—
History—20th century. 4. Nurses—United States—History—20th century. 5. United
States. Army—Nurses—History—20th century. 6. United States. Army Nurse Corps—
History. 7. United States. Army Air Forces—History. 8. World War, 1939–1945—
Participation, Female. I. Title.
  D807.U6B37 2013
  940.54'75—dc23

                                2012048161

17 16 15 14 13   5 4 3 2 1

She follows the soldier where danger is dire.

She crawls as he crawls under barriers of wire.

She sails where he sails and she flies where he flies

And sometimes in battle beside him she dies.

—*From "The Nurse" by Edgar A. Guest*

CONTENTS

MAPS AND ILLUSTRATIONS

Maps

Illustrations

PREFACE

At the height of World War II, five hundred army flight nurses served with the army air forces as members of thirty-one medical air evacuation squadrons located throughout the world.[1] Flight nurses participated in the major campaigns on both the European and Pacific fronts as soon as it was feasible to send in transport planes. Their work was not insignificant: over 1 million patients were evacuated by air between January 1943 and May 1945. Air surgeon of the army air forces David N. W. Grant credited air evacuation among the five wartime achievements that were great lifesaving measures; blood plasma, front-line surgery, penicillin, and sulfa drugs completed his list.[2]

Faced with casualty rates growing from about five thousand a month in 1943 to eighty-one thousand a month by the end of 1944, military leaders were quick to realize the value of flight nurses and enlisted technicians in making the newly organized air evacuation program a success. "We found afterwards that the use of nurses was probably the wisest thing the air evacuation [program] ever had," remarked Colonel Ehrling Bergquist after the war. Bergquist, who had been command surgeon for the 9th Troop Carrier Command and later the 1st Troop Carrier Command in Europe during the war, continued: "The young ladies were highly enthusiastic, and they sold the air evacuation program. They wore distinctive uniforms, and people knew who they were. The result was that whenever people wanted to talk about air evacuation they said, 'Oh, yes, you are part of the outfit that has those nurses.' That may sound silly, but it was one of the selling points of the program."[3] These specially trained army nurses had met the challenge and taken nursing to new heights. Often decorated for their accomplishments, they exemplify the ability of a group of nurses to cope successfully with the challenges of war.

The venerable history of the United States Army Nurse Corps, of which these women were a part, has been told elsewhere.[4] Beginning in late 1944, the United States Navy trained and deployed its own flight nurses, but this is not their history.[5] This book chronicles the story of army flight nursing in World War II from the years preceding the war when pilot Lauretta Schimmoler founded the civilian Aerial Nurse Corps of America with intent to provide flight nurses for a military program, to the establishment of the air evacuation program in the United States Army Air Forces and the training of the army nurses who provided in-flight patient care, to the participation of flight nurses in air evacuation missions overseas.

A unique feature of the book is the inclusion of firsthand accounts by twenty-five of these remarkable women, whom I was privileged to interview in 1986 when their recall for events of their flight nurse duty was still remarkably vivid and informative. I was on active duty as an air force nurse at the time, living in San Antonio, Texas, where military colleagues helped me locate a handful of former army flight nurses in the city and one out of state. I met some of them at luncheons for retired military nurses in the city. These women gave me names and contact information for others who had been in their squadrons during the war. I contacted them by telephone, and in some cases by letter as well, to seek their participation in a study about coping with war. Those who declined cited their own or their spouse's health, a busy schedule, travel distance and expense for me, and the feeling that their experiences would not prove helpful. I conducted all interviews in person with those who agreed to take part, traveling at my own expense to a location of their choice. Most interviews were in the women's homes, though several took place at a hotel in Cocoa Beach, Florida, where I was asked to speak at a World War II Flight Nurses Association reunion. I had served as a flight nurse myself, assigned to the 9th Aeromedical

Evacuation Group at Clark Air Base in the Philippines from 1973 to 1975, logging over 1,260 flight hours on air evacuation missions with patients throughout the Pacific.

The stories the women shared with me often confirmed and occasionally contradicted the literature about army flight nursing in World War II found in unit and medical histories, air evacuation histories, human-interest stories written during and shortly after the war, and oral histories recorded years later. But always the interviewees' accounts are insightful, offering a glimpse of what it was really like to serve as a flight nurse in World War II and to cope with the exigencies of wartime nursing. Their stories are both humorous ("It is possible for a nurse with slacks on to aim at the pilot's relief tube, but, believe me, it's very difficult, and you have to hope that the plane is going to fly steady while you're there!") and heartfelt ("But you feel so helpless when your patient's going out and there isn't anything you can do. . . . We had no oxygen on board, no IVs to give him—nothing to help a patient like that. And all I could do was just watch him."), entertaining ("One time one of the planes I got was just covered with glossy prints, and they were all nudes. . . . So I took my Band-Aids, and I dressed the entire ceiling of the plane.") and revealing ("I was petrified of flying. I was scared to death to fly. I was scared on every trip.").[6] The recorded experiences of these World War II army flight nurses give new meaning to the phrase in the Flight Nurse Creed, written in 1943: "I will be faithful to my training, and to the wisdom handed down to me by those who have gone before me."[7]

By the time I completed this book, only five of the twenty-five flight nurses whom I had interviewed were known to be living. I tried repeatedly to obtain their consent to include material from their interviews with me, but not all responded. As other authors have found when recounting the stories of World War II veterans, over the intervening years some of the interviewees had been lost to declining health, changes in living arrangements, and unknown exigencies that come with the passage of time.

I am grateful to staffs of the following agencies for permitting me access to documents and photographs held in their archives between 1974 and 1986 and in some cases again in 2006 and 2007: the Air Force Historical

Research Agency at Maxwell Air Force Base in Montgomery, Alabama (medical air evacuation squadron histories and Reba Whittle diary); the National Archives and the National Headquarters of the American Red Cross, both in Washington, D.C. (correspondence pertaining to the American Red Cross); and the Edward White II Aerospace Medical Museum (Hangar 9) located at Brooks Air Force Base—later Brooks City Base—in San Antonio, Texas (documents about Elsie Ott). The Hangar 9 materials are now located at the Air Force Research Laboratory at Wright-Patterson Air Force Base, near Dayton Ohio. Thanks also to staffs of the United States Army Medical Department Museum at Fort Sam Houston in San Antonio, Texas (Leora Stroup papers) and the Bucyrus Historical Society in Bucyrus, Ohio (Lauretta Schimmoler papers) for permitting me access to documents and photographs held in their archives, and to the Oral History Research Office of Columbia University for granting me permission to cite and quote excerpts from Kenneth Leish's interview with Ellen Church in its collection. The staff of the Central Arkansas Library System interlibrary loan office was consistently helpful in locating published materials not available locally. I am also indebted to Ethel Carlson Cerasale and Helena Ilic Tynan, who let me reprint photographs from their private collections, and to Micah Jones and Robert Skinner, who clarified some research matters. Chris Robinson prepared the maps for the book. A special thank you goes to Joyce Harrison, acquisitions editor for Kent State University Press, for guiding this book through the publishing process with such grace and good will.

Finally, I extend a special thank you to the twenty-five women, all former United States Army flight nurses, who gave so generously of their time and experiences during my interviews with them: Anonymous, Ethel Carlson Cerasale, Hilda Halverson Chamberlain, Mary Eileen Newbeck Christian, Frances Sandstrom Crabtree, Blanche Solomon Creesy, Adele Edmonds Daly, Louise Anthony de Flon, Dorothy White Errair, Ivalee (Lee) Holtz, Jocie French Huston, Lucy Wilson Jopling, Alice Krieble, Agnes Jensen Mangerich, Dorothy Vancil Morgan, Clara Morrey Murphy, Josephine (Jo) Malito Nabors, Denzil (Denny) Nagle, Elizabeth Pukas, Sara Ann (Sally) Jones Sharp, Jenevieve (Jenny) Boyle Silk, Helena Ilic

Tynan, Brooxie Mowery Unick, Miranda (Randy) Rast Weinrich, and Grace Dunnam Wichtendahl. The date and location of each interview are found in the appendix.

PROLOGUE

E thel Carlson was "scared to death" and "wanted to turn around and go back" when she and her footlocker boarded a Chicago–to–Saint Louis train in the middle of the night in April 1943. The twenty-one-year-old, who never had been away from her hometown of Chicago except on family vacations, had earned her diploma in nursing from Englewood Hospital on the city's south side in 1942 and recently had joined the army. She was on her way to her first duty assignment at Jefferson Barracks, an army air corps training base near Saint Louis.[1]

Carlson was one of more than fifty-nine thousand nurses who voluntarily joined or were already serving in the army during World War II. Some worked in stateside army hospitals where they helped wounded soldiers through the definitive surgeries and rehabilitation necessitated by combat wounds. Other nurses served overseas, often close to the front lines of battle, in the chain of field, evacuation, station, and general hospitals that met the surgical and medical needs of American and Allied troops in all the military theaters of operation. Fewer army nurses staffed hospital ships and hospital trains. Specially trained army nurses served with the army air forces aboard airplanes on medical air evacuation flights. Carlson wanted to be a flight nurse, and as her train left Chicago's south side station, that dream and her resolve that, as she put it, "I had never been a quitter, and I had said I was going to do it" finally quelled her fears.[2] Carlson's determination paid off, for she eventually got her dream assignment as a flight nurse.

This book is about the army flight nurses of World War II. When twenty-five of these women, including Carlson, shared their wartime experiences with the author in 1986, they were in their mid-sixties to late seventies. Their experiences augment the broader history of army flight nursing, offering firsthand accounts of the personal and professional challenges faced by women who served in air evacuation assignments during the war. All were registered nurses and had attended diploma schools of nursing located in thirteen states, mostly in the Midwest. All but one nurse had graduated between 1935 and 1942; the oldest among them graduated in 1929. Their work experiences prior to military service varied, with hospital, clinic, private duty, and industrial nursing all represented. Dorothy White, who had this last type of job, considered it ideal preparation for flight nursing, because it involved emergency cases and responses when a physician was not in attendance and supplies were limited.[3] Eleven of the nurses already knew they wanted to be flight nurses when they entered the military; the others learned about this new field of nursing when at their first duty assignments.

Information was filtering down through official channels to army and army air forces hospitals, and nurses often learned about the new flight nurse program from notices and sign-up sheets on bulletin boards. For Carlson, Lee Holtz, Helena Ilic, Sally Jones, Eileen Newbeck, and White, the chance to be a flight nurse was the impetus for joining the military. For other more pragmatic nurses, like Jo Nabors and Blanche Solomon, it was a ticket out of an unpleasant hospital assignment; they wrote their names on every roster promising duty elsewhere. Clara Morrey signed up for the cadres deploying to war zones, specifying "air ambulance only" before the flight nurse program had even begun, having heard about it from military contacts. Jenny Boyle, who heard about flight nursing on the radio, wrote directly to the office of the air surgeon, army air forces, for information and an application.[4] All but one of the twenty-five nurses interviewed graduated from the army air forces flight nurse course at Bowman Field, Kentucky, prior to starting air evacuation duties. Morrey, who was sent overseas with her squadron before the formal training course began, attended after completion of her overseas tour of duty.

Assignment to Bowman Field to train as a flight nurse was not automatic on entering the army, though Newbeck, who had prior experience as a civilian flight nurse in the Aerial Nurse Corps of America (ANCOA), was assigned directly to attend the flight nurse course at Bowman Field. The other twenty-four nurses interviewed were assigned first to army or army air force bases, where they worked until accepted for flight nurse training. Boyle, Carlson, Denny Nagle, and an interviewee who wished to remain anonymous all began their military service in overlapping assignments at Jefferson Barracks. For White, who was stationed at George Field in Illinois, the wait for flight nurse training was only five months, but for many nurses the wait was longer.

After completion of their training, the nurses deployed to several theaters of operation. Louise Anthony, Boyle, Carlson, Grace Dunnam, Jocie French, Brooxie Mowery, Nagle, and Frances Sandstrom all went to Europe; the anonymous flight nurse, Hilda Chamberlain, Adele Edmonds, Holtz, Ilic, Jones, Alice Krieble, Nabors, Elizabeth Pukas, and Lucy Wilson went to the Pacific; Agnes Jensen, Morrey, and White began their tours in North Africa and the Mediterranean; and Newbeck flew in Alaska, Dorothy Vancil in Central Africa, Randy Rast in the China-Burma-India Theater, and Solomon in the North Atlantic. Their assignments represented at least fifteen of the thirty-one medical air evacuation transport squadrons, later renamed medical air evacuation squadrons, activated during World War II; assignments sometimes changed so quickly that flight nurses were never quite sure to which squadron they belonged.[5] Dunnam, Pukas, and Wilson were the chief nurses of their respective squadrons.

The nurses gave many reasons for joining the Army Nurse Corps and volunteering for flight nurse duty. Ilic and Mowery had wanted to be flight attendants, but those plans fell through when the airlines stopped hiring nurses, who were urgently needed in the military, at the beginning of the war.[6] For these two women, flight nursing was a logical plan B. For Jensen, the chance to travel and see the world provided the incentive; Solomon, who had to help support her mother, appreciated the financial security of army pay, which she said was $150 a month at the time. Newbeck, who had two brothers in the service, felt that she should be in the service too, and air evacuation meant flying, something she really loved.[7] But by far the leading motive was one's patriotic duty. It was not a question of whether to volunteer for military service, said Carlson. Men were drafted, but everyone did what they could. "And if your training put you in a spot like being in the Army Nurse Corps, this is where you went."[8]

That military flight nursing was an option for them had much to do with the exigencies of a war that separated casualties from medical facilities able to treat them. But flight nursing itself had appeared in the previous decade in the civilian sector as ANCOA. Because of that organization's attempts to forge a military link, and because some ANCOA nurses, Newbeck among them, traded their civilian wings for those of the army air forces, the story of flight nursing begins with the events that foreshadowed the program in which army nurses participated.

Origin of Flight Nursing

O n remote World War II battlefields scattered throughout Europe and the Pacific, thousands of soldiers in the U.S. military were being shot and wounded and experiencing the usual and more exotic illnesses associated with military duty overseas. Staffs of military facilities in the army and navy chains of evacuation worked admirably to treat these casualties of war within their capabilities, but the sheer number of patients as well as the severity of their wounds and the time, supplies, and equipment required could exhaust already limited medical resources. Ground transportation, too, was a problem. Because terrain in many locations, such as Alaska, Burma, and New Guinea, made surface transportation of sick and wounded soldiers to medical facilities impractical, evacuation by air became a military and a medical necessity. And flight nurses, the air surgeon of the army air forces decided, were the most highly trained medical personnel available to provide essential in-flight patient care.[1]

The decision to employ nurses for flight duty, however, first had to overcome opposition from high-ranking officials in the army—the branch of service from which the flight nurses would be selected—who, even before America's entrance into the war, anticipated a resulting shortage of nurses available for other kinds of work. Colonel Bergquist, command surgeon for the 9th and later the 1st Troop Carrier Command, supported the use of female flight nurses for air evacuation: "We felt that if in this country a group of healthy individuals could fly around in commercial airlines having a nurse attend them, our wounded certainly were entitled to the same consideration."[2] He was referring to the prewar airline policy to hire only registered nurses as flight attendants. When the need for nurses to work in civilian hospitals and serve in the armed forces became urgent during World War II, the airlines substituted college education for a nursing diploma as a prerequisite for work as a stewardess.[3]

Military leaders eventually worked out their differences of opinion on the use of nurses, and on 30 November 1942, not quite a year after the Japanese attack on Pearl Harbor had thrust the United States into World War II, the office of the air surgeon, United States Army Air Forces, made an urgent appeal for nurses to volunteer for air evacuation duty.[4] The military flight nurse program met its next challenge not from within its ranks but from a civilian source.

Aerial Nurse Corps of America

As early as 1930, before flight nursing in the U.S. military was a reality, Lauretta M. Schimmoler, a pilot, shown in illustration 1.1, foresaw a need for flight nurses. Born in Fort Jennings, Ohio, in 1900, Schimmoler, who graduated with honors from the Bliss Business College of Columbus, tried her hand at various pursuits—working as a court stenographer, studying law, raising chickens—before settling on the business of aviation. By the age of thirty she had learned to fly, obtained her pilot's license, and established and managed the Port Bucyrus Municipal Airport in Ohio. As the first female pilot in Crawford County, Ohio, Schimmoler was a "favorite daughter" of the local press. "From Chickens to Flying: Lauretta Schimmoler Quit Poultry Raising to Pilot Planes," began one account, typical in its admiration of her achievements. After chronicling Schimmoler's career, the reporter concluded:

> It is not hard to understand why Miss Schimmoler has risen so rapidly in the flying world. Her extraordinary capacity for activity, her quick movement, her orderly mind and her keen sense of values are outstanding. She never is too busy to help a student flyer. She isn't

afraid to climb into overalls and to find out what causes an unnatural knock in an engine. She keeps her head when at the controls and so far has not had a crack-up.

Lauretta Schimmoler looks responsibility and hard work straight in the eye.[5]

In 1932 in recognition of her aviation activities, Schimmoler was inducted into the Ninety-Nines, the national organization of licensed women pilots.[6] But she had even loftier ambitions. While continuing to participate in air shows and aerial exhibitions as part of this prestigious group of flyers, she contemplated the use of aircraft for a more compassionate purpose, one that would involve flying nurses.

The idea of nurses in airplanes was not entirely new. Nurses had first become airborne in 1930, when a group of women selected and organized by Ellen Church, a nurse from Iowa who was working at a San Francisco hospital, formed the initial cadre of registered nurse stewardesses for Boeing Air Transport, the predecessor to United Airlines. Church had never been on a commercial plane when she stopped by the Boeing Air Transport office in February 1930, ostensibly to book a flight home to Iowa. Mr. Stephen Stimson, passenger traffic manager for the Oakland, California, to Cheyenne, Wyoming, route, chatted with her about the new planes capable of transporting eighteen passengers. Church, who had learned to fly and had thirteen solo hours to her credit, wanted to combine her love of flying and her love of nursing in some way to earn a living. Like Schimmoler, she envisioned a need for air ambulances in outlying districts far removed from hospitals. In her conversation, Church mentioned that she had learned to fly, and she and the excited Stimson began to talk about "the boys" Boeing had recently hired for different jobs, at least some obviously involving air travel. "Why couldn't a girl with nursing do that?" Church asked. As she recalled in 1960, Stimson "got real enthusiastic" about the possibility, promising to pursue the idea and get back with her.[7]

Two or three weeks later Stimson called to arrange an interview with Church and one of the company vice presidents "about this stewardess

1.1 Lauretta M. Schimmoler, circa 1932 (Bucyrus, Ohio, Historical Society)

proposition if you are still interested." The vice president was "totally unenthusiastic about the whole thing," but Stimson, sold on the idea, got approval from William E. Boeing himself for a three-month trial with home base at Cheyenne. Church, who had once wanted to be a copilot, found her true calling in the airplane's cabin, not its cockpit.[8]

Finding the first seven nurses for stewardess duty was not easy for Church because of height and weight requirements, although many women were interested. She eventually found three women in San Francisco and four in Chicago. Concerning their training as steward-esses, Church recalled that they had "nothing to go on" and had to learn initially by trial and error.[9]

Tasked with providing safety and comfort for the traveling public, these eight women, whose number included Church as chief stewardess, did much to boost the image and reputation of the budding commer-cial airline industry as they attended to the needs of the occasionally apprehensive but for the most part healthy passengers. In the air, the stewardesses served their passengers a cold picnic-type meal with hot coffee or hot tea, supplied reading materials, sent telegrams and dispatched letters, furnished pillows and blankets, pointed out sights of interest below, and spent time talking with them.[10]

Church had been a stewardess for only eighteen months when she was grounded following an automobile accident. She returned to school to earn her nursing degree and resumed her nursing career on the ground. Meanwhile, the stewardess program took off, with most of the airlines following Boeing's lead. The idea of stewardesses had caught on not only with air passengers but also with America's nurses, who applied by the thousands for the chance to take their nursing into the skies.

Schimmoler, however, had a different idea. Flying her new plane from Akron to Lorain, Ohio, in 1930, she had seen the residual destruction caused by a tornado that had swept through that area about a year before. What if nurses could have been flown to the scene after the storm to render immediate aid to its victims on the ground and accompany them by air to medical treatment elsewhere, she wondered. Later, when she noted the inadequate emergency care provided to a fellow pilot following an accident at an air show, her idea took more definite form.[11] By 1932 Schimmoler, who was living in Cleveland, had begun preparations for her civilian flight nurse organization. She gathered together a group of nurses interested in her idea and formed the Emergency Flight Corps, whose initial task was to research and develop the aerial nurse concept further. After her 1933 move to Los Angeles, where she worked in the first of several aviation-related jobs, Schimmoler pressed on with her plan for aerial nurses. For the National Air Races held in that city in 1936 she provided ten registered nurses to staff two field hospitals for the four-day event. The Emergency Flight Corps, renamed the Aerial Nurse Corps of America (ANCOA), was now operational.[12] By 1940, ANCOA structure, objectives, routines, and course of study were spelled out in the sixty-three-page *Regulations Manual* and other supporting organizational directives.

According to ANCOA literature, no other organization was providing nurses with essential aeronautical education. Whether Schimmoler knew about the American Nurses Aviation Service, Inc., formed in New York City in 1931, is uncertain. Her research, detailed in statements and speeches, identified aerial nurses in France, Chile, and England but not in her own country. With its purposes to foster and promote air-mindedness in its registered nurse and licensed physician members, to give courses and lectures in aeronautics and allied subjects to qualify members as attendants to patients in air ambulances, and to institute chapters throughout the country leading to a national aviation nursing service, the American Nurses Aviation Service, Inc.'s goals were similar to those Schimmoler developed for her own organization.[13] The *Journal of Aviation Medicine*, a publication of the Aerospace Medical Association, endorsed the New York organization and welcomed news of its progress within its issues for 1931, 1932, and 1933.[14] News of the American Nurses Aviation Service, Inc. had faded from the pages of the journal by 1934, about the time Schimmoler's aerial organization was attracting media attention elsewhere.

From when she first launched ANCOA, Schimmoler worked steadily to have the organization endorsed and recognized as the flight nurse unit of various service organizations, both civilian and, ultimately, military. Believing that actions speak louder than words, ANCOA members offered their services at air shows and other aviation activities, gaining some local and national exposure in the press. When the need and opportunity arose, the nurses accompanied patients on flights as well. Media coverage that followed had more impact than advertising in bringing ANCOA's work to the public's attention. National ANCOA officers then referred to these activities in their speeches to nursing and aviation organizations.

In the late 1930s, the Los Angeles Sheriff's Aero Squadron recognized ANCOA as a voluntary auxiliary unit for emergency and disaster work.[15] In 1938 the National Aeronautic Association endorsed ANCOA as its official nursing organization, and in April 1940 Gill Robb Wilson, the National Aeronautic Association president, wrote to Mary Beard of the American Red Cross (ARC) asking that society to "take a constructive interest" in ANCOA, a "valued affiliate of the National Aeronautic Association."[16] One must wonder whether Wilson's letter was intended to reconcile differences between Schimmoler and Beard since, as shown below, the interest the ARC had shown in ANCOA up to this point had been anything *but* constructive. Schimmoler recalled Beard telling her, "You have a wonderful idea, but you are ten years ahead of us. If you were only a nurse we could find a place for you."[17]

ANCOA's association with Relief Wings, Inc., a civilian program begun in 1941 for the humanitarian use of airplanes during war or in peacetime disasters at home and overseas, for which Schimmoler served on the advisory committee for technical aeronautical problems, was strained at best.[18] Relief Wings planned to establish and maintain a voluntary corps of flight nurses, but in 1941 Ruth Nichols, its executive director and a licensed pilot, wrote to Harriet Fleming, a member of the California State Nurses Association, "Although I have felt that Miss Schimmoler has evolved a fine detailed piece of training program for aerial nurses, we have not found any basis upon which she was willing to co-operate with Relief Wings."[19]

Nichols thought they had an agreement that Schimmoler was not honoring. In short, Nichols would help ANCOA obtain more members if those members would be available for disaster service under Relief Wings, but Schimmoler apparently was not encouraging this collabo-ration.[20] At stake was each woman's control over the limited number of nurses available for civilian aerial work during time of war and her claim to the uniqueness of that work. Their differences may not have been reconciled. Nichols's 1942 letter to Fleming suggests that Relief Wings did not know the present status of ANCOA; Nichols had heard, however, that it "had died a natural death."[21]

ANCOA had not died, but the ultimate association Schimmoler sought for it—to form a unit of the U.S. military—was beyond her control. ANCOA had as one of its purposes "to provide technically trained and physically qualified personnel to fulfill the requirements of the Medical Department of the United States Army and Navy Nurse Corps, under their supervision, in national emergencies, for nursing duty in air trans-ports, at airports and air bases of the Army, Navy, and Marine Corps in time of national and civic emergencies."[22] Schimmoler, who founded her flight nurse organization independent of the other service organizations such as the United States Army and the ARC, nevertheless intended that ANCOA would become the air unit of the ARC, which in turn provided nurses for the military.

Undaunted in the face of the skepticism she encountered when promoting her new organization to nursing officials, Schimmoler relentlessly pursued her goals. Rivalry between ANCOA and ARC, in contention to provide the nurses for a flight nurse program, marked the formative years of flight nursing prior to the development of the program in the United States Army Air Forces. This rivalry highlights an issue that has plagued nursing from its beginning: that nurses should control their own profession.

Although a civilian organization, ANCOA was organized according to military command structure, with national headquarters in Burbank, California. It was divided into three wings, subdivided into nine divisions, each corresponding to corps area boundaries found in the United States Army. The divisions were subdivided into companies. The military analogy went even further: Schimmoler, the national commander and president, held the honorary rank of colonel; a lieutenant colonel commanded a wing; a major commanded a division; and a captain commanded a company. Most of the nurses held the rank of first or second lieutenant or cadet, which was the lowest grade for a registered nurse.[23]

Like their military counterparts, ANCOA nurses took an oath of office, the words differing slightly in various ANCOA documents, "to support and defend the Constitution of the United States of America and the Aerial Nurse Corps of America against all their enemies whomsoever" and "to bear true faith and allegiance to the same."[24] The oath-taking had the fervor of a religious ceremony when, in the presence of the American flag and at least two ANCOA members, the recruit first made a ten-question pledge, responding at each prompt, "I am" or "I do."[25]

An ANCOA nurse had to be a single female American citizen twenty-one to thirty-five years old with a height between five feet two and five feet eight inches and a weight within set guidelines corresponding to her age and height. She had to pass a physical examination to determine her fitness for air duty. The applicant also had to be a member of her state nurses association and a member of the First Reserve of the ARC, which provided the pool of applicants from which military nurses were drawn.

1.2 ANCOA nurses Margaret Gudobba (left) and Eileen Newbeck (right) display new flag (USAF photo)

Nurses joining ANCOA served on active duty for three years and agreed to perform nursing duties in any airworthy aircraft. They also attended two-hour classes and lectures one night each week—divided into medical subjects the first year, aeronautical subjects the second year, and theoretical subjects the third year. After six months, having made the necessary passing score of eighty on the *Regulations Manual* examination and earned a third-grade radio telephone operator's license, the new nurses joined the active duty roster and were promoted from cadet to second lieutenant.[26] With the promotion in rank, these nurses wore the blue-gray ANCOA uniform, with its overseas cap and military-like insignia, shown in illustration 1.2, supplied by a California clothing manufacturer.[27]

Unlike military nursing, work as an ANCOA nurse was not full-time but rather was limited to part-time volunteer participation in evening classes and weekend activities that included providing first aid for national air races and smaller air events. Occasionally ANCOA nurses accompanied a patient on a flight to provide nursing care en route. Members held other nursing jobs and paid for the privilege of being part of ANCOA with a $5 enrollment fee and monthly dues of fifty cents.[28]

Schimmoler's optimistic goal of ten thousand ANCOA nurses trained and ready, reported in a 1941 issue of *Trained Nurse and Hospital Review*, was unrealistic, given the projected need of ten thousand nurses for the Army Nurse Corps alone as the United States headed into war.[29] Equally unrealistic was her undated prediction of an adequate supply of ANCOA nurses for aviation duty within ten years.[30] Yet, in its early days ANCOA showed a modest growth, with twelve companies formed by 1940 and others planned in several large cities.[31] By April 1941, ANCOA had chapters in twenty-two cities spread over fifteen states.[32] Writing to medical historian Hubert A. Coleman in 1945, Schimmoler cited a roster numbering between six and seven hundred ANCOA members.[33]

Detroit Company A of the Third Wing, Fifth Division was one of the more active ANCOA units.[34] Its success may be attributed in large part to the efforts of company commander Captain Leora B. Stroup. A registered nurse employed in nursing education, Stroup knew when she saw the female pilots at the National Air Races in Cleveland in 1929 that she, too, wanted to fly. A few years later, in 1933, she earned her pilot's license at the Cleveland airport, where she met Lauretta Schimmoler and, like her, later was inducted into the Ninety-Nines.[35] Stroup was also a member of the Civil Air Patrol and the National Aeronautic Association and held national offices in ANCOA, serving first as its treasurer and quartermaster and later as its director of nursing. In 1941, Schimmoler appointed Stroup ANCOA president.

The first in the Midwest, Detroit Company A of ANCOA was one of Stroup's pet projects, and by 1939 it had its full quota of fifty-six women, of whom thirty were registered nurses.[36] The rest of the women filled supportive roles in first aid and communications. Members met every Wednesday night in the Saint Joseph's Hospital Training School auditorium for their classes and on Sunday afternoons at the local airport to make flights with Stroup or an army reserve pilot who assisted the ANCOA unit. Eight of the nurses were themselves pilots, but piloting planes was not an ANCOA duty. Rather, members were taught enough about aviation to determine by ground inspection whether a plane was airworthy and learned about weather conditions relevant to flight as well.[37]

Declining membership in ANCOA in general and in Detroit Company A in particular may have been a problem as early as 1939, for Stroup told a reporter for the *Detroit Evening Times* that "the corps served as a recruiting agency for airline hostesses."[38] A year later, Margaret Quinn, a private-duty nurse in Detroit Company A, wrote to the War Department, Michigan Military Area, indicating her willingness to serve her country as part of the United States Army Air Corps, citing her air ambulance work as justification.[39] Her wording suggests the possibility of an ANCOA campaign to seek military flight nurse positions for its members. By 1941 ANCOA had lost Quinn to the United States Army; she was a nurse stationed at Michigan's Fort Custer.[40] In his January 1941 reply to a letter from Stroup, John G. Slevin, medical officer for the United States Army, Headquarters Michigan Military Area, told her, "No doubt, within the next year the first Reserve will be badly depleted by call to extended active duty with the Army. Hence, your organization will lose many of its present members." He suggested that ANCOA should continue to function, filling its ranks with ARC Second Reserve nurses as an important valuable aid to home defense work.[41]

With units like Detroit Company A leading the way, by 1936 ANCOA had become an active organization, and in 1937 Schimmoler began to contact key personnel in the United States Army to seek recognition of her flight nurse organization. She went straight to the top in an apparent effort to discuss her plans with Brigadier General Henry H. "Hap" Arnold, acting chief of the air corps, who regretted not having had a chance to "talk over the program of the Aerial Nurse Corps of America" with her while he was on the west coast. "I believe there is a place in the scheme of things for such an organization," he wrote her, "but just what that place is I will be unable to definitely decide until I know more of the details."[42]

Although Schimmoler surely found Arnold's reply encouraging, it was destined to be short lived, for a month later when Arnold had learned more of the details, he advised her to work in conjunction with the ARC, which by law was designated as an auxiliary aid to the medical department of the army in time of emergency.[43] Arnold enclosed a copy of Army Regulation 850–75 "Employment of American National Red Cross" to acquaint Schimmoler with its provisions. Arnold's advice apparently had come indirectly from Major Julia O. Flikke, Army Nurse Corps superintendent. When Arnold asked Colonel Malcolm C. Grow, chief of the medical section, to draft a reply, Grow in turn sought input from Flikke, whose memo to him used wording that Arnold incorporated into his final letter. Not appearing in Arnold's letter was Flikke's belief that "Miss Schimmoler's plan is very complete and would be of great value if it could be used but it would conflict with the present set up if carried on independently."[44]

American Red Cross

Army Regulation 850–75 stated that "the Red Cross serving with the armed forces and under the orders of the President is the only voluntary society authorized to render aid to the Medical Department of the Army. Any other society desiring to render similar aid can do so only through the Red Cross."[45] It was under the aegis of this regulation that the ARC worked closely with the Army Nurse Corps to recruit nurses for service in the army. Nurses enrolled in the First Reserve of the ARC constituted the pool of qualified applicants from which nurses were drawn to expand the nursing service of the Army as needed. Requirements for enrollment in the ARC First Reserve were stated in that organization's literature.[46]

Nurse leaders of the ARC, who were aware of ANCOA and following its activities closely, voiced concerns about Schimmoler in correspondence Ida F. Butler, director of nursing for the ARC, initiated in 1937.[47] First, Schimmoler was a pilot directing an organization of nurses. In a letter to Gladyce L. Badger, director of nursing for the Pacific branch of the ARC, Butler, who had seen Schimmoler described as "a great promoter with the ability to attract because of her personality" but lacking in culture and education, expressed surprise that nurses enrolled in the Red Cross nursing service would "organize with a leader who is not one of their professional group."[48] And second, although Schimmoler had not yet contacted the ARC about her organization, she had made enrollment in the First Reserve of the ARC a requirement for membership in ANCOA. Because of her position on the American Nurses Association (ANA) board of directors, Butler had read all the confidential information on ANCOA filed at ANA headquarters. From it she learned that ANCOA nurses were also required to complete the ARC first aid and life saving courses.[49] That these requirements implied a connection between the two organizations that in fact did not exist may have prompted Butler to ask Mrs. Alma H. Scott, director of the ANA whether the ARC should or the ANA would recognize ANCOA officially.[50]

According to Butler, Schimmoler had not contacted the ARC about ANCOA, but Schimmoler recalled that she *had* communicated with the ARC as early as 1932 in a letter to Clara Noyes, director of the ARC nursing service at the time, to inquire "if I were to assemble a number of nurses for the purpose of giving them aeronautical training to equip them for air ambulance duties, if I would be contributing to the service of my country." Noyes allegedly replied "that it was doubtful that nurses would ever fly, if so they would probably fly in government airplanes and would not require special training."[51]

The ARC legal advisor, Mr. Hughes, had advised Butler not to write to Schimmoler directly, since the letter "might be misconstrued and might be used for publicity in a way of which we would not approve."[52] Butler thus asked Badger to obtain more information about ANCOA, particularly an application form. In her letter to Badger, Butler took the official stance of the Army Nurse Corps and the ARC to express no interest in ANCOA, but she confidentially thought, "We might have stepped into this breach and made an offer ahead of this woman to help the commercial planes in selecting well trained nurses for this service."[53]

Butler wrote Mrs. Maynard L. Carter, chief of the nursing division, League of Red Cross Societies in Paris, that she had spoken with Major Flikke about ANCOA's similarity to the army organization. Butler understood that Flikke's commanding officer had advised her to ignore ANCOA and its use of army terms for the time being.[54]

The growing distress over the activities of Schimmoler and ANCOA prompted Butler to discuss the matter with the chairman of the ARC, Admiral Cary T. Grayson. At his request, Butler drafted a letter for his signature to the surgeon general of the army, Major General Charles R. Reynolds, stating that the Red Cross stood ready to organize an aerial corps of their nurses if the surgeon general thought it would be a good plan toward preparedness.[55] Reynolds discouraged pursuing this option for the time being but allowed that in time of war, "especially in the secondary evacuation in the rear area or the theater of operations and in home territory there may be a need for specially trained nurses. However, this need will not exist, in my opinion, in the combat zone, or at least the employment of women nurses for front line evacuation will not be required." He did recommend that he and Grayson discuss the matter in more detail "first to provide adequately and reasonably to meet known conditions or those to be expected and, more particularly, to forestall activities on the part of unaffiliated auxiliaries in this country in the field which offers more romance than war has ever seen before."[56] This early use of "romance" in conjunction with flight nurse duties is noteworthy, indicating concern that the work might be chosen for reasons other than service to one's country.

A few months later, Schimmoler, who continued to seek army ANCOA recognition, appealed to Major Flikke for support. In her letter Schimmoler included a four-page summary of ANCOA's objectives and accomplishments and ended her correspondence with the hope that Flikke would take an interest in the organization and provide for its nurses a definite place "in the scheme of national defense in the event of a major national emergency."[57] Flikke's reply to Schimmoler was not encouraging. Flikke did not dispute that air travel was vitally important and would become more so in the future; she even acknowledged that Schimmoler's organization seemed "well planned" and could be successful in commercial air transportation. But she foresaw no military application, since the army had its own well-organized nurse corps. Many army nurses had traveled with a physician on board a plane to transport a patient to a distant hospital. Like Reynolds, she believed that any well-trained nurse could serve on a plane, "so that at the present time at least there seems to be no factual justification for a group of nurses being segregated and called aerial nurses. Nor does it seem advisable to have two organizations with such similar nomenclature that confusion may result therefrom."[58] Flikke expressed her expectation that the ARC would continue to supply nurses for the military with the usual efficient service.

Again, the military did not grant recognition to ANCOA, but the rejection of her coveted goal only made Schimmoler more determined, as Beard, who had succeeded Butler as director of nursing of the ARC, soon discovered. Beard again consulted legal advisor Hughes, with concern that the ANCOA organization's activities "have been growing more and more aggressive. Miss Schimmoler, who is not a nurse, is being almost Deified as the great founder of this organization. The disconcerting thing is that she is using the Red Cross to advertise her project, using it in little 'un-get-at-able' ways such as a notice of a meeting, when on the first line appears 'Red Cross Nurses' and then in smaller print 'are interested in ***.'"[59]

Beard must then have heard directly from Schimmoler, because a memo Beard wrote to Hughes dated a month later expressed the double bind in which she found herself regarding manipulative tactics employed by the ANCOA leader and requested his help. "Miss Schimmoler seems determined to 'draw' us in regard to this aerial service," she wrote, and would use either ARC approval or disapproval for publicity purposes. Beard did not like either position.[60]

Shortly thereafter, Virginia Dunbar, Beard's assistant at ARC headquarters, sent her boss a summary of statements made about ANCOA in literature and letters, shedding additional light on Schimmoler's public relations efforts. Dunbar's cover letter revealed her own opinion that although the references to the ARC were impressive, they were "decidedly misleading as they certainly inferred a connection with the Red Cross (and the Army)."[61] Armed with the latest information on ANCOA, Beard wrote Schimmoler, stressing the separateness of the two organizations and the role of the Red Cross alone to provide nurses for the military, even for aviation duty.[62]

American Nurses Association

To avoid possible misunderstandings of ANCOA activities, by 1939 Schimmoler had appointed a registered nurse, Ruth G. Mitchell, as chief of staff. The plan had always been to have someone direct the nursing activities in accordance with nursing standards, Mitchell told delegates of the California State Nurses Association (CSNA) meeting in San Francisco in August of that year. ANCOA was "wholly a nursing project . . . designed to serve the daily needs of the public through aeronautical means," Mitchell emphasized, glossing over the fact that Schimmoler was a pilot but not a nurse. After reviewing ANCOA aims, Mitchell outlined a plan to form committees from representatives of state nurses associations that would advise ANCOA on professional requirements and mediate on its behalf in issues regarding nursing and aviation. She then recommended that the CSNA establish an advisory council to investigate ANCOA, accept it as a nursing project, and endorse its activities, with recognition by the ANA as the ultimate goal.[63]

While Mitchell was courting the CSNA, Beard continued to express her concern about ANCOA activities. In her report at a meeting of the ANA board of directors in January 1940, she reiterated that Schimmoler, who founded ANCOA, was not a nurse. Beard stressed that no connection, formal or informal, existed between the ARC and ANCOA, despite statements such as "The Aerial Nurse Corps should be called into service through the American Red Cross, the Army, the Navy, or any other civic or military group placed in charge at the time the emergency should arise" found in ANCOA literature. Beard wrote that Schimmoler had sought the ANA's backing in at least two states and closed her report with a reference to the military's view that "neither the Army nor the Navy wishes to request any special action in regard to the services of nurses in the air."[64]

As Mitchell recommended, the CSNA appointed an advisory committee to ANCOA. A copy of the committee report on ANCOA letterhead dated 14 October 1940 reflects the ambitious Schimmoler's influence. Its list of seven recommendations included approval and recognition of ANCOA "for the development of an aviation department for the nursing profession under the National Defense Program" and creation of an ANCOA roster "in the Red Cross Nursing files for any and all forms of aviation duty for national emergency under the direction of the American Red Cross."[65]

Badger, who was a member of the CSNA advisory committee, refused to sign the document, because, as she told Beard, only ANCOA should represent itself before the ANA.[66] In the interim, according to Badger, Schimmoler was "working the crowd," suggesting that nurses who applied for enrollment in the Red Cross reserves should indicate preference for service in ANCOA.[67] There was, of course, no such ANCOA reserve in the ARC.

A special committee of the ANA to confer with ANCOA, chaired by Emily Eck, met six times to investigate that organization, study the need for trained aerial nurses, and determine if ANCOA prepared its nurses adequately. Of particular interest in the notes of one meeting was Schimmoler's apparent willingness to step down from her leadership of ANCOA and leave it in the hands of nurses as soon as she felt the organization could take care of itself. Schimmoler was not likely to disappear from the scene, however, Dunbar explained, because "the nurses in the group are quite concerned to find the proper way for Miss Schimmoler to continue to give what they consider her great contribution, especially in the field of the construction of aeroplanes for transporting sick people safely. A great deal was made of the fact that the ideal place for Miss Schimmoler would be on a national advisory committee to the Red Cross on the use of planes in disaster."[68]

After very carefully considering the information obtained from correspondence with ANCOA, organizational and other aviation literature, and superintendents of the Army and Navy Nurse Corps, the special committee recommended that formal recognition of the organization be withheld, because ANCOA was nonprofessional with a pilot instead of a nurse as president. Furthermore, the training it provided was inadequate for disaster nursing service. If, however, ANCOA should reorganize and select a qualified nurse as its president, the ANA would consider developing a close affiliation with that organization. But for the time being, the ANA expected the ARC, not ANCOA, to organize the reserve of nurses qualified "for any and all forms of nursing duties in aviation, in the event of civic or national emergencies."[69] The committee submitted its report to Julia C. Stimson, president of the ANA, on 16 May 1941.

About a week later, Schimmoler appointed Leora Stroup president of ANCOA. Eileen Newbeck replaced Stroup as Detroit Company A commander.[70] Stroup submitted a reorganization plan for ANCOA that would, in part, revise the constitution and bylaws; make ANCOA an all-nurse group; and seek guidance, support, and approval of the ANA.[71]

The Civil Air Patrol, which had been created in December 1941 as a noncombat voluntary auxiliary of the U.S. military, was a focus of ANCOA collaboration. Stroup, the deputy medical officer of the Detroit women's squadron of the Civil Air Patrol, likely used that platform to coordinate ANCOA activities with this national defense organization. By 1942, ANCOA members had joined the ranks of the Civil Air Patrol but maintained some degree of autonomy by gaining permission to wear their own uniforms, on which Civil Air Patrol insignia was displayed.[72] Changes in the ANCOA organization were likely too little, too late. The ANA did not revisit ANCOA's status. Whether this had anything to do with a possible rift between Schimmoler and Stroup involving the ANCOA presidency to which Nichols of Relief Wings alluded in a letter to Fleming in 1942 is uncertain; a letter from Schimmoler to Stroup in June 1942 implies a possible "falling out."[73]

Perhaps the lingering discontent of ANA leaders with ANCOA was not only that Schimmoler was not a nurse but also that, as was the case with Relief Wings, ANCOA threatened to exert unwarranted control over the limited number of nurses available for wartime needs. And the need to mobilize the ARC First Reserve of nurses for military service and to fill resulting civilian vacancies would have taken precedence over continued study of the ANCOA situation. With articles such as "American Nurses— We Are at War!," "First Reserve Quotas!," "Nurses, to the Colors!," and "The Time Is Now!" appearing in 1942 in the *American Journal of Nursing,* the ANA clearly had more pressing issues occupying its time.[74]

Schimmoler had failed to achieve formal recognition of ANCOA by the ANA. Ultimately the rivalry between the two organizations was much ado about nothing. But the deliberations and decisions of nurse leaders of the ARC and the ANA concerning Schimmoler and ANCOA offer insight into how nurses sought to maintain control of their profession as America headed toward its involvement in World War II.

Army Air Forces Flight Nurse Program

Undeterred by the ANA rejection, Schimmoler again set her sights on military support of ANCOA. In July 1942, with approximately four hundred ANCOA nurses on duty with the armed forces, Schimmoler wrote

Brigadier General David N. W. Grant, air surgeon for the army air forces, United States Army, shown in illustration 1.3:

> Frankly, General, I have almost begun to think that I am another Billy Mitchell. I have not, however, given up hope that some how some way that your department will embark upon the creation of a school for nurses for air ambulance duty and that we [ANCOA] might be accorded the consideration of doing our part in the operations of this school. I feel this department should be separate apart from the regular Army Nurse Corps and be attached as a special unit of the Air Forces. . . .
>
> There isn't a question in my mind, with the interest there exists in this field, that if we had the support and authority needed, that we could create an Air ambulance unit that you could well be proud of.[75]

In his reply, Grant told Schimmoler that mass evacuation of casualties from combat zones was now in the "formative stage" in the armed forces. Nurses, especially those with prior experience in the airlines, would be assigned from the Army Nurse Corps for this duty. He suggested that ANCOA nurses could join the army but could not be guaranteed a flying assignment. They would be earmarked for flight nurse duty, however, when the need arose.[76]

A month later, Grant and members of the army surgeon general's office accepted a plan for a workable air evacuation system that Colonel Wood S. Woolford, the first Air Transport Command (ATC) surgeon, had designed. Grant submitted the plan to the air staff in July 1942 and received approval to begin its implementation. Because airplanes were in short supply, evacuation of casualties was split between the Troop Carrier Command, whose tactical mission was to fly men and equipment into combat areas, and the ATC, responsible for strategic flights between overseas locations and the United States. These transport planes, when outfitted with litter installations, could be converted into air ambulances for the return trip once troops and cargo were offloaded, putting to humanitarian use planes that would have returned to their bases empty. An interesting feature of Woolford's plan was the employment of 103 female flight nurses.[77] At the time, only women served as army nurses. Although the army had

1.3 David N. W. Grant, air
surgeon, army air forces
(USAF photo)

male nurses, they were not commissioned as officers but rather were classified as nurses at the induction centers and assigned in the medical department of the army as enlisted medical technicians.[78] Like the army nurses assigned to ground medical facilities, the flight nurses would hold the relative initial rank and wear the insignia of second lieutenant. Not until 10 July 1944 did a presidential executive order appoint nurses as commissioned officers of the United States Army with the corresponding rights, benefits, and privileges accorded male officers.

Over the next five months, events happened quickly in the development of the air evacuation system in which army flight nurses would participate. In September 1942 the 38th Medical Air Ambulance Squadron, a "paperwork" organization with only one officer and a few enlisted men that had been activated at Fort Benning, Georgia, the previous May, was transferred to Bowman Field in Louisville, Kentucky. Bowman Field was chosen because of its proximity to the 1st Troop Carrier Command headquarters in Indianapolis just over a hundred miles north and because it already had some facilities in place as the former site of the Medical Officer Training School.[79]

Upon its arrival the squadron, now with two officers and 138 enlisted men, fell under the army air forces 1st Troop Carrier Command responsible for organizing and training air evacuation groups and was attached to the base hospital. Renamed the 507th Air Evacuation Squadron, the unit now had flight nurses among its personnel and served as the nucleus for the air evacuation system. The 349th Air Evacuation Group activated at Bowman Field on 7 October incorporated the 507th and three additional units—the 620th, 621st, and 622nd Air Evacuation Squadrons, all activated on 11 November.[80] Table of Organization 8-447, issued in tentative form in November 1942 and finalized in February of the next year, established the medical air evacuation transport squadron (MAETS) with a headquarters section that included a flight surgeon commander, administrative officer, chief nurse, and four evacuation flights of six flight nurses and six enlisted surgical technicians. A flight surgeon commanded each flight. Flight teams of one flight nurse and one surgical technician would staff transport planes as needed, and when personnel were short or when casualty loads exceeded available teams, the flight nurse and the surgical technician could fly in separate planes.[81]

During the months when the air evacuation program was being organized, the office of the air surgeon received letters from nurses both in and out of the military inquiring about air evacuation duty. Replies to United Airlines stewardesses from California, a nurse from New York who was working toward her private pilot's license, nurses from Georgia, Louisiana, and Nebraska, and a congressman in Washington, D.C.—likely on behalf of constituents—all contained essentially the same information: All nurses for air evacuation units would come from the pool of nurses who joined the Army Nurse Corps through the usual channels. Volunteers then would be assigned to this duty at a later date when the need arose. War Department Memorandum No. W40-10-42, dated 21 December 1942, spelled out the qualifications for air evacuation nurses and the application procedure to be followed. Only those applicants who were members of the Army Nurse Corps would be favorably considered. Applicants had to be twenty-one to thirty-six years old, weigh between 105 and 135 pounds, be physically qualified for flying, and certify willingness "to be placed under orders requiring frequent and regular participation in aerial flights."[82]

As the war continued, the need for an air evacuation system overseas became more urgent. At Bowman Field on 10 December 1942, the 507th, 620th, and 621st Aeromedical Evacuation Squadrons became the 801, 802, and 803 MAETS as outlined in Table of Organization 8-447.[83] The 801 and 802 MAETS trained hastily in the essentials of air evacuation—an "admittedly meager and inadequate" preparation for the work ahead.[84] As Morrey, whose request for "air ambulance only" finally resulted in assignment as a flight nurse with the 802 MAETS, recalled, the curriculum was "nowhere near complete," except for chemical warfare. "GAS will be used in this war," she remembered Captain Gray emphatically repeating time and again, and the flight nurses "learned all there was about the recognition of the various gases, how to put on a gas mask and how to treat patients who were contaminated. That class, physical exercises, and marching rounded out our brief education."[85]

On Christmas Day 1942 the 802 MAETS departed Bowman Field for North Africa to provide air evacuation support for the Tunisian campaign. Former chief stewardess Ellen Church, now recovered from her automobile accident and a lieutenant in the United States Army, was among the flight nurses in that organization, as was Morrey. Just over three weeks later the 801 MAETS left Bowman Field for the South Pacific, where American troops were still engaged in the battle of Guadalcanal.[86]

ANCOA Grounded

ANCOA essentially now was grounded. Despite Schimmoler's pronouncement to Stroup in January 1942 that "ANCOA shall never die," the organization apparently *did* die a slow death.[87] After the outbreak of World War II, as part of the national defense program, civilian aircraft relocated from the West Coast to inland bases, thus eliminating ANCOA training flights, and air shows were put on hold.[88] ANCOA nurses, who by regulation were members of the ARC First Reserve, were mobilized for active duty with the military. Some one hundred of them, including Stroup, according to an uncorroborated newspaper account, served with distinction as flight nurses with the army air forces.[89] Schimmoler, in her early forties by then, was past the age limit for government flying in the Women Airforce Service Pilots (WASP) program.[90] Not being a nurse, military flight nursing was not an option for her.

In fact, the closest Schimmoler came to being a flight nurse was on the big screen with the 1942 release of *Parachute Nurse,* a Columbia Pictures film for which she was technical director. In this fictional wartime melodrama, nurses are in training for a newly formed corps of parachute nurses to be dropped at sites inaccessible to medical care. Schimmoler was cast in the role of Jane Morgan, commander of the Parachute Corps, "a very efficient, good-looking, plump, graying, motherly sort of woman, with a hardboiled exterior and a heart as big as her frame, which is ample."[91] Sixty-two ANCOA members of Los Angeles Company A, First Division were used in the marching scenes, shown in illustration 1.4.[92] Schimmoler's personal correspondence suggests that she dreamed of follow-on movie contracts as a character actress, but the *Hollywood Reporter* did not ensure her potential success in Tinsel Town when in its review of *Parachute Nurse* Schimmoler was included only among those nameless others having "lesser chances to score."[93] Off the movie set, Schimmoler had researched the idea of parachute nurses as a possible opportunity for ANCOA, but, as she told *R.N.* magazine, "even with the present war developments, it seems unnecessary for women nurses to run the risks of being dragged in rough terrain, of being impaled in a tree, in landing in water, or of suffering some other casualty."[94] She then hinted of the movie soon to be released.[95]

After her film debut, with ANCOA no longer a viable organization, Schimmoler closed her offices in Burbank, turned her clerical staff over to the war operations center of the Los Angeles County Sheriff's Department, and considered her next step. Not willing to sever her connections with aviation, she worked in the civilian sector before enlisting in the Army as a Women's Army Corps (WAC) member in 1944. After completing basic training in Des Moines, Iowa, Private Schimmoler reported to California's Fairfield-Suisun Army Air Base—renamed Travis Air Force

1.4 Marching scene from movie *Parachute Nurse* (USAF photo)

Base in 1951—where she worked in base operations as a dispatcher, "since they could not find a place for me to serve direct in Air Evac."[96] Schimmoler was alone on duty one night in 1944 when the first C-54 Skymaster air evacuation flight from the Pacific theater of operations touched down safely on her watch. She recalled that the arrival of this plane "was gratification which no amount of money could purchase."[97] She continued: "When the first stretcher made its appearance in the open door of the plane and they began to move slowly down the ladder, I was overcome by it all for the moment. I said aloud, 'And they said it wouldn't be done.'"[98] It may have been a bittersweet moment for Schimmoler, however, to see that her dream had become a reality—but not for ANCOA.

02

Military Air Evacuation Tries Its Wings

A ir evacuation began shortly after the invention of the airplane, when two officers at an army base in Florida constructed and in 1910 flew the first known air ambulance, but the War Department chose not to allocate funds for further development of the airplane for medical transport. As early as 1919, patients were transported to hospitals by airplane in both civilian and military life using improvised methods. Some of the larger air force bases were equipped with small airplanes, painted white with the Geneva Red Cross insignia and specially equipped for air evacuation of two to four patients, but these operations were on a small scale. Even during World War I, the airplane was used only to a minor extent to evacuate casualties. Air evacuation as an accepted means of patient transport had to await improvement in airplane design to accommodate patients and their caregivers and military necessity based on distance, lack of medical care, and inaccessibility via ground transportation. The medical personnel for these early flights with patients were volunteers, largely untrained; they were not nurses.[1]

In an irony of military logic, the first nurse on a military air evacuation mission was not a flight nurse and had never flown before. She might not even have been a volunteer for flying duty but rather simply the nurse available for what was to be the first major test of the evacuation of patients from an overseas location to the United States on ATC aircraft. The ATC was the middle link in the chain of worldwide air evacuation. The Troop Carrier Command brought patients back from the active fronts to hospitals in the rear areas overseas, after which ATC then transported patients to hospitals on the east and west coasts of the United States as soon as they could be moved. From there, the ferrying division distributed patients to convalescent centers throughout the United States.[2]

The modus operandi for the transoceanic mission, which occurred before the first MAETS had arrived at its overseas location, was more a continuation of the previous policy regarding nurses on patient transport flights stated in 1938 by Major Julia Flikke, superintendent of the Army Nurse Corps than of the new policy for air evacuation nurses implemented by the air surgeon, Brigadier General Grant, in 1942.[3] Oliver La Farge, chief historian for ATC during the war, had the impression that the trip was "bootlegged."[4] Brigadier General Harold F. Funsch, who as a major was the wing surgeon of the South Atlantic Wing of ATC in Natal, Brazil, one of the stops along the air evacuation route, later stated that the trip was kept confidential, "since the Army Air Corps did not want the army Surgeon General to be aware of this flight until it was successfully completed."[5] Air evacuation's reputation was at stake.

The Karachi to Washington, D.C., air evacuation mission was, by a later account, "poorly planned and poorly coordinated."[6] But if its implementation was questionable at times, the trip's purpose was sound. In addition to the therapeutic effect of returning sick and wounded soldiers home for lengthy treatment and recovery, air evacuation of patients from overseas hospitals meant a major savings in manpower and supplies. Medical authorities had calculated that the care of a patient overseas occupied the time of six people and represented ten tons of supplies.[7]

Although not the primary mission of ATC, air evacuation "was a task at which no one could help but work with enthusiasm"; this shows the compassionate side of combat while also serving as an example of military practicality.[8] One of the most enthusiastic supporters of air evacuation at the conclusion of the mission was Lieutenant Elsie Ott, the nurse pioneer on this historic trip. Enthusiasm might not have been her first reaction, however, when Ott learned of the task she was being assigned.

Unexpected Orders

On 16 January 1943, Ott, an army nurse assigned to the 159th Station Hospital at Karachi, Pakistan (then part of India), learned she was to be prepared to leave within twenty-four hours for the United States on an ATC plane to provide nursing care for five patients. Ott, twenty-nine years old and a graduate of Lenox Hill Hospital School of Nursing in New York City, had entered the army in 1941. Following an initial assignment at Barksdale Field in Louisiana, she was sent to Fort Story, Virginia, from where she traveled overseas in March 1942, arriving at Karachi two months later.[9] The five patients scheduled for her flight in January 1943, two on litters and three ambulatory, represented a variety of medical conditions—chronic poliomyelitis and partial paralysis, multiple fractures and bedsores, early active tuberculosis, glaucoma, and manic depression.[10]

No flight surgeon assessed preflight the patients' ability to withstand the stresses of air travel. Ott received no special instructions or medical supplies for her patients prior to departure. Falling back on her nursing initiative, she gathered up a few dressings and medications from the ward where she worked—"a few sodium amytal capsules, aspirin tablets and a few PAC [phenacetin, aspirin, caffeine] capsules, plus one bedpan and one urinal."[11] The ward furnished two cots, mattresses, and blankets for the litter patients. A medical department staff sergeant with chronic arthritis, who had recently been a patient himself, accompanied Ott on the flight as her medical attendant. One wonders what must have been going through Ott's mind that last night in Karachi as she prepared to take her first airplane ride under such novel and demanding circumstances.

The flight from Karachi began the morning of 17 January on either a commercial DC-3 airliner or its military version, the C-47 transport plane—more affectionately nicknamed the "Gooney Bird," after the clumsy black-footed albatross of the same name that inhabited Pacific islands—under ATC control. Sources differ on this detail. Because the Germans and Italians held all of North Africa from the Mediterranean Sea to the Sahara Desert, the only air route open for military aircraft at the time was through Central Africa to the Sudan and down the Nile River.[12]

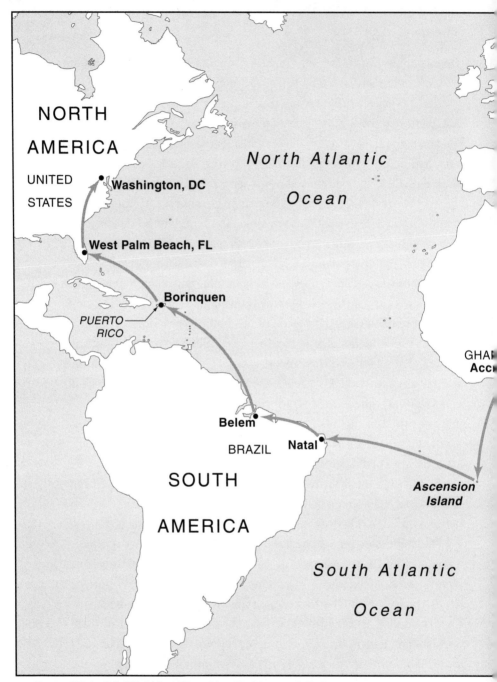

2.1 Route of Elsie Ott's Flight from Karachi to Washington, D.C., January 1943

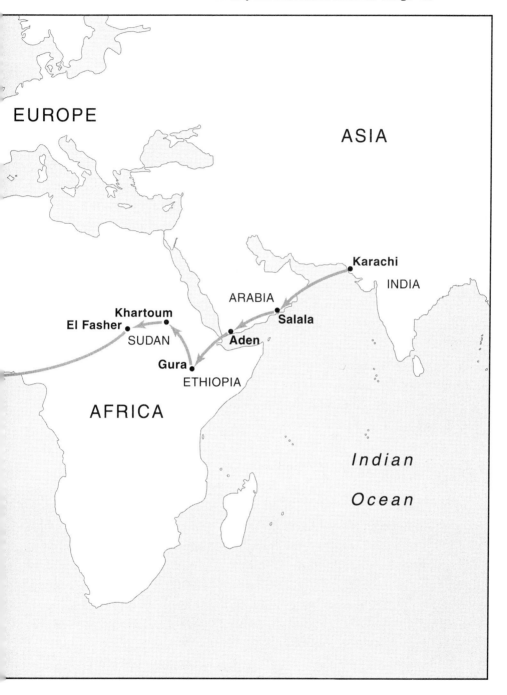

On the first day of its air evacuation mission, the plane stopped at Salala and Aden in Arabia (now in Oman and Yemen, respectively). At Aden the patients were taken to the British hospital for the night and two meals, at the cost of $2 per patient. Ott stayed in the room with the two litter patients to provide their nursing care; the staff sergeant stayed with the manic depressive patient.

The patients and nursing crew departed Aden the next morning on the same plane, stopping at Gura, Ethiopia, to refuel. They arrived at Khartoum, Sudan, where they ate box lunches during their hour layover, en route to El Fasher. Here the patients stayed at a Sudanese hospital overnight, with two meals, again for $2. Staff members of the hospital, who were more helpful than their British counterparts of the previous night, changed dressings, bathed the patients, irrigated wounds, and replaced an indwelling urinary catheter.

The third day was even more tiring on the patients and the nursing crew. Other than stops for refueling, they were in the air well over thirty hours from just before seven in the morning until five the next evening, when they reached Accra, Ghana. Here, the 67th Station Hospital provided the patient care.

For the flight from Accra, which departed at midnight, the patients traveled on a C-87—a B-24 Liberator bomber converted for transport. The plane configuration provided seating for the ambulatory patients, nursing crew, and eleven passengers; the litter patients had to lie on mattresses on the plane's floor, because there was no way to secure litters. Ott had only two thermoses of coffee to sustain the patients en route until a two-hour stopover on Ascension Island. After a rather unpalatable breakfast, the patients were airborne again, this time winging toward Natal, Brazil.

When the plane reached Natal just over eight-and-a-half hours later, Ott and the patients encountered the bright spot of their trip in the person of Major Harold Funsch, wing surgeon for the South Atlantic Wing of ATC. He had received advance word of the air evacuation flight and was prepared to make their stay a pleasant one. Speaking to a graduating class of United States Air Force flight nurses in 1965, Funsch recalled:

As it [the C-87] lumbered to a rolling stop, I climbed aboard and there stood an attractive, but very weary and bedraggled, nurse with 5 very sick patients. Two were paralyzed from spinal cord injuries and one was psychotic. I don't recall the diagnoses of the other 2, but they all required constant attention. There were no Aeromedical Technicians in those days. Our Medical Group at Natal assumed the care of the patients.

We bathed them, fed them, medicated them and rested them. After Lt Ott was assured her patients were properly cared for she rested and showered, and we then took her to dinner. She was most appreciative of our interest and concern for the patients entrusted to her. She stated that this was the first relief she had received since starting her trip six days ago. She had been attending these patients all this time alone. She had been mother, nurse, chef, finance officer, housemaid, and latrine orderly.[13]

Refreshed for their continuing journey, Ott and her patients departed Natal that evening, headed for Belem, Brazil. Here the patients were cared for in the hallway of the hospital, because the doors to the patient rooms were too narrow to accommodate the stretchers without tilting them. They left Belem shortly after their arrival and stopped next at Borinquen, Puerto Rico. Because of the cool weather, the patients remained on the plane, where they were treated to a hearty breakfast. After a two-and-a-half-hour layover, patients and crew were once again airborne, destined at last for the United States.

Arrival in the United States

On the evening of 23 January, the travel-weary patients and crew arrived at Morrison Field, West Palm Beach, Florida. Their welcome did not bode well for the success of air evacuation as Grant and his staff had envisioned it. Ambulances that met the plane did not have enough personnel to remove the two litter patients from the aircraft, and once the patients arrived at the admitting room of the base hospital, they had to wait approximately an hour before settling into beds on a ward. When Ott visited her patients a few hours later, she discovered that the private with the multiple fractures had not been bathed, nor had his dressings been changed. He had, however, been fed. He is reported to have told Ott that they had received better care from the Sudanese hospital at El Fasher than from this American one. When no enlisted men were available to unload the mattresses and bedding from the plane, Ott had to do it herself. Concerning this reception, Major Richard L. Meiling, chief of the operations division, office of the air surgeon, summed up the impressions of both the air surgeon's staff and the members of the air evacuation flight team. Reporting to Colonel Walter Jensen, assistant to and acting air surgeon, 1st Troop Carrier Command, he wrote, "In general no appreciation was shown of the trip the patients had just made or the fact that these patients were casualties returning home after months on a front."[14]

But Ott's problems at Morrison Field had only begun. She was the one who had to make arrangements for the flight from Morrison Field to Bolling Field in Washington, D.C.—the patients' final stop—the next morning. Her first phone call was not productive. She then called the operations officer at Morrison Field to tell him the priority rating of her mission and to request the needed air transportation for the five patients, the staff sergeant medical attendant, and herself. He gave her a tentative eleven o'clock departure time, which was delayed by an hour. Ott had difficulty obtaining the patients' medical records, which she had turned over to the hospital at Morrison Field, and no records of treatment while at that facility were forthcoming. After delays, the patients and their attendants left Morrison Field on a DC-3 at noon on 24 January, with the patient with multiple fractures placed on a Stokes litter for the flight. Eight hours later, the plane touched down at Bolling Field, Washington, D.C. Medical attendants meeting the plane transported the patients to Walter Reed Army Hospital, where all the patients recovered satisfactorily.[15]

In 1965, Ott recalled just how exhausted she had been at the conclusion of her first flight. Reporting to the head nurse at Walter Reed, she was given a form to fill out. "The first line asked my name. I could not remember it. The girl asked me where I had come from, and I avoided answering her because I could not remember. I asked if I could fill the form the next morning, and was told to put my name on top and do the rest later, and I had to surreptitiously pull out my dog tag to find out what my name was."[16]

The morning after her arrival, Ott met with military officials to report on the air evacuation mission. All ATC wing surgeons subsequently received a letter identifying both the problems she related at various en route stops and the means to prevent their recurrence.[17] Natal, the only medical facility that received a "glowing" report for the care Ott's patients received, was obviously the standard to which all other en route locations were held.[18] Recommendations Ott made during her debriefing eventually were implemented as part of air evacuation policy and included slacks as part of the flight nurse uniform, medical kits with supplies for in-flight patient care, onboard food and beverages when feasible, financial arrangements for patients and nurses to cover or defray travel expenses, and transcripts of medical care given at en route stops to accompany patients.[19]

Award of Air Medal

Major Meiling summarized the significance of this historic flight that brought patients halfway around the world within a week's time, attended by a nurse to provide their care: "The future success and development of air evacuation certainly rested in the hands of Lt. Ott during those seven days, for had she failed it would be difficult to regain the lost confidence of all concerned."[20]

But Ott did not fail, and in recognition of her accomplishment, she received the Air Medal—and was the first woman in the history of the United States Army to be awarded this military decoration. The citation accompanying the award read:

Second Lieutenant *Elsie S. Ott*, Army Nurse Corps, United States Army. For meritorious achievement while participating in an aerial flight from India to the United States January 17 to 23, 1943. During this flight,

Lieutenant *Ott* served as nurse for five patients who were being evacuated from India to Washington, D.C. This was the pioneer movement of hospitalized personnel by air over such a great distance. Several of these patients were suffering from serious ailments which required constant attendance and vigilance on the part of Lieutenant *Ott*. In addition to her nursing duties, she was responsible for arranging for the feeding and housing of the patients en route, the transportation and stowing of their baggage, as well as making all financial arrangements involving their feeding and care while at ground bases not under the control of the Army Air Forces. The successful transportation of these patients was made possible largely by the efficiency and professional skill of Lieutenant *Ott* and her unflagging devotion to duty. It further demonstrated the practicability of long-range evacuation by air of seriously ill and wounded military personnel from theaters of operations and reflected great credit upon Lieutenant *Ott* and the Army Nurse Corps.[21]

At a press meeting at Bowman Field marking the occasion, Ott gave a more personal insight into her role aboard the aircraft. When asked about the treatment she rendered, she said with a smile that she had given the patients "pills for whatever ailed them. They didn't know it, but it was all aspirin," since the drugs prescribed for them could not be administered because of the effects of high altitude. The same pills were not as effective on Ott, who was "terribly air sick" the first day. "I couldn't persuade myself that they would do any good. My patients were all better fliers than I."[22]

Ott, shown in illustration 2.1, received her Air Medal on 26 March 1943 at the ceremonies of the second class of flight nurses to graduate from the School of Air Evacuation at Bowman Field. Seven weeks later, she was among the graduates of the third class to earn their flight nurse wings, having been granted her request to attend the flight nurse course. Ott was sent eventually to China-Burma-India (CBI), where she worked from Chabua, India, taking patients out of Burma by plane as a member of the 803 MAES.[23] She earned a second Air Medal—an oak leaf cluster in lieu of the actual medal—for her participation in more than 150 hours of "operational flight in transport aircraft" as a flight nurse from

2.1 Elsie Ott receives Air Medal from Brigadier General Fred Borum, 26 March 1943 (USAF photo)

23 February to 27 August 1944 through combat zones in Upper Assam (India), Burma, and Southwest China.[24]

The publicity value of Ott's trip should not be underestimated. The media coverage was good for launching a successful air evacuation system and aided in the recruitment of nurses to provide in-flight patient care. Ott's flight, which made good copy for the base public relations office, was chronicled in the local newspaper and in civilian and military publications in the days and months after the event.[25] Her flight even was the subject of a five-page color cartoon targeted at young readers. "Flying Nurse," described as "A True Picture Story: The true story of Elsie Ott, Nurse of the U.S. Army Air Forces," appeared in the September 1943 issue of *Calling All Girls*, a monthly publication of the Parents Magazine Press. The pictures are not true to life—one shows tiers of litters with curtains surrounding them in the aircraft interior, for example—but the accompanying text gives a fairly accurate account of the event.

Ott's Historic Flight Revisited

Years later, in 1960, the story of Elsie Ott resurfaced when staff members were reviewing historical materials archived in the Military Air Transport Service (MATS) headquarters at Scott Air Force Base, Illinois. These materials gave Irving H. Breslauer, chief of public information for MATS the idea of a national made-for-TV movie of the first transoceanic air evacuation flight.[26] Breslauer was unable to locate Ott at this time, however. Five years later, Ott's role in this historic flight was again a subject of interest, when Brigadier General Funsch, then command surgeon of the Military Airlift Command, wanted to invite Ott to participate in the roll-out of the C-9A Nightingale, a military version of the DC-9 aircraft dedicated exclusively to transporting patients. With the help of colleagues in the Air Force Nurse Corps, Funsch successfully located her. Around the same time, a movie company eager to capitalize on a revival of Ott's story—"since aeromedical evacuation is a topical subject again due to the South Vietnam conflict"—contacted Funsch.[27]

The story of a World War II flight nurse offered a pleasant change from the standard media depiction of nurses in the late 1960s. During World War II, the American public considered nursing "the most distinctive and heroic of all possible occupations," a viewpoint films tended to reflect.[28] Early in World War II, filmmakers portrayed individual nurses as nonessential military personnel who inspired the male leads to manly action and achieved romantic fulfillment as their reward. By the 1942 release of *Parachute Nurse*, however, nurses were forging a group identity as a military unit. This positive wartime image of nursing reached its peak in the 1943 Paramount release *So Proudly We Hail*, a film based on true stories of the nurse POWs imprisoned by the Japanese in the Philippines.[29]

In 1943, disgruntled army GIs slandered female soldiers with intent to degrade them and drive them out of a perceived all-male domain. These unfounded allegations spread to the national media and to the American public, seriously undermining these women's patriotism and tarnishing their character. The smear campaign was aimed primarily at Women's Army Auxiliary Corps members (WAACs). Army nurses for the most part were exempt from the salacious comments and cartoons, though they had experienced similar antagonism when the Army Nurse Corps was founded, approximately forty years earlier.[30]

Although in movies the military provided the nurse with the ideal environment to meet and become romantically involved with a soldier, the focus remained on her more laudable contributions to the war effort, so as not to weaken the favorable image of nurses the film industry wanted to convey. Romance took a backseat to bravery in the daily lives of wartime female nurse characters on the screen. Such portrayals of military nurses during World War II advanced the profession of nursing and served as an important recruiting tool.[31]

In the mid-1960s, when Ott's story was being considered as a motion picture or television special, the film depiction of nurses and nursing had shifted. The media portrayed nurses as "sensual, romantic, hedonistic, frivolous, irresponsible, and promiscuous."[32] Nurses' private lives overshadowed their professional activities, and sexual liaisons substituted for acts of courage in film plots. Judging from the extant copy of the screenplay in manuscript, if produced, the Elsie Ott story would have shown a nurse in the more favorable light of a World War II heroine.[33] The screenwriters did not stop eliciting emotional responses in the prospective audiences, however. To satisfy the conventions for a successful screenplay, the writers hinted at a budding romance between Ott and one of the patients on her flight and developed the character of the psychiatric patient to set up more obstacles impeding the success of her mission. The writers even found a way to introduce nudity, by including a bath scene. This last enhancement, designed to titillate the viewers' senses and enacted within a military setting, undermined the credibility of the film version of this true story and raised some official eyebrows. For example, Funsch, who was given the opportunity to review the draft of the screenplay, took issue: "The bath scene??? This should be modified. Perhaps a gesture or veiled threat of giving her a bath if she didn't do it herself would be adequate, to spice it up a bit. I think the scene as is reflects adversely upon the military establishment."[34] The scene in question took liberties with the military conduct of Ott and Funsch during the stopover at Natal, Brazil.

Ott is portrayed as a maverick whose unruly behavior causes her chief nurse to send a resentful Ott on the Karachi to Washington, D.C., mission out of spite. The script plays up Ott's airsickness and her latrine duties. She is portrayed as an assertive nurse who does not hesitate to use the gambit of the potentially violent behavior of her manic patient, Sergeant Ed Spellman, to secure flights for her patients when aircraft are grounded or nonexistent. Straitlaced officers and cocky pilots are no match for this super-nurse. When Spellman predictably escapes from the barracks on Ascension Island to which he has been taken, Ott heroically searches him out in a mountainous cave. True to convention, the final scene hints that Ott has found her future husband in Captain Ray Dower, the burn patient on her historic flight.[35]

The introduction to the movie script categorized the conditions Ott encountered as "almost beyond belief."[36] Perhaps the screenplay itself was beyond belief—the outcome of this Hollywood media venture is uncertain. The production is not included in the comprehensive bibliography of motion pictures and television series with one or more nurse characters Philip Kalisch and Beatrice Kalisch compiled in *The Changing Image of the Nurse*.[37] A Fox Movietone film of Ott's award of the Air Medal wound up on the cutting room floor; perhaps the film of her air evacuation mission suffered the same fate.[38]

03

Flight Nurse Training

Thanks for the memories of drilling in the sun
And making it seem fun and eating sand
And killing flies and guarding with a gun
Oh thank you so much.

Thanks for the memories of swimming every week
Of forming in the street of scrubbing clothes
And dusting doors and bathing in the creek
Oh thank you so much.

Flight nurse training at Bowman Field, Kentucky, was a memorable event for those army nurses selected for air evacuation duty. Class songs such as this one written by members of the fifth class, which graduated in August 1943, often commemorated this time of rigorous military preparation with a hint of nostalgia. Air evacuation itself was relatively new, and the use of flight nurses to provide in-flight patient care was unprecedented in the U.S. military. Training of flight nurses was thus a priority.

This training evolved and became more relevant over the course of the war as input from air evacuation squadrons overseas helped determine what was most useful to include in coursework and practical instruction. The first two squadrons received minimal training because of the need for immediate deployment overseas, but by January 1943, members of the other squadrons being formed benefited from a didactic course of study under the direction of the 349th Air Evacuation Group, with responsibility for the actual training of the flight nurses delegated to Leora B. Stroup, shown in illustration 3.1.

349th Air Evacuation Group

The American Journal of Nursing kept its readers updated on the latest military needs and news relevant to nurses. Thus the August 1942 issue began with a plea for more nurses to enroll in the ARC First Reserve to

3.1 Leora B. Stroup, 1942 (AMEDD)

meet wartime requirements on the battlefront and on the home front. To help nurses determine where their skills could be used most effectively, the journal provided an easily read guide to whether nurses should serve with the armed forces or at home, based on marital status, age, and civilian nursing position. In brief, unmarried nurses under age forty engaged in private duty or office nursing, in nonessential head nurse or public health positions, or in non-nursing jobs should enter military service. Older nurses in essential teaching, supervisory, or public health positions should remain at home in their current employment.[1]

Leora Stroup, who had already enrolled in the ARC First Reserve, must have read with particular interest the article in the same issue titled "Army Nurses in the Air," which spelled out the initial plans for air evacuation in the army air forces, especially the final three sentences: "It is the plan of the War Department to assign nurses who have had flying experience to hospitals at air fields. They will be on call for duty in connection with transportation of patients by plane. Experience as pilots is an asset but not a requirement."[2]

At forty-one, Stroup may have wondered if she was too old to be mobilized for military service, though by June 1943 the age limit for joining the Army Nurse Corps had been raised to forty-five.[3] Her answer came two months later, in the form of military orders to report to Walter Reed General Hospital in Washington, D.C., as a member of the Army Nurse Corps. As a nurse, aviator, and educator, Stroup had a background of special interest to the army air forces, and she expected an air evacuation assignment. A photograph in the *Detroit Free Press* over the caption "Ordered to Active Service" shows a radiant Stroup, who obviously was optimistic about what lay ahead.[4]

When Stroup reported for active duty in the United States Army, she was already an experienced and highly educated nurse. Following high school graduation, she had attended a year of college before entering Lakeside Hospital School of Nursing—renamed the Frances Payne Bolton School of Nursing at Case Western University—from which she earned her nursing diploma in 1923. She had become a licensed nurse that same year. And she was among the Jubilee Class of 1927 when she earned her Bachelor of Science in Education and a certificate in public health nursing from Ohio State University. A letter to her mother from the Dean of the College of Education indicates that Stroup had shown unusual scholarship and ability and had earned high grades during her four years of academic work.[5]

Stroup taught health education for about ten years before earning her master of arts in education from Western Reserve University. She then moved to Detroit to serve as director of special programs in nursing at Wayne University and pursued her interests in aviation and ANCOA until called to active duty with the military.

Although Stroup entered the United States Army as a second lieutenant in October 1942, she was promoted to first lieutenant only a month later. It appears that her work at Walter Reed as ward nurse, head nurse, and assistant chief nurse was for the purpose of obtaining her chief nurse rating. According to one source, Stroup was made chief of the air evacuation unit at Walter Reed, which would have been beneficial, for she was already designated for flight nurse instructor duty, confirmed by her transfer to Bowman Field, Kentucky, at the end of 1942.[6] She would oversee the training of flight nurses who would serve with the army air forces in air evacuation units.

The 349th Air Evacuation Group, which had been activated at Bowman Field in October 1942, was responsible for training the flight nurses and other personnel in MAES activated at the beginning of the war. The original plan was to activate, train, and deploy several groups composed of four squadrons each, but because air evacuation squadrons were urgently needed, military leaders abandoned this plan in favor of sending individual squadrons overseas as soon as they were trained. Thirty-one MAETS, redesignated medical air evacuation squadrons (MAES) in July 1944, were activated during the war.[7] Personnel in the first two MAES—the 801 and 802—received an abbreviated course of training before immediate departure for overseas assignments. Time permitted only brief instruction in first aid, medical and surgical care of patients en route by air, and loading and unloading patients from the planes, as well as a course on chemical warfare.[8] But the 803 and additional MAES benefitted from more thorough training in preparation for their work.

After the 802 MAES had left but while the 801 MAES was still at Bowman Field, staff and students on base made time to introduce the air evacuation training program and its flight nurses to the press and to the American people. The four-minute radio segment of NBC's *Army Hour* on 28 December 1942 featured jobs performed by women in wartime, and some of these women now were flight nurses. Lieutenant Colonel Ralph Stevenson, commandant of the 349th Air Evacuation Group, chose to focus on the importance of speed in saving lives. Lieutenant Grace Mundell, the first chief nurse of the 349th, introduced the segment.[9] The dramatization that followed included speed in converting an airplane for evacuation of patients and in placing them on board in the best location to facilitate their care. "The trick of being a good nurse in Air Evacuation is to be able to make instant decisions calmly even in the most critical situations," Stevenson explained to listeners. He then gave Stroup, who was among the participants on the radio program, a strong endorsement. In reply to her scripted comment, "This war is certainly bringing nurses into their own, isn't it, Col?" Stevenson replied, "Yes, Miss Stroup and women pilots, too, as *you* can testify. 1st Lieutenant Leora Stroup has been with us here about one week, coming to us from the Army Medical Center at Washington, D.C., where she worked with war casualties, chiefly cases involving burns. She is both pilot and nurse and a real addition to our Group."[10]

The physicians and surgical technicians assigned to the MAES had previous military experience from their respective basic military training courses; many of the flight surgeons were also pilots. The nurses, however, had come into the military straight from civilian life, where most had worked in hospitals or as airline stewardesses. The main focus of training for air evacuation in the early stages, therefore, was to indoctrinate nurses into the military way of doing things. These women knew how to be nurses—now they needed to learn how to be *military* nurses. As the supply of nurses for air evacuation duty caught up with initial demand, however, those selected for this work were drawn from among nurses with more experience in army hospitals and thus had a better grasp of military life.

Flight Nurse Training Program

Anticipating the establishment of a school of air evacuation, Brigadier General Grant prepared a tentative outline for training flight nurses and enlisted surgical technicians. He forwarded a copy to Colonel Eugen G. Reinartz, commandant of the School of Aviation Medicine at Randolph Field in San Antonio, Texas, where flight surgeons were currently trained, for his review in August 1942. Courses that Grant outlined covered a wide spectrum of subjects relevant to air evacuation overseas. Aeromedical nursing, physiology, and classification of patients headed the syllabus, followed by air evacuation records, operations, and logistics, tropical and arctic medicine, tactics of air evacuation, special studies, and field sanitation and hygiene. The greatest number of hours would be devoted to special studies—mental hygiene and its relation to air evacuation, air routes of the world, climate studies in the theaters of operation, desert medicine, and oxygen indoctrination. Instruction would span four weeks of lectures, demonstrations, and field problems.[11]

Missing from this first training outline was the subject of courtesies and customs of military service, which was incorporated into the training program beginning with the first graduating class of flight nurses.

The students received military indoctrination outside the classroom in the form of marches, drills, and parades, as shown in illustration 3.2. The nurses put all of their training to the test when they went out on maneuvers that introduced them to simulated wartime scenarios.

Interviewed for *Skyways* magazine, Lieutenant Colonel Stevenson explained that the purpose of the school was to teach the flight nurse students "to be officers who can take care of any emergency. That's our biggest problem. As nurses, they have never before been made to stand on their own feet—there's always been a doctor or a chief nurse they could run to for instructions. But not where they are going! Once the plane with its load of patients takes off, those girls are in absolute charge and the lives of the men are in their hands. The speed and sureness of their decisions may make the difference between life and death to more than one boy. So we concentrate on mental discipline and also on the ability to command."[12]

How to salute was one of the first military courtesies the flight nurse students were taught. A reporter for the *Cincinnati Enquirer* wrote that Stroup's account "of how the students learned to salute might rate a Broadway or Hollywood laugh: It seems some of them couldn't stage a salute without an oomph wiggle or almost a jitterbug act."[13] The lesson must have been a challenging one indeed, since the women were not used to the military way of life. Ethel Carlson, a flight nurse who graduated on 21 January 1944, remembered her first attempt at saluting before she arrived at Bowman Field for training. She was on her way to her first day of ward duty as an army nurse at Jefferson Barracks in April 1943 when an enlisted soldier walked toward her. Flustered, Carlson returned his salute with the one she remembered from her days as a Girl Scout.[14]

The first nurses to benefit from an organized course for the study of air evacuation duties began their rigorous program in January 1943. Former ANCOA nurse Eileen Newbeck, a member of the first class, recalled the inaugural course that she and her classmates experienced as jungle, desert, and arctic medicine "practically read out of medical books to us—because there were no books for us to study from—in order to acquaint us with the different diseases we would have in the various

3.2 Flight nurses on parade at Bowman Field (USAF photo)

countries where we might be sent." As the first class of nurses to have military drill, they were shown off to visiting generals. The media caught on to this novelty, Newbeck continued: "They came with their cameras, and we ended up in the [British] Pathé News up on the screen in the theaters in Louisville."[15]

Training was fast paced, and four weeks later a formal graduation ceremony, held in Bowman Field's base chapel on 18 February 1943, marked successful completion of their studies. The occasion was a milestone for both the thirty-nine army nurses who had earned the coveted title of flight nurse and the school that had offered them the knowledge and skills to reach this point. The air of excitement, created in part by the music of the 67th Army Air Forces band and by the presence of a host of local and visiting dignitaries, was evident in the remarks of air surgeon Brigadier General Grant, the graduation speaker:

Your graduation as the first class of nurses from the first organized course for air evacuation marks the beginning of a new chapter in the history of nursing. For me, it is the realization of a dream which we, in the Air Forces, have had for many years. For you, this day contains great implications. You stand on the threshold of a new era in nursing, one which will put into actual practice lessons which we have previously learned concerning the care of the sick and wounded during war. . . .

Surely the spirit of Florence Nightingale must glow with enthusiasm at the new worlds to conquer which have been opened to you.[16]

At the conclusion of the address, Brigadier General Fred S. Borum, commanding general of the 1st Troop Carrier Command, awarded diplomas to the new flight nurses. The honor graduate of the class was Geraldine Dishroon, in illustration 3.3, who later flew with the 806 MAES in Europe.[17]

The first graduates did not receive the coveted flight nurse wings worn by later flight nurses, because no badge to distinguish this branch of nursing had been authorized yet. Perhaps to correct this oversight on the part of the air surgeon's staff, Grant made sure that at least the honor graduate received a pair of wings. In *Medical Support of the Army Air Forces in World War II*, Mae Mills Link and Hubert Coleman, medical historians of the air force and the army air forces, respectively, give Grant's version of the situation: "General Grant—on the spur of the moment—realizing that no one had thought of an insignia for the flight nurses, unpinned his own miniature flight surgeon's insignia, and pinned it on the honor graduate remarking that from that moment on, the insignia of the flight nurses would be similar to that of the flight surgeons, with the addition of a small "N" superimposed."[18] Reporters for the *Bowman Bomber* base newspaper and the *Louisville Courier-Journal* saw it differently: Lieutenant Dishroon, whose final rating was 96.5, was awarded a pair of miniature gold wings from Grant, but Borum made the presentation and expressed the hope that perhaps later the wings might be made regulation for all air evacuation nurses.[19]

Grace Dunnam, later Dishroon's chief nurse in the 806 MAES, downplayed this much-publicized story with a bit of humor. Jerry—as they called her—was bright, Dunnam remembered, but she thought it more likely that Jerry just happened to be standing there when Grant decided to present his wings to a flight nurse.[20] Whoever did the pinning, Grant's

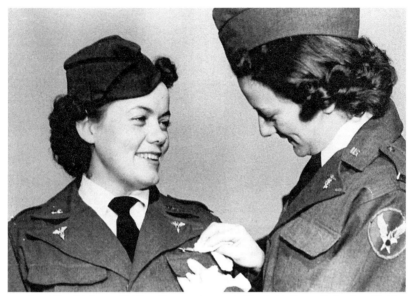

3.3 Geraldine Dishroon (left) smiles as classmate Wanda Fulton polishes her flight nurse wings on graduation day, 18 February 1943 (USAF photo)

gesture offered a fitting highlight to the occasion in general and to Dishroon in particular and set in motion the process by which all flight nurses would wear wings.

A formal parade and retreat in the afternoon in honor of Grant and the other invited guests followed the chapel ceremony. Borum was so impressed with what he had observed that after returning to his base he wrote to Stevenson to compliment him and his staff on their "excellent showing" during his visit. "The instructors as well as the nurses, deserve a great deal of credit for the proficiency attained in so short a time in close order drill, military discipline, and ceremonies," he wrote. New-beck and her classmates would have been pleased to read, "Retreat and the review closely approximated the performance of a seasoned unit."[21]

Stroup, who had arrived at Bowman Field near the end of December 1942 in preparation for her position as flight nurse instructor, likely witnessed this historic occasion as a member of the training staff. Beginning that week, she was both instructor for and student of the second organized class of flight nurses. Like many nurses selected for the flight nurse course, Stroup had arrived before the actual start of her training class. Because all military time must be accounted for, nurses who arrived early participated in a number of activities. Hikes helped condition their bodies for the physical labor of air evacuation. Training manuals on military courtesies military sanitation, equipment, clothing, and tent pitching prepared nurses for what they could expect once the coursework began. Some nurses went to the base hospital to assist with drawing blood. Others spent time in a Link Trainer to familiarize themselves with airplane controls. When planes were available, some flying time might be had. Nurses already assigned to an air evacuation squadron also spent time getting their uniforms and other government-issue items such as gas masks. And of course there were the required immunizations.[22]

A pleasant surprise awaited Stroup at Bowman Field—two former ANCOA members from Detroit Company A were on base. Lieutenant Newbeck arrived for the first flight nurse class, which graduated on 18 February 1943, and Lieutenant Margaret Gudobba began her flight nurse training in the same class as Stroup. The local newspaper, always eager for details about the flight nurses, made much of the "Three Aerial Nurse Pioneers Reunited at Bowman Field."[23]

Beginning with the second class, of which Stroup and Gudobba were members, the flight nurse course was extended to six weeks. As had been the case for the four-week program, the lengthened course focused on academic education and practical training in air evacuation and military indoctrination in six eight-hour days a week. In addition to military courtesies and customs, military art and logistics covered rules of land warfare; camouflage; chemical warfare; arctic, desert, jungle, and ocean survival; map reading; booby traps; and plane recognition. In military medicine and sanitation, the flight nurses learned emergency medical treatment, tropical medical nursing, mental hygiene, pharmacology, and the loading and unloading of litters. For this last subject, the fuselage of a troop carrier C-47 that had crashed was given new life as a valuable training aid—and the name "Limited Service." Topics of aviation medicine and nursing included air evacuation operations, tactics, aeromedical physiology, oxygen indoctrination, and religious procedures in an emergency. The nurses also accrued at least eighteen hours of flying time during the course.[24]

Classes in aeromedical physiology held the key to how patient care differed in the air from on the ground. Flight nurse students learned that the higher the plane flew, the lower the atmospheric pressure in the aircraft cabin and the lower the oxygen in the air. As a result, oxygen content in the body decreased, and air or gasses trapped inside body cavities expanded. Before beginning their air evacuation assignments, flight nurses and enlisted technicians spent time in a low-pressure chamber—also known as the altitude chamber—to identify their own reactions to hypoxia, or decreased oxygen. During air evacuation missions, they were alert to their patients' reactions to hypoxia, especially those with head and chest injuries, and to the effects of air expanding at altitude in patients with abdominal and other wounds.

An element of the training that officials of the 349th Air Evacuation Group and the public relations office continued to use to sell the air evacuation program was the speed with which the flight nurses and enlisted surgical technicians in training could load litter patients in demonstrations staged for visiting dignitaries and the press. One such demonstration took place in Washington, D.C., in May 1943, with Lieutenant Colonel Stevenson as moderator. After briefly relating the history of air evacuation and of the Troop Carrier Command, he turned to a description of the School of Air Evacuation and focused on the flight nurses trained there, mentioning their course of instruction and their appearance. Some of these nurses were participating in this combat scenario, which began with the arrival of a C-47. "So, get out your watches and let's go!" Stevenson told the observers. He then explained the configuration of the aircraft interior, procedure for loading litters, in-flight duties of the flight nurse, and equipment with which she provided patient care, while onlookers watched mock casualties being loaded onto the plane. As the last litter was loaded, Stevenson announced, "And that was the twenty-fourth litter! Time, eight minutes and a half—about twenty seconds per litter! That, ladies and gentlemen, you'll have to admit, is fast work." He gave the enlisted personnel the lion's share of the credit not only for loading patients quickly and efficiently but also for the success of air evacuation, adding, "Together with the flight nurses and the flight surgeons, they're making history—medical history, and world history."[25]

Of special interest to the press were the maneuvers in which the flight nurses took part, an aspect of training that provided numerous "photo ops," many undoubtedly arranged by the base's public relations office. In the first phase of training, the flight nurses participated in a weekend bivouac to learn tent-pitching, military sanitation, and camp discipline. In the second phase they went out on three-day maneuvers to apply the practical aspects of their didactic instruction, but now experienced under simulated combat conditions, shown in illustration 3.4.[26] Humorous incidents of flour bombs dropped on troops not sufficiently camouflaged and nighttime raids on unsuspecting sentries taught the flight nurses serious lessons about protecting themselves from the enemy once overseas.

Bivouac, with its opportunity to apply classroom lessons on "principles of medical field service, field sanitation, first aid, mess management and group living," was only one type of maneuvers or military training exercises in which flight nurse students participated. The sec-

3.4 Camouflaged flight nurses on bivouac (USAF photo)

ond flight nurse class, of which Stroup was a member, went on bivouac 23 to 24 March 1943, a few days before its graduation ceremony; the critique prepared by Stroup and classmate Grace Dunnam offers a first-hand account. While marching approximately five miles with field equipment, the nurses encountered two surprise "gas" attacks requiring use of chemical warfare gear. Upon arriving at their campsite, the foot-weary women pitched their tents after watching a tent-pitching demonstration. They did not have to dig their own latrine but did dig an "ablution trench," filling it with water brought in buckets from a nearby farmhouse. They received on-the-spot instruction about mess management and "chow line" formation. Other demonstrations covered the Lyster bag for chemically purified water, improvised first aid, and guard duty.[27]

At the end of bivouac, officers took down their own tents. Six nurses who did not report for roll call at six-fifteen that morning had to police the nurses' area for trash. Before departing, all officers walked the length of their area in line, picking up paper and lost articles. They then returned to base. Two of the problems Dunnam and Stroup identified in their critique were missing tent ropes, which would have been caught had equipment been checked before starting, and the need for more practical clothing such as thick-soled shoes for marching, two-piece coveralls for women, and bed socks.[28] Once Stroup had progressed from the student role to that of instructor, she added "Recreation—singing by campfire" to the bivouac activities for the third flight nurse class.[29]

Graduation marked the culmination of the flight nurses' time at Bowman Field, and the right to wear flight nurse wings. As 819 MAES unit historian June Sanders, who graduated from the course in January 1944, wrote, "Believe me! They weren't handed to us on a silver platter. We wear them with the knowledge that we successfully completed a difficult course."[30] After graduation, many of the new flight nurses were assigned to one of the recently activated MAES at Bowman Field awaiting orders for shipment overseas. Because deployment was not immediate, prior to mobilization these post-graduate flight nurses worked in their squadrons and participated in other activities such as flights to Stout Field in Indianapolis; laboratory work at the base hospital, Louisville General Hospital downtown, and Fort Knox down the road; and visits to the radio tower in Louisville. Newbeck was one of six post-graduate flight nurses sent to Thermal, California, to evacuate ill and injured soldiers—"the troops that Patton left behind"—who had participated in a training exercise prior to the invasion of North Africa.[31]

New graduates still participated in physical training with the flight nurse students every afternoon, but they were exempt from the Saturday morning inspections of barracks.[32] Inspections were no small matter, so to be exempt from them was reward indeed. These inspections taught the nurses military discipline, sanitation, and how to conduct inspections as officers in charge of enlisted troops. Beds, furniture, floors, windows, clothing, and extraneous articles all had to be made up, cleaned, and arranged the GI way, in accordance with illustrated instructions given to each flight nurse. On 20 March 1943, fifteen members of the 803, 804, and 805 MAES learned just how particular the inspectors could be. Nine of the women were written up for their beds, five for shoes improperly placed, and someone had forgotten to remove the laundry hanging in the second-floor bathroom.[33]

Some graduate flight nurses replaced flight nurses already serving overseas; departed Bowman Field on temporary detached duty, as was Newbeck; or, much later in the war, reported to army air forces hospitals elsewhere while awaiting the call for air evacuation duty.[34] They were still without official flight nurse wings, however.

Having created flight nurse wings on his own, without approval or authorization of the War Department, Grant encountered difficulty making good his word. No insignia manufacturer would make them, so flight nurses made do with the gold flight surgeon's wings, to which they had a dentist solder an "N," shown in illustration 3.5. A memorandum for the chief of staff on the subject "Special Badge for Flight Nurses" cited among the reasons army nurses designated as flight nurses should have a distinctive badge was that flight nurse wings would serve as a reward and compensation for the flight nurse, whose work required "special training, special knowledge, and regular and frequent aerial flights" over and beyond that of other army nurses.[35] Grant finally received approval for flight nurse insignia from Major General Arnold, chief of staff of the army air forces, after a delay of about six months, when the two officers

3.5 Flight nurse wings, 1943 (USAF photo)

landed at Bowman Field and Grant brought up the subject.[36] In 1944, to conform to other aviation badges, silver replaced the gold metal for the insignia.[37]

School of Air Evacuation

Because the 349th Air Evacuation Group was classified technically as a tactical unit, it had difficulty securing the needed support for training purposes. For this reason, in June 1943 the War Department dissolved it and created the Army Air Forces School of Air Evacuation—an administrative change only—to make the necessary resources more readily available for teaching "professional, technical, tactical and administrative procedures involved in the air evacuation of the sick and wounded."[38] The six-week course acquainted the flight nurses, enlisted surgical technicians and medical and administrative officers, now trained as complete squadrons, with their special responsibilities for "administering medical treatment, classifying patients, loading patients on the plane, and treatment while in the air."[39] At the conclusion of training, these personnel were ready as a group for further training or assignment overseas.

In 1943 the School of Air Evacuation had only two nurses on its staff. Lieutenant Mary Leontine, who had been in the army since 1940 and at

Bowman Field since January 1943 to help organize the school, was the chief nurse and handled administrative matters concerning the nurses in training.[40] Like Stroup, Leontine had been assigned to her staff position in the school before attending the flight nurse course; she graduated with the third class on 14 May 1943. As the sole nurse instructor of flight nurses, Lieutenant Stroup was responsible for their training at Bowman Field. Both nurses eventually pinned on captain's rank in recognition of their outstanding work in the School of Air Evacuation. In addition, Stroup was promoted from instructor to assistant superintendent, based on the recommendation of Lieutenant Colonel Stevenson, who, as commandant of the School of Air Evacuation, wrote: "Lt. Stroup is reliable, intelligent, has initiative, is persevering, conscientious and is an excellent organizaer [sic] and leader."[41]

Along with the new School of Air Evacuation designation came delineation of Stroup's duties. As instructor of flight nurses for the department of aviation medicine and nursing, she was responsible for planning, supervising, and teaching the daily flight nurse training program in the classroom, on scheduled flights, and in the field.[42] An undated document from the Army Air Forces School of Air Evacuation, Bowman Field, Kentucky, possibly written by Stroup herself, lists and describes in detail fifteen duties pertaining to the office of the nurse in the department of training. It was a demanding and diverse job description for one individual, which was perhaps the point of spelling out the duties, for the anonymous writer added a note at the bottom of the list: "An assistant nurse in the Department of Training seems indicated by the above numerous duties."[43] Orders issued from the School of Air Evacuation in June 1944 reflected a realignment of staff personnel and duties. Captain Stroup became assistant to the principal chief nurse, and Lieutenant Anne M. Baran was named officer in charge of the nurses section in the department of training.[44] Baran, a 13 August 1943 flight nurse graduate, took over Stroup's classes on aeromedical nursing.[45]

Swimming class was added to flight nurse training in the summer of 1943. "What is gained if, after months of costly training, a soldier is lost in two minutes with the capsizing of a ship or while trying to reach shore from an invasion barge?" air forces officials asked. These same officials reasoned that "a soldier psychologically prepared to overcome fear of deep water, even when fully dressed and heavily equipped," and who has knowledge of functional swimming, has more confidence and "is far less likely to become a casualty of drowning."[46] For flight and medical crews whose aircraft might have to ditch at sea, water survival was an ongoing concern. "Kicks from Nurses," read the caption above a picture of flight nurses in swimsuits and caps practicing their kicks in a Louisville pool.[47] A historian for the 803 MAES wrote of the compulsory swimming classes: "Some of the nurses and men had no desire to swim, but there is no place for crocheters in this group, so all learned to swim or sink. None sank."[48]

The flight nurse course continued with no major changes in the program of study over the next several months. A master schedule dated 1 August 1943 outlined the training at that time for flight nurses of the Army Air Forces School of Air Evacuation in detail.[49] Adele Edmonds, a member of the seventh class of flight nurses, which graduated on 26 November 1943, recalled that the course was "very rugged. Very rugged. You knew that everything you participated in would make or break you. . . . And bivouacking and marching and constantly being on the run to go to class or to do something—your day was just terrifically full. You'd be exhausted at night. . . . And we just used to talk about these things and wondered how you could ever survive war, actual war, which we knew we were eventually going to be in when we finished."[50]

A glance at the weekly schedule for Edmonds's class confirms her assessment. Mondays through Fridays were filled with classroom work, practical demonstrations, swimming, physical training and drill, occasional examinations, and retreats and parades. Saturday morning classroom work was followed by the weekly inspection.[51] Saturday afternoons might be filled with flying time or field maneuvers. One Saturday was spent at Maxwell Field in Montgomery, Alabama, where students spent time in the low-pressure chamber during which all but one nurse started out wearing oxygen masks. To demonstrate the effects of hypoxia or oxygen deprivation at high altitude, a lone nurse volunteer left her mask off for the "flight" up to thirty-thousand feet, then she donned her own mask. Dorothy Vancil, in the same class as Edmonds, recalled her experience in the low-pressure chamber, for she feared it might have gotten her a third demerit; she already had one for putting her hands in her pockets and another for returning late from pass. It was a large class of one hundred students, and word had gotten out that only fifty would graduate. "We saluted our shadow. We were scared silly!" Vancil recalled. She explained that when her ears started bothering her, the technician asked her if they hurt. She replied, "Not really, they are just a little uncomfortable." He then "put her out" of the chamber, but not the girls who were crying from ear pain. "And, oh, I thought, *My gosh, I should have cried,*" Vancil recalled, instead of trying to yawn and blow her nose to clear her ears. But it did not count as a demerit after all.[52] The class went out on bivouac for three days in the final week of training. Then it was time to prepare for graduation.

At the end of each course, the new graduates received their flight nurse designations in ceremonies attended by visiting dignitaries, one of whom delivered the graduation address. On 26 November 1943, the speaker was again the air surgeon, now Major General Grant. In his speech, Grant remarked that the flight nurses who had been trained carefully and had mastered successfully the instructions given them now had an understanding of the problems of nursing and knowledge of the theory of nursing in the air. He concluded:

Now you go to the greatest adventure, the greatest experience, the greatest work of all—actually doing the job.

And so you must go beyond your training—beyond the line of duty when called upon—cheerfully, willingly, gloriously. I know you will. You have pledged yourselves to a nurse's creed, a noble way of life. May I suggest a further resolve for each of you flight nurses in this great school?

I will summon every resource to prevent the triumph of death over life.

I will stand guard over the medicines and equipment entrusted to my care and insure their proper use.

I will be untiring in the performance of my duties, and will remember that upon my disposition and spirit will in large measure depend the morale of my patients.

I will be faithful to my training and to the wisdom handed down to me by those who have gone before me.

I have taken a nurse's oath reverent in man's mind because of the spirit and work of its creator, Florence Nightingale. She, I remember, was called the "lady with the lamp."

It is now my privilege to lift this lamp of hope and faith and courage in my profession to heights not known by her in her time. Together with the help of flight surgeons and surgical technicians I can set the very skies ablaze with life and promise for the sick, injured and wounded who are my sacred charge.

This I will do. I will not falter. In war or in peace.[53]

These words became known as the Flight Nurse's Creed and were printed on the graduation program of the seventh and later classes.

Lengthening the flight nurse course to eight weeks in 1943 gave time for instruction on ward management and operating room technique and two weeks of specialized training at cooperating hospitals in Louisville. Each nurse was teamed with an enlisted surgical technician and taught him about intravenous therapy, catheterization, oxygen administration, and other emergency procedures.[54] The work also served as a refresher course for the nurses who had not worked in hospitals recently. Dorothy White, a member of the flight nurse class graduating on 2 July 1943, assigned to the 807 MAES, recalled the benefits of the hospital practicum for her three enlisted surgical technicians—who had been "mechanics or printers or plumbers or something in civilian life"—at Louisville General Hospital. Together with the help of White and a willing patient, the men learned how to care for a patient with a tracheotomy. Each of White's technicians eventually encountered such a patient when he was the only attendant on an air evacuation flight and told her afterward, as White recalled, "Thanks, Whitey, for teaching me how to do that, because I knew what to do when I saw that metal tube hanging out of that fellow's throat."[55]

Not all squadron members embraced this opportunity to return to the hospital setting, however. Members of the 815 MAES, who spent half-days at local hospitals while in training at the School of Air Evacuation, found the work "distasteful," because few of the patients on the wards were the type likely to be encountered in the air evacuation of war casualties.[56]

In theory at least, a nurse would always fly with the same technician, so the training dyad was a way of strengthening this working relationship. It also offered much-needed practical experience for the enlisted surgical technicians who lacked some of the nursing skills required of them on air evacuation flights. Beginning in 1944, enlisted technicians had already completed a six-week course in field medicine at another base before starting their specialized air evacuation training.[57]

Chief Nurse Leontine's request that the flight nurse graduates write to her about their air evacuation experiences once they had left Bowman Field helped her determine how training could prepare students best for the situations they actually would encounter in their work overseas and stateside. After explaining how the nurses worked out flight assignments along their air evacuation route, Lieutenant Miriam Britton, whose squadron—the 805 MAES—flew with the ATC in Alaska, told Captain Leontine in August 1943 about one of her trips. "We find that one of the hardest things to do is to keep the boys entertained on the 6 hr trip from our station," Britton wrote. Magazines and playing cards, food and coffee all helped pass the time in flight. Few problems that her squadron encountered merited attention in the training program, Britton said. "The problem of property exchange is probably the biggest headache, for someone is always wanting to give something inferior to what they are getting." Experience had taught her that the large ambulance chest was not necessary on all trips: "We usually know the type of cases and the Officers Medical Kit is sufficient; but we do take it on all emergencies."[58]

"Fortunately, or unfortunately depending on how you look at it, I had no nursing to do outside of giving the sum total of four A.P.C.s [aspirin, phenacetin, caffeine]," wrote Lieutenant Bernice Stick, a flight nurse with the 808 MAES, to Leontine about her ATC flight from the CBI to Miami in October 1943. "It was a pleasure, however to watch the joy displayed by the boys returning home," she continued. Stick had thought airsickness would be a problem out of Puerto Rico, the first stop in more than sixteen hours of flying that offered fresh milk, malts, and Cokes, but the patients were fine. "All in all, I was not much more than a stewardess without the agony of serving meals but it *is* a beginning. . . . I'm sure as the trips become more frequent, there will be more to report that will be of more interest," the flight nurse concluded.[59]

Louise Anthony, Jenny Boyle, Ethel Carlson, Brooxie Mowery, Denny Nagle, and Frances Sandstrom were among the students graduating from the flight nurse course and marching in a retreat parade on 21 January 1944. Two of their classmates, Stephany J. Kozak and Dymphna M. Van Gorp, were the only United States Navy nurses to attend the army air forces flight nurse course, before the start of the navy's flight nurse program. As with previous classes, training emphasized bivouac as a means to apply didactic classroom instruction to simulated combat conditions in the field. Anthony gave a humorous account of her classmates pitching their tents in the frigid January temperature. It took all day to issue the field equipment—tent pegs, shelter halves, mess kits, canteen and its holder, flashlights, clothing, "everything imaginable"—to the large class.

Then they announce, "All right, fall out in the morning with all your field equipment, and we will show you how to put it together." The weather was so cold, we all wore at least two sets of underwear and our slacks, plus any outer clothing we could put on top. And we fell out. It was dark. These four squadrons lined up . . . and frequently someone would drop a tent peg, and we'd giggle. And they'd bend over to pick up the tent peg and drop their canteen or something else. And then somebody else would try to help pick up one of the things dropped, and she would drop something. And [Edith] Jackson was standing out in front. Each of the flight leaders was standing in front of the squadrons to take the morning report and turn and give it to Jackson, who would turn and give it to the captain standing behind. And Jackson was yelling out periodically, "Attention!" which couldn't be had under the circumstances very easily. And finally she yelled out, "You are supposed to fall in at attention!" And then she added, "To the best of your ability." The captain behind Jackson doubled up laughing—was almost on the ground laughing. . . .

Then when we did go out, . . . the captain who was in charge said . . . , "Is anyone cold?" And there were about twenty of the girls [who] said, "Oh, I'm freezing! Oh, it's so cold, I'm dying!" And I thought, *Jiminy Christmas, why can't they keep their mouths shut?* And all of a sudden he said, "All right. Everybody fall into line." And he ran us around the field about four times—to warm us up.[60]

The flight nurses of Anthony's 816 MAES, who included Boyle, Mowery, and Sandstrom, and those of the 815 MAES, who included Carlson and Nagle, eventually found themselves dealing with a cold British winter during the buildup to D Day and Operation Overlord.

The flight nurse class that began training in January 1944 was the largest to date, though class size had been increasing steadily.[61] Nurses of the 821 MAES who were in the class recalled this "day of days" as "more thrilling than when we graduated from our hospital nurses training, if possible. For on this day we were presented with these coveted little gold wings of a Flight Nurse. It really was a super special occasion. We had been drilled, briefed, rehearsed, lectured, inspected, and cautioned to within an inch of our lives, and well so for our wings were presented to us by Lt. Colonel Nellie V. Close of the Air Surgeon's office."[62] Lieutenant Colonel John McGraw, commandant of the Army Air Forces School of Air Evacuation, and the visiting dignitaries were particularly pleased with the showing of the flight nurses in the celebratory passing in review, which McGraw claimed "was one of the best it has ever been my privilege to witness."[63] Alice Krieble and Blanche Solomon were among the new flight nurses on parade.

School of Aviation Medicine

In October 1944 the responsibility for training flight nurses and enlisted surgical technicians was transferred from the School of Air Evacuation, which was subsequently closed, to the Army Air Forces School of Aviation Medicine at Randolph Field in San Antonio, Texas. This school was already preparing flight surgeons and aviation medical examiners and was prepared to absorb the activity of the former School of Air Evacuation as the division of air evacuation training.[64]

After its relocation, the flight nurse course was lengthened from eight weeks to nine, divided into three equal phases. The first two covered subjects required of all medical personnel plus material specific to air evacuation and concluded with a four-day bivouac. As was the case with previous classes, to test their physical fitness and adaptability to the primitive field conditions found in forward areas of battle zones, the nurses experienced simulated ground and air attacks on their march to the campsite. Once at their destination, they had to camouflage the entire area, complete an exercise in map and compass reading, protect themselves against simulated chemical warfare attacks, and engage in an evacuation exercise.[65]

During the final phase of the program, flight nurses and enlisted technicians flew on missions transporting sick and wounded soldiers to hospitals within the continental United States under the watchful eye of an accompanying instructor. Using what they had learned about aeromedical physiology and the effects of altitude, nurse-technician teams bandaged wounds; treated patients for shock; administered plasma, drugs, and oxygen; and helped with in-flight feeding.[66] Given the high numbers of neuropsychiatric patients evacuated by air, especially from the Pacific, their treatment in flight was an important focus of instruction.[67]

Staff considered these training flights "the most important part" of the flight nurse course, because they helped determine a student's suitability for air evacuation duty in support of the actual mission of patient transport. In 1945, Captain Ellen Church, who had flown with the 802 MAES on the European front, coordinated the flight nurse training for the division of air evacuation training. Several flight nurses who had returned from overseas duty or had flown in the United States augmented Church's staff to provide the nurse supervision on training flights.[68]

As information reached the school from air evacuation squadrons overseas, flight nurse training was revised to reflect problems addressed. The course favored practical instruction in the field over didactic teaching of the same material. The hours devoted to patient litter loading and simulated evacuation were doubled from nine to eighteen, for example, and a class titled "Personal Safety in Aircraft Emergencies" was added to the curriculum.[69]

While training the first thousand flight nurses during her two years as instructor and assistant plans and training officer at Bowman Field, Captain Stroup must have longed more than once to join the departing squadrons mobilized for air evacuation duty overseas. The war was still in progress on both the European and Pacific fronts, and Stroup, like other patriotic nurses, may have wanted to experience it firsthand. In 1943 the *Cincinnati Enquirer* reported, Stroup "looks forward to the day when her orders send her to lead a group of nurses to a battlefield to bring back wounded."[70] At last she was given an opportunity to apply the training she had coordinated beyond the class setting when she received orders for duty overseas. She went to Hickam Field, Hawaii, with the newly activated 828 MAES in August 1944. The squadron was disbanded in October of that year and absorbed into the 830 MAES.[71] Stroup's ultimate position, which she assumed in December 1944, was as chief flight nurse of the Pacific division of ATC.[72]

In August 1945, after the American bombing of Hiroshima and Nagasaki brought the war in the Pacific to an end, the flight nurse course was cut back to six weeks—with two weeks for each of the three phases—in anticipation of the increased number of flight nurses needed in the Pacific. Between December 1942 and October 1944, 1,079 flight nurses had trained at Bowman Field. Another 330 earned their wings from the course at Randolph Field between November 1944 and September 1945.[73] Only 15 of 435 flight nurse students failed to graduate with their classes between November 1944 and June 1946, for reasons of airsickness, physical disqualification, and academic failure. Most of the other nongraduates simply had decided against a flying job.[74]

"Many are called, but few are chosen" was the description Lieutenant Colonel Meiling, chief, operations division, office of the air surgeon, gave regarding the selection and preparation of personnel for air evacuation duty.[75] His use of the biblical analogy was particularly apt in the case of flight nurse training: in 1943, the first year of the program, twenty times more nurses volunteered than were selected for the course.[76] During World War II only five hundred or so nurses served with air evacuation squadrons.[77] The other wartime graduates of the flight nurse course returned to ground duty while awaiting the opportunity to put their new training to use in the air. Members of earlier classes had a better chance of reaching that goal, since nurses typically received air evacuation assignments in order of their graduation dates.[78]

★ ★ ★ **04**

From Flight Nurse Graduation to Arrival Overseas

For some flight nurses, the interim between earning their wings and participating in air evacuation in the real world seemed like an eternity. The first verse of the "803rd Lament," written by Lieutenants Elsie Ott and Georgia Insley "while lying on cot waiting final movement orders at Bowman Field, Kentucky, July, 1943" and sung to the tune "It Ain't Necessarily So," depicts the sense of limbo in which the newly minted flight nurses sometimes found themselves:

> The Squadron is ready to go
> But orders are coming in slow.
> We wait without ranker
> To get on a Tanker
> Because we are ready to go.[1]

Orders *could* be slow in coming, as the eleven verses of this lament suggest. But the 803 MAES, like the squadrons that would follow, eventually did depart Bowman Field for the actual work of air evacuation overseas. Of the thirty-one MAES activated between 11 November 1942 and 8 November 1944, ten went to the United Kingdom in preparation for D Day—the 806, 810, and 811 MAES, and the 813 through 819 MAES. Nine—the 801, 804, 809, 812, 820, and 828 through 831 MAES—went to various locations in the Pacific, most of them flying with ATC. Another eleven were assigned as needed to Alaska; Africa; China, Burma, and India; Sicily and Italy; the North Atlantic; the South Atlantic; and the United States. The 826 MAES was disbanded while still at Bowman Field and its members incorporated into the 830 MAES for eventual duty in the Pacific.

Getting to those locations often involved shared discomforts of troop trains, staging for overseas shipment, and transport across potentially hazardous seas. Before relating the experiences of flight nurses engaged in air evacuation duty, beginning with their journeys overseas, it is helpful to understand how the medical air evacuation squadrons were formed and where they were assigned, how flight nurses spent their time between being assigned to a squadron and departing Bowman Field, and what flight nurses encountered initially on arrival at their overseas locations.

Medical Air Evacuation Squadrons

Air evacuation duty usually began with a nurse's assignment, either before or after her flight nurse training, to one of the twenty-nine MAES activated at Bowman Field.[2] The former plan, which began after June 1943, gave the squadron of flight surgeons, flight nurses, enlisted technicians, and support personnel a longer time to gel—to build esprit de corps—and become acquainted with each other and with their duties before shipment overseas. Together they accomplished administrative tasks, post-graduate training while still at Bowman Field that included additional bivouacs and other field maneuvers, and procurement and preparation of equipment and supplies for overseas shipment. For flight surgeon Morris Kaplan, 803 MAES commander whose squadron was destined for the CBI, it was "an opportunity to weed the boys from the men, and the crocheter from the real women."[3] The time could also provide opportunities for squadrons to perfect their air evacuation skills on stateside missions.

Chief nurses were appointed and flight nurses selected for each squadron while at Bowman Field, though the squadron to which a nurse was assigned initially was not necessarily the squadron with which she would depart for overseas. Transfers among squadrons were common to bring squadrons nearing deployment up to their authorized number of personnel. Occasionally such a transfer was life-changing. Agnes Jensen had been assigned initially to the 809 MAES, which had only about twelve of its twenty-five nurses at the time. She was not very happy waiting at Bowman Field for the nurses who would fill out the squadron quota. When the commanding officer and chief nurse of the 807 MAES offered her a transfer, Jensen gladly accepted the chance to deploy sooner. She was among the 807 MAES nurses on a plane that crashed in enemy-occupied Albania (see chapter 6).[4]

Some of the newly formed squadrons participated in final maneuvers before departing Bowman Field for distant shores. Lieutenant Katherine Hack of the 821 MAES recalled her squadron's three-day bivouac, which began on 13 March 1944, two days after the flight nurses had graduated. The exercise followed the usual pattern of a long march punctuated by simulated attacks, setting up the campsite, walking guard, and participating in field problems, terminating with an informal program around a campfire on the last night. "Hot dogs and coffee were served, the fire began to die out and we all reluctantly took leave, knowing it would be a long time before we could enjoy this sort of thing in the U.S. again."[5]

Even more demanding than these wartime scenarios encountered during bivouac may have been the daytime infiltration course at nearby Fort Knox. Hack related the 821 MAES flight nurses' performance on that course the day after the squadron's return. Members of the press had arrived to "take in the atmosphere. One, a Mr. Parsonette, connected with one of the film studios, was invited to join us. For he had been flickering off and on in the background since bivouac, and some time before that. He very suavely replied that being a man he would be unable to truly capture a feminine reaction to going through the infiltration course. He was assured that the experience he would find there knew no sex." The nurses "rolled, crawled, wiggled and slithered through the mud, under barbed wire through the [ditches] abundant with water, to the staccato refrains of the machine guns. When the final ditch was completed, we truly were a sight to behold. Our fatigues were soaked with a most tenacious variety of Kentucky mud. From this day on we ceased to refer to ourselves as 'Female Cadets' thinking 'Female Commandos' more fitting."[6] Successful completion of this difficult rite of passage was a point of pride among the flight nurses and a boost to squadron morale and sportsmanship.[7]

Kaplan, who observed the progress of the 803 MAES flight nurses through the infiltration course following their graduation from training in May 1943, concluded: "I felt that if all 25 girls could take that beating, then I could take them anywhere. I had just finished it myself through much less dust than they and had wanted to quit a dozen times. It was certainly the hardest physical work I had ever done as it consisted essentially of doing 150 pushups and the temperature was 105."[8] The 803 MAES flight nurses filled their remaining days at Bowman Field gaining proficiency on the firing range and learning to drive jeeps and trucks. They also learned the intricacies of packing a parachute. Months later one nurse in that squadron had reason to recall this lesson—and the instructor's sarcastic comment that she could always exchange her parachute if it failed—when she had to put it to the ultimate test over the mountains of China (see chapter 10).[9]

Destination Overseas

The time finally arrived when each MAES left Bowman Field—often under cover of darkness—on secret orders to a staging base on the east or west coast to await shipment overseas. Travel across the United States was usually by troop train. Lee Holtz, assigned to the 801 MAES, remembered that her name was among twelve called out one day to report to the office, where they received overseas orders. Specific instructions on what to take with them followed, but no word on where they were being sent. Holtz thought the middle-of-the-night departure in a truck "ridiculous." Once on the train, the nurses still did not know where they were going, but in daylight they discovered they were heading west, to Camp Stoneman in California.[10]

Ethel Carlson, whose 815 MAES traveled by troop train to the east coast, remembered the time spent at Camp Kilmer, New Jersey, as filled with passing physical examinations; getting all kinds of shots; receiving new olive-drab uniforms, field packs, and other equipment; and "having a ball" taking the train into New York City to enjoy Broadway shows.[11] It was also a time to get one's personal affairs—such as allotments, power of attorney, and life insurance—in order and to check and recheck one's military records, clothing, and equipment. Blood types were checked and dog tags restamped. The flight nurses of the 816 MAES, who with the 815 MAES also awaited shipment overseas from Camp Kilmer, found that their chief nurse had a sense of humor when dealing with some of the more unrealistic demands of military life. The squadron was at Camp Kilmer during winter, when it was very cold, and someone complained to the chief nurse that her flight nurses were not standing reveille in the mornings. Louise Anthony continued the story: "And she said, 'Well, we're shipping out overseas. And if you think I'm going to make them stand it out in the cold, and they'll catch pneumonia or something else—they're standing it inside.' So she called a meeting and told us about it, and she said, 'You are standing reveille every morning.' She said, 'I don't care if you stand it in bed. But you are standing reveille.'"[12]

A squadron's stay at the staging area could last from days to weeks; regardless, the wait seemed endless to some nurses who were impatient to start their new duties. One nurse thought, "We're never going to get out of here. . . . Let's quit and do something—do some nursing." She talked it over with her chief nurse and decided to stay when she heard that the squadron would be alerted for shipment the next day. But she remembered, "We had heard that so many times."[13]

The day of overseas deployment for a squadron's flight nurses finally did arrive, and they reported to the port of embarkation. When the 821 MAES personnel arrived at Hampton Roads, Virginia, the morning of 23 May 1944 to depart on the USS *General George M. Randall,* gay tunes played by a swing band on the dock greeted them, "Presumably to reinforce spirits lagging at the realization they were about to leave the U.S.A." Other kind gestures were a bit impractical, however: "Red Cross women were eagerly offering hot coffee right and left, but what could we take with both hands full?"[14]

Although some squadrons activated late in 1943 and in 1944 made the trip by plane, most made lengthy ocean voyages on crowded troop ships zigzagging through potentially dangerous seas in convoy or alone, with or without air cover. Clara Morrey, whose 802 MAES was the first to travel overseas by ship, recalled, "They always told us that we were in 'coffin corner,' in other words, the one [ship] that was most likely to be hit."[15] Troops took daily lifeboat drills seriously, in case of an "Abandon Ship" alert. The unit historian of the 801 MAES, the second squadron to embark on an ocean crossing, held a similarly dreary view of that squadron's "wretched" twenty-day sea journey on the *Tisadane*, an old Dutch merchant ship. A rumor circulated that the ship was sunk on a later voyage, "but the consensus of all who were on her this trip, was that it should have happened long before and saved a lot of suffering."[16]

Seasickness was a problem for some flight nurses. Carlson of the 815 MAES was sick for what she remembered as four days of her ship's four-and-a-half-day journey: "I was so seasick I wanted to die, and I was afraid I wasn't going to."[17] Other nurses, determined not to get seasick, found more pleasant ways to occupy their time aboard ship. Fresh air, shipboard romances, card games, shuffleboard, and working in the ship dispensary kept them healthy during their sea journey. Daily lectures and calisthenics rounded out the 803 MAES flight nurses' activities while in transit.[18]

Several women vividly remembered arrival at their overseas locations. The sound of bagpipes greeted them in Scotland; in London the effect of a recent bombing raid was evident in the broken glass at Paddington Station. A nurse who expected North Africa to be hot and full of steamy jungles encountered bitterly cold temperatures at a location still under air attack following a siege. Another found beauty in the contrasting colors and sounds of Central Africa. A blackout greeted nurses arriving in the Pacific. Nabors of the 812 MAES recalled her reluctant attendance at a colonel's afternoon tea the day after her arrival in Hawaii. Tired from her ocean voyage, she had not heeded the invitation. She was sleeping when a knock on the door was followed by the message: "Well, it wasn't an invitation. It's a command performance—you must go to this."[19]

Once the flight nurses had arrived for overseas duty, their locations often determined their experiences. Living conditions were not the same in a converted English mansion as in a Pacific Quonset hut; flying the skies above Alaska differed markedly from flying over the Hump. But they all had in common the nuts and bolts of their airborne work environment, the crewmembers with whom they performed their missions, other squadron personnel, and the protocol to be followed in performance of air evacuation.

Air Evacuation Aircraft

The most commonly used plane for air evacuation was the C-47 Skytrain, shown in illustration 4.1. This almost indestructible two-engine airplane, a military version of the DC-3 commercial airliner, was the reliable workhorse of the army air forces during World War II. Able to withstand inclement weather and enemy fire, the C-47 could fly into primitive airfields constructed in recently secured Allied territory. Fully loaded, it could carry twenty-five ambulatory patients, eighteen to twenty-four litter patients, or a combination of both. Metal litter brackets that attached to the bulkhead were standard aircraft equipment early in the war, but they added considerable weight to the plane and allowed only eighteen litter patients. The sturdy webbing strips that replaced the metal brackets beginning in 1944 attached to the ceiling and the floor of the plane and could accommodate twenty-four litter patients. Litters were arranged in tiers of three to maximize available space, shown in illustration 4.2; the "walking wounded" sat in the standard aircraft bucket seats.[20]

The flight nurses of the 821 MAES in the CBI had the good fortune to fly air evacuation missions on the *Miss Nightingale II,* one of three C-47 aircraft the Women's International Bowling Congress purchased and presented to the army air forces for use as air ambulances. Funded by female bowlers in response to the "Give Your Dollar Wings of Mercy" campaign, the aircraft made its maiden flight on 15 March 1945 with Lieutenants Clara Dillon, Jane Haynes, and Laura Revel on board as flight nurses.[21] This aircraft, the *Holly Cholly II,* and four other airplanes used by the 803 MAES apparently were unique in their exterior display of the Geneva Red Cross, perhaps because the cargo on the inbound flight consisted of medical supplies and equipment. Although two flight nurses with the 812 MAES in the Pacific recalled flying in planes identified with a red cross, by Geneva Convention regulations, any plane also used to transport war matériél and personnel could not fly under the protection of the Geneva Red Cross.

The C-46 Commando was the largest two-engine transport plane in the army air forces' inventory during World War II. This aircraft achieved its fame flying cargo from India over the Himalayan Mountains—the Hump—into China. As an air evacuation aircraft, the C-46 could transport up to thirty-three litter patients, thirty-seven ambulatory patients, or a combination of both.[22] The C-46 allegedly flew better in rough weather and on one engine than the C-47, but some aircrew members nicknamed it the "flying coffin" because of its shape and the occasional tendency of its gas-powered heaters to malfunction with disastrous results.[23]

The 820 MAES flight nurses in the Pacific did much of their flying in the C-46 with inexperienced pilots who did not attempt to hide their criticism and distrust of the aircraft. The continued disparaging remarks troubled the squadron's flight surgeon because they drained the flight nurses' morale. Such behavior needed to be checked, he said, because it could affect the success of air evacuation missions adversely.[24]

The C-54 Skymaster, the military version of the DC-4 civilian aircraft, was the airplane of choice for the longer air evacuation flights over water. With its four engines, large cargo space, great range, and high speed, the C-54 was well suited for flights from overseas to the United States. It could accommodate more patients than could the smaller C-46 and C-47—as many as thirty-six litter patients, thirty-one to forty-five ambulatory patients, or a combination of both, depending on the fuel requirement for the trip.[25]

Although it was a high-flying, long-range bomber rather than a cargo aircraft, if necessary the durable four-engine B-17 Flying Fortress could be outfitted with web strips to carry ten litter patients and up to twenty ambulatory patients. Air evacuation squadrons in both Europe and the Pacific transported patients on the B-17 when other aircraft were unavailable.

The CG-4A glider was an aircraft without motor or propellers; it became airborne when the hook at the end of a cable on a low-flying

4.1 C-47 Skytrain in Europe (author's collection)

4.2 Aircraft interior configured for air evacuation (author's collection)

C-47 tow plane snagged a towrope on the stationary CG-4A, sweeping it into the air. The glider was then released in flight, and a pilot guided it to the designated landing site. During the war, the Allies used the CG-4A to transport military supplies, equipment, and personnel into areas with no airstrip. On 22 March 1945, two CG-4A gliders transported wounded soldiers from the Remagen bridgehead, the point of the first successful Allied crossing of the Rhine River into Germany. Flight nurse Suella Bernard and flight surgeon Albert Haug, both from the 816 MAES, each rode in a glider modified to accommodate litter and ambulatory patients and towed by C-47s. Both flights were successful, and within fifteen minutes the patients arrived at the door of an evacuation hospital at Euskirchen, on the west side of the Rhine.[26]

In a 1984 letter to her colleague Louise Anthony, Suella Bernard recalled her air evacuation mission on a glider. They had to wait "quite a long time" for the patients to arrive, and when the C-47 tow ship lifted the glider, one of the ropes holding a tier of three patients broke. Two men struggled to resecure it. Bernard was "terribly concerned" about her patients, one of whom had a completely bandaged head. One of the wheels on the glider collapsed on what was an otherwise smooth landing, and the aircraft came to a stop near a fence, but all the patients tolerated the flight well.[27]

Crewmembers and Squadron Personnel

In addition to the pilot and copilot, the C-47 included among its crew a navigator, radio operator, and crew chief. Other cargo aircraft had essentially the same complement of crewmembers. On air evacuation missions, these nonmedical personnel were boons to the flight nurse in numerous ways. Pilots considered flight nurses' requests to fly at lower altitudes when a patient's condition necessitated it and even diverted the aircraft to the nearest airfield where a patient could be rushed to a hospital for immediate emergency care. But some pilots apparently honored these requests begrudgingly and others not at all. By regulation, when a plane was carrying patients with chest wounds, the pilot was not to fly above three thousand feet, but lower altitudes often required flying through low clouds and turbulent air, which were equally bad for wounded men. In addition, when litter patients were on board, pilots were not to bank their planes at more than a twenty-degree angle, which necessitated much slower approaches to landing strips.[28]

Although it might not have been their first choice of assignment, some pilots enjoyed flying missions with flight nurses on board, as this excerpt from "Troop Carrier Song—New Guinea" reveals:

> I'd rather fly a fighter than a transport any day
> I'd rather fly a fortress than a biscuit-bomb at Lae
> But when I see the Nurses you can bet I'll always say
> I'll fly the Nurses home.
>
> Chorus
> Glory, Glory, that's the way I want to fight
> Glory, Glory, that's the way I want to fight
> Glory, Glory, that's the way I want to fight
> Just flying the Nurses home.[29]

Radio operators provided the means for the flight nurse to ask for a flight surgeon and ambulance to be waiting at a patient's destination. The crew chief helped load patients and scrounge for equipment and supplies on board for improvised medical uses. In some cases, they provided the brawn required to subdue an out-of-control patient. After the war, Martin Wolfe, who had been a radio operator on a C-47, wrote, "There was one job no one ever had to command us to do: help handle wounded soldiers."[30] When there were not enough enlisted surgical technicians and ambulance crews to load and off-load the patients for an air evacuation mission, the flight crews would hang around, glad to pitch in when needed.

Less has been written about the enlisted surgical technicians assigned to MAES than about the flight nurses, but their work on air evacuation missions was no less important or heroic. When selected for this duty, these men held the rating of technician third grade (T/3), the pay-grade equivalent of staff sergeant. Some flight surgeons thought "surgical technician" was an erroneous designation, since most of the men had only basic training or very limited operating room training before joining the MAES. They were more correctly classified as nursing orderlies or medical technicians.[31]

Early in the war, air evacuation technicians were recruited from military medical installations and brought to the Army Air Forces School of Air Evacuation at Bowman Field for training. They had already completed a basic three-week course in first aid, camouflage, and other aspects of fieldwork prior to their arrival. Work at the School of Air Evacuation was both didactic and practical. Courses in emergency medical treatment of patients, using metal brackets or web strips to convert cargo planes to ambulance planes, loading and unloading patients, and equipment use provided the skills fundamental to their new work. The care of psychotic patients was another important aspect of instruction. Training flights, maneuvers, and bivouacs rounded out their program of study.

The training of air evacuation technicians, like that of flight nurses, went through changes in length and content to meet the needs of students and the wartime situations in which they would work. With the October 1944 move of air evacuation training from Bowman Field to Randolph Field, the course for enlisted technicians placed increased emphasis on aerospace medicine and therapeutics, particularly the effects of altitude on patient care. At the School of Aviation Medicine, as had been the case at the School of Air Evacuation, training flights in which flight nurse–enlisted technician teams engaged in the actual transportation of patients within the United States let the medical crews apply their knowledge to the work they would undertake as members of MAES overseas.[32]

In reality, the enlisted technicians often worked as the sole medical crewmember on an air evacuation flight. Although they were trained to work with flight nurses, the number of patients needing transport sometimes required that nurse and technician fly in separate planes to accommodate them. When the medical teams were split, the flight nurse usually attended the more seriously wounded litter patients on one plane, and the technician provided the care for the less critical ambulatory patients on another. And a much-contested policy in effect in some theaters of operation dictated that because of the danger associated with air evacuation flights into some forward combat areas, only male attendants, not female flight nurses, could staff these missions.[33]

Transforming these enlisted technicians from "farmers, cowboys, carpenters, truck drivers and factory workers" into medical technicians to whom the flight surgeons could entrust the nursing care of battle casualties was often a tedious process, according to an unnamed flight surgeon whose 804 MAES was preparing to leave the United States for overseas deployment.[34] MAES commanders typically organized a program of continuing education for squadron members once they arrived at their overseas duty assignment to augment training received at Bowman Field or Randolph Field. When setting up new campsites on Pacific islands, these commanders were often thankful, however, for their enlisted men's diversity of backgrounds. Leopold Snyder, who headed a detachment of the 804 MAES sent to Biak, reported that thanks to their civilian life skills, the men could do anything. "Carpentering, construction, plumbing, blasting, wiring for electricity, running cement mixers all found someone able to handle the job. . . . I can excuse these men of many past and future sins after working thru this period with them."[35]

In addition to the twenty-four enlisted technicians assigned to flying duties, each MAES was authorized thirty-seven more enlisted men who provided the essential ground support to keep the squadron operating at peak efficiency. These unsung heroes of mess, motor pool, and supply—the cooks, bakers, drivers, mechanics, clerks, typists, and guards—were the backbone of the MAES and performed the myriad tasks that allowed the organization to function independently. It was they who, with flight surgeons, comprised the advance cadre of personnel at a new campsite that cleared the land and erected the tents and other portable structures to house and feed the squadron members, store equipment, and provide administrative space. Cooks were praised for their ability to turn wartime food rations into culinary feasts and the supply personnel for their ability to buy, beg, borrow, and barter—or obtain through "midnight requisition" when all else failed—for the comforts and necessities of life and work. The officers of the 816 MAES in Europe credited the nonflying personnel for their squadron's successes, and the unit historian offered an apt football analogy. These men were like linesmen, he said, without whose fundamental and vitally important role the "spectacular" flying personnel backfield would be unable to accomplish their missions.[36] In gestures of appreciation, the flight nurses and flight surgeons in various MAES wined and dined their enlisted men and gave parties and dances in their honor. On one such occasion the officers and nurses of the 803 MAES put themselves on KP duty, to the delight of their enlisted guests.[37]

Mission Protocol

Each MAES set up its operations in coordination with the officials of the command to which it was assigned for operational purposes, whether serving on the European or the Pacific front. Flight surgeons did not routinely fly on air evacuation missions but rather served as liaisons on the ground between the ground and air forces to provide an efficient system of air evacuation at the earliest opportunity.

The air evacuation mission began when the respective MAES head-quarters received word of the number of patients requiring evacuation. The flight nurse selected for the mission, perhaps joined by an enlisted technician, gathered up her gear—medical kit, helmet, gas mask, and canteen. Although Geneva Convention dictated that medical personnel could not be armed, in some locations flight nurses carried pistols as well. Nabors, who flew with the 812 MAES in the Pacific, recalled carrying a gun on missions to Eniwetok, Okinawa, and Leyte. The flight nurses of her squadron had been told to use their guns on themselves if they were captured rather than be taken prisoner, she explained. But she thought it "a terrible thing to have somebody say . . . 'Now use this gun on yourself.'"[38] Holtz of the 801 MAES also remembered having "the pistol under the arm" as part of her equipment for air evacuation missions in the Southwest Pacific.[39] One flight nurse assigned in the Pacific and two assigned to the CBI whose interviews appear in Diane Fessler's *No Time for Fear: Voices of American Military Nurses in World War II* (1996) also recalled carrying guns for protection.[40]

Each plane carried a medical ambulance chest stocked with equipment, supplies, and medications that might be needed for patient care in flight. Some squadrons modified this chest to suit their own particular needs. Content of these kits was essentially standard: portable oxygen; blood plasma; bedpan and urinal; tourniquet and dressing supplies; catheters and lubricating jelly; stethoscope, blood pressure cuff, and thermometer; and alcohol, iodine, and aromatic ammonia. Medications included aspirin and other analgesics; antiemetics; sedatives; quinine; sulfa tablets and powder; and nasal spray. Each flight nurse carried a small medical kit with additional dressing supplies and medications in a canvas musette bag. But because of an incident that had occurred earlier in the war, she carried the most important drug—morphine—in her pocket. Early in the war, the plane in which a flight surgeon from the 801 MAES was attendant on an air evacuation mission crashed. He was thrown from the plane, which immediately caught fire, and was unable to return for supplies and medications to treat the survivors.[41]

What to wear on air evacuation missions was initially a problem for flight nurses overseas. The first flight nurses were expected to wear skirts, like their sister nurses assigned to hospital duty on the ground, even though such a uniform was impractical for air duty. Out of necessity, flight nurses came up with their own, unauthorized uniforms, sometimes modifying men's flight suits to fit them. A humorous story of how the flight nurses finally received authorization to wear slacks as part of their official uniform reveals some savvy and ultimately successful manipulation by the staff of the School of Air Evacuation at Bowman Field after letters submitted through official channels had failed. Two versions of the story differ slightly but have the same outcome.

As part of her job in the office of the army surgeon general, Colonel Florence Blanchfield, who was appointed superintendent of the Army Nurse Corps in July 1943, determined what uniforms her nurses should wear. Because the nurses flying with the army air forces were still army nurses, they fell under her authority on this matter, despite the difference in their assignment. When Blanchfield, wearing a dress uniform that included skirt and high heels, visited Bowman Field, the staff of the School of Air Evacuation took her on a demonstration flight. In one version of the story, the staff members demonstrated how they reached up to the highest litters and down to the lowest ones while dressed in regulation skirt and high heels. In both versions, Blanchfield and the other nurses donned their parachutes for the flight. In the second version of the story, the parachute initially was worn without the mandatory straps fastened between the legs, but when shortly into the flight an engine faltered, the pilot directed all aboard to prepare to jump. At that point, Blanchfield learned firsthand how the straps could not be fastened gracefully while one wore a skirt. With that point made, a few moments later the engine miraculously restarted, and the plane landed smoothly back at the base. Not long afterward, the flight nurses had a new authorized uniform—with slacks.[42]

Dressed for flight duty with gear in hand, the flight nurse and enlisted technician joined combat troops or cargo on board an available cargo plane that flew to the airfield nearest to where the patients were waiting. The cargo could have been anything: mail, money, aircraft parts, cans of gasoline, hand grenades, ammunition, pigs, chickens, ducks, rabbits, horses, or—another efficient means of transporting supplies, especially in mountainous regions—mules.

When a plane's cargo had been removed, the crew quickly converted the aircraft cabin for air evacuation use. Having learned and practiced this at Bowman Field, the enlisted technicians prided themselves on the speed with which they could make an aircraft ready to receive patients. The 803 MAES in the CBI boasted the "crack loading team" that could set up a plane, load eighteen litter patients, and close the doors in a short six minutes.[43] The team snapped unneeded bucket seats back against the walls then secured the metal arms used early in the war or pulled down the strips of sturdy webbing from the ceiling where they had been stored and attached them to the floor.

Before boarding began, the flight surgeon at the loading point screened the patients in the holding area who had been brought to the airstrip, occasionally straight from the battlefield. More typically, patients arrived from field and evacuation hospitals near the front line or, if the airstrip was farther from the fighting, from station and general hospitals. In the absence of a flight surgeon, the flight nurse screened the patients. Although the nurse could refuse any patient who might not survive the flight, she turned few away. On an airstrip under attack, for example, patients would be kept onboard. Flight nurses were scattered across several continents in their duty assignments, but the patients they evacuated by air had injuries that remained relatively consistent: battlefield gunshot and shrapnel wounds; lacerations, fractures, and amputations, often evacuated postoperatively while still under the effects of general anesthesia; burns; and medical problems that included malaria, tuberculosis, respiratory and cardiovascular diseases, and a variety of gastrointestinal complaints.[44] Patients with psychiatric disorders and dermatological conditions were numerous in some combat zones.

After observing a wide range of wounds and illnesses early in the war, flight surgeons determined that most patients could survive air travel at low altitudes with trained medical personnel on board if properly prepared preflight by controlling shock and bleeding, reinforcing dressings, medicating for pain, administering oxygen, sedating and restraining as needed, feeding, and attending to emptying bladders and bowels.[45] As shown in illustration 4.3, the flight nurses supervised while loading teams positioned patients in the aircraft cabin to facilitate their nursing care—head injuries and other serious cases forward, in the most stable part of the plane; bulky casts low because of their weight; injured limbs on the aisle side for easy access.

Although policy dictated that mentally disturbed patients could be accepted for air travel when placed on litters, restrained adequately, and sedated properly, experience showed that these patients presented particular concerns on air evacuation missions. The School of Air Evacuation addressed the need for a standard, reliable, safe form of in-flight restraint for them. Flight surgeons considered the presence of the female flight nurse on flights with mentally disturbed patients therapeutic, as it allayed these patients' fear of air travel.[46]

Nursing care during an air evacuation mission varied according to the length of the trip. Flights removing patients from areas of combat to hospitals farther from the fighting could be as short as twenty minutes. With each successive trip in the chain of evacuation to medical facilities offering more specialized care for patients, flights were longer. Far less could be accomplished in a cross-Channel flight in Europe, lasting under an hour, than in a transoceanic flight in the Pacific, lasting several hours.

4.3 Ada Endres of 801 MAES supervises patient loading at Bougainville, July 1944 (author's collection)

America was fighting two wars geographically, and although its war began and ended in the Pacific, the earliest offensive action was planned to stop Hitler, not avenge the Japanese attacks. The first group of flight nurses sent overseas, therefore, set foot not on a Pacific island, but rather on North African soil in support of the war in Europe. The stories that follow in chapters 5 through 8 recount the role of army flight nurses in the build-up to D Day and the invasion of Fortress Europe that took them from North Africa to Italy, from England to France, and, ultimately, into Germany itself. The experiences of flight nurses assigned to the Pacific front on the islands, in Alaska, and China-Burma-India follow in chapters 9 and 10.

★ ★ ★ 05

Flight Nursing on the European Front: North Africa, Sicily, Italy

The growing importance of air evacuation, improvised during the early months of the war, led the War Department to charge the army air forces officially with developing a comprehensive medical air evacuation system that incorporated intra-theater, inter-theater, and theater–to–United States movements and, in the last months of the war, movement of patients within the United States.[1] MAES provided organization and personnel for all four types of air evacuation. The 802 MAES, which arrived in North Africa a month after Elsie Ott's historic flight from Karachi to the United States, was the first squadron to use flight nurses in day-to-day operations within a theater of war.

Flight Nurses in North Africa

The 802 MAES sailed to North Africa to support the Allies, who were fighting the Italians and the Germans to prevent Axis domination of the Mediterranean. The Operation Torch landings in French North Africa in November 1942 marked the first planned offensive of the war for American troops, and military planners anticipated casualties would need air evacuation in that vast country marked by mountains and desert. Although air evacuation of patients was already under way, with enlisted medics serving as attendants on the planes, flight nurses brought better training and sound, often lifesaving medical decisions, as well as a psychological boost to patients.[2]

Simultaneous amphibious Allied landings on 8 November 1942 in Morocco and Algeria targeted the key ports of Casablanca, Oran, and Algiers. Allied troops then pressed their way into Tunisia, through the Kasserine Pass, on their way to Tunis and Bizerte. In the series of Tunisian campaign offensives and counteroffensives over the next several months, the Allies eventually prevailed, leading to complete surrender of Axis forces in North Africa in May 1943 and setting the stage for the Italian campaign and the invasion of Sicily, which began on 10 July of that year.

When the 802 MAES flight nurses disembarked from the USS *Lyons* at a harbor in Oran on 21 February 1943 after a two-week journey by sea, they scrambled down their ship's debarkation ladder to the dock in full combat gear, because the Algiers docks were still prime targets for air attacks.[3] After a night in a villa in Oran, the flight nurses traveled by truck to a bivouac area where the next night, while dozing warm and dry in their sleeping bags, "they listened to what was then identified as rifle shots in the distance, but which proved, less dramatically in the morning to be the crack of dropping latrine seats." Cold showers every third day in a facility with no roof, chow lines for meals eaten without convenience of a table, and long hikes introduced the newcomers to life in a war zone. Watching outdoor movies and taking photographs of Arabs provided brief respites from the primitive living conditions.[4]

Ten days later, on 3 March 1943, the squadron arrived by plane at its first permanent duty location at Maison Blanche a few miles from Algiers. Clara Morrey laughed as she recalled how the airport personnel reacted to what the flight nurses thought was their arrival at the front lines of battle. The flight nurses had considered themselves "going forward," so had donned all the fleece-lined clothes they had been issued. "And we put our gas masks on. And we noticed everybody out on the deck looking at us, and we found out later that they really got a lot of enjoyment out of seeing us in all that gear."[5]

The soldiers were pleased to have the flight nurses at their base and treated them royally. They had cleaned out the cement French barracks where the flight nurses would stay, Morrey remembered. "And right about ten paces out the back door, they had built us a beautiful private air raid shelter. So we all got down in there and looked around, and that air raid

5.1 The Mediterranean Region

shelter collapsed before we had our first air raid."[6] Air raids were frequent on the docks and harbors nearby. Personnel bombs left for unsuspecting Allied soldiers to discover were another threat to safety, and the flight nurses heeded the warning against picking up stray fountain pens, pencils, cigarette lighters, and other small devices on the ground.[7]

Work was heavy for the 802 MAES, and on shorter flights, the nurses made up to three thirty-minute trips a day with patients. Other flights were longer. The flight nurses and enlisted technicians typically started their flying days at four o'clock in the morning, and after eating breakfast they assembled at the airfield to wait until they were assigned to board planes already loaded with cargo. They did not fly at night, so air evacuation crews often remained away overnight during longer missions. Gunfire and flashes of light at forward airstrips reminded the flight nurses and enlisted technicians just how close they and their patients were to the fighting. Fighter escorts en route during flights immediately following an invasion were a welcome sight in skies in which the flight nurses occasionally viewed aerial dogfights.[8] By the end of May 1943, the squadron had evacuated more than seventeen thousand patients on C-47 and, in the case of walking wounded, C-53 Skytrooper aircraft.[9]

These patients were American and British but also South African, Australian, Indian, Russian, and French soldiers, some fresh from the battlefield.[10] Yet, as flight nurse Henrietta Richardson of the 802 MAES observed, they never complained. "You ask them if they need anything, but you practically have to beat them over the head before they'll admit they would feel better with a dressing changed. 'I'm all right,' they will say. 'Maybe somebody else wants something.'"[11] When time and medical condition allowed, all were fed in flight with Spam sandwiches or K- and C-rations, fruit juice, coffee, and water.[12] Flight nurses changed dressings, gave pain medications, and administered oxygen and blood plasma while taking time to listen to those soldiers who were ready to talk about their wounds. Richardson realized that her presence was just as important to her patients as was attention to their physical comfort; with her listening ear, for the moment, she embodied the mother, wife, sister, and girlfriend they had left behind.[13]

For some flight nurses, the most difficult air evacuation patients were not the physical or mental casualties of the war but rather the enemy prisoners of war (POWs). The 802 MAES had both Italians and Germans as patients. Mixing Allied and enemy patients on board an airplane could have potentially perilous results. *Trained Nurse and Hospital Review* reprinted an act by a flight nurse in the 802 MAES as one of intense human interest and of good nursing: A seriously wounded soldier just hours from the battlefield was one of twenty patients on an air evacuation flight. Suddenly, he left his litter and crawled toward that of a terrified German prisoner. The flight nurse quickly removed the kerchief from her head and blindfolded the soldier, who lacked the strength to remove it. With the situation under control, she removed the blindfold, covered the soldier with a blanket where he lay, and spent the rest of the trip sitting beside him, stroking his head. "He didn't say a word, just clung to her thumb the way small boys do."[14]

As the war progressed, requirements for air evacuation changed, and the 802 MAES responded, sometimes very quickly, to support these shifts in priorities by moving its headquarters and maintaining detachments in other locations as needed.[15] Flight nurse Dorothy Lonergan left Maison Blanche, Algiers, where the 802 MAES was initially headquartered, on a short flight one day in July 1943, and when she returned the same day, her squadron had moved without her knowledge, taking all her belongings with them. Not knowing what would happen next, she sat down and began to read. A pilot who passed by flew her to her squadron's new location at Foch Field, Tunis.[16] Frequent moves were not unique to flying squadrons. June Wandrey, an army surgical nurse assigned to a frontline hospital in the Mediterranean theater, recalled that some hospital platoons moved twenty-eight times in the first thirty-two days after the invasion of southern France and had moved sixty-three times by the end of that invasion.[17]

Licata, Sicily, served as home base for the 802 MAES two months later, and Palermo, Sicily, followed the next month; the 807 MAES joined it there. From this location, the 802 MAES evacuated its fifty-thousandth patient on 30 December 1943 and began evacuating patients from Anzio.[18] Just before the D-Day invasion of Normandy, the squadron moved again, to Frattamaggiore near Naples, and two months after that to Lido di Roma, a resort village built by Mussolini ten to fifteen miles outside Rome. Here the 802 MAES evacuated 851 patients on 30 September 1944, the most they had evacuated in one day while overseas. Less than two months later, total number of patients evacuated by the 802 MAES had exceeded a hundred thousand.[19]

Squadron moves necessitated changes of living quarters, and the flight nurses of the 802 MAES found themselves in tents in Maison Blanche; a French villa with "atrocious plumbing," a foxhole in the backyard, and a religious shrine nearby in Tunis—"very appropriate in case prayers were in order"; and a lighthouse keeper's house on the bay in Licata.[20] An apartment building near the opera house was home to the flight nurses in Palermo, and Morrey recalled attending the Sunday matinee, rushing to the mess hall nearby for dinner during intermission, and returning in time for the opera's next act. A baroness's villa with a view of Mount Vesuvius was home in Naples.[21]

The 802 MAES flight nurses flew without regulation uniforms much of this time. Having left for overseas duty before uniforms were available, they each took with them two pairs of navy slacks and blue regulation shirts to wear on duty. The hot African sun had bleached their makeshift uniforms to purple before the eagerly awaited official articles of clothing finally arrived in June 1944—three previous shipments had been lost at sea.[22]

Life in North Africa, Sicily, and Italy was not all work. The flight nurses made the most of down time, giving and attending parties, watching movies, dancing, relaxing on the beach, and sightseeing. MAES commanders, all flight surgeons, were alert to signs and symptoms of flying fatigue among their flight nurses and enlisted technicians and did their utmost to send personnel to rest camps during lulls between campaigns. A favorite spot in Italy was the Isle of Capri, which was to Morrey "like stepping into heaven" with no evidence of the war.[23] Like flight nurses in other theaters of war, those in the 802 MAES never passed up an opportunity to dine on navy ships docked in harbor, where meals were excellent and served in civilized splendor among great company.[24]

Morrey initially took for granted the availability of aircraft and presence of patients ready for air evacuation at forward airfields. She soon gained respect for the flight surgeons and enlisted technicians who coordinated the system from the various detachments separated from the squadron's headquarters. Of the routine problems encountered— communication lapses, shortages of litters and blankets for property exchange, unpredictable weather—weather was the most devastating enemy to the 802 MAES flying mission, for it could not be controlled. Bad weather was, in fact, the cause of the death of a flight nurse.[25]

Beginning in August 1944, when the 802 MAES was headquartered near Rome, about half of its nurses went on two-week detached duty to Istres, France, where they evacuated patients within France and from France to Italy.[26] Adela "Lutzie" Lutz had been with the 802 MAES since its arrival overseas and had led her squadron in number of missions flown, total flying hours overseas, and number of patients evacuated. She was on an air evacuation mission with fifteen patients en route from Luxeuil in the Belfort Gap on the German border to Istres on 1 November 1944, when the aircraft in which she was traveling encountered a severe storm, went out of control, and crashed at Saint-Chamond, France, near Lyon. Lutz died from extensive third degree burns; the fifteen patients died as well. As a tribute to her life and service, two medical facilities—one floating and one fixed—were named for her posthumously: the former French luxury liner *Columbie,* converted into an army hospital ship in 1945, and the Veterans Administration Medical Center established in 1950 in Saginaw, Michigan, Lutz's hometown.[27]

The original flight nurses of the 802 MAES had understood they would rotate back to the United States after a year overseas, when they would attend the flight nurse course and officially earn the wings they already were wearing. This did not happen. Not until May 1945, after V-E Day, did orders send them to the States with the option to attend the course, then at Randolph Field, so they could continue wearing their wings.[28] The victory in Europe resulted in a reshuffling of the 802 and 807 MAES. Flight nurses with enough points—determined by months in service, months overseas, and combat decorations—were sent home for thirty days of rest and recuperation followed by discharge from the military or reassignment. Those 802 MAES flight nurses lacking adequate points who remained in Italy were now attached to the 807 MAES and preparing for a voyage to Manila when word of an imminent Japanese surrender cancelled their orders for the Pacific.[29]

From Sicily to Italy with the 807 MAES

On 3 September 1943, the British military invaded the toe of Italy, and the Italian government surrendered to the Allies. American soldiers landed at Salerno on 9 September and liberated Naples on 1 October 1943.

The 807 MAES, which had been activated in May 1943 at Bowman Field, arrived overseas on 4 September 1943 after a two-week ocean voyage on board a crowded troop ship. Grace Stakeman, the squadron's chief nurse and historian, recalled the evening at sea when, passing into the Mediterranean on 1 September, her squadron mates became seasoned wartime veterans: "Just about dusk all the officers and nurses were spending their time as usual on boat deck, speculating on time for Garbage dumping, when someone noticed some beautiful red sky-rockets being sent up from the other ships of the convoy. Being blissfully ignorant of their significance, everyone ah-ed and oh-ed, but it wasn't long until the accompanying gun fire, diving planes overhead, and jarring of the ship made everyone realize this was no game but a bitter struggle in which all were participants, whether we liked it or not. Thus did the 807th receive its baptism of fire."[30]

The squadron debarked on 4 September at Bizerte, Tunisia, where male soldiers greeted the flight nurses with gasps and whistles. The women spent the next six days in a bivouac area nearby. Here a pleasant surprise awaited them, for a tent had been pitched for them—outfitted with electric lights and cots supplied for sleeping—and a latrine dug. British soldiers across the road offered the flight nurses use of their shower and invited them to tea. Time spent in foxholes during air raids, however, introduced the flight nurses to the less civilized aspects of living in a war zone. On 10 September, the squadron was on the move again, to Foch Field, Tunis, where it initially worked under the supervision of the veteran 802 MAES. Four weeks later, in early October, the 807 MAES departed for Catania, Sicily, where they began evacuating patients from Corsica to Algiers. They evacuated more than sixteen hundred patients that month.[31]

Allied soldiers had begun fighting in the Italian campaign that same month, with landings near Reggio on 3 September, and Stakeman recalled air evacuation trips her flight nurses made while the squadron was stationed in Catania as filled with the satisfaction of doing the work for which they had been trained. By November, flight nurses and enlisted technicians were going out as fast as they came in to get another load.[32] They flew the patients to Naples, a trip of about an hour, and the air evacuation teams often made five trips in one day, transporting as many as one hundred patients. These were severe battle casualties who, with the speed of air evacuation, reached hospitals within thirty-six hours of being wounded. Loading and placing patients on the airplane was not always easy, however. Since so many of the soldiers were encased in plaster, "sometimes almost from head to foot," the plane passageway at times resembled "a hopscotch court." But despite the bulky casts, crews managed to settle everyone on board in less than thirty minutes.[33]

Like other MAES, the 807 accommodated the constantly changing need for air evacuation as a campaign progressed by opening detachments in more forward areas. On 8 November 1943, about half of the squadron's flight nurses and enlisted technicians departed Catania by air for detached duty at new locations opened the previous month in Bari and Grottaglie, Italy, but their plane landed in enemy-occupied Albania instead.[34] Months passed before they returned to Italy, and in their absence the squadron functioned on half strength until replacements arrived just ten days before the first group returned (see chapter 6).

Dorothy White, shown in illustration 5.1, was among the squadron members left behind in relative safety in Catania. She remembered it as a very busy time, since twelve flight nurses were doing the work of twenty-five, and a "very lonely time. Every place you looked you saw empty chairs, empty cots, the emptiness." The worst place was the mess hall, where no one would eat at the long tables. "We'd all get over at this one little table in the corner and eat there, because at least you were close to somebody." By the second month, squadron members knew their colleagues were alive but not when they would see them again. "So we just looked, many times standing on the coast of the Adriatic Sea, and you looked across, and you knew they were over there someplace. And it was like you were willing them to come home, and making a bridge—a little air bridge sort of like a rainbow—so that they could climb over." The hard work helped the squadron members deal with the stress of their missing colleagues. But, as White said, "in the back of your mind, you always knew, you just kind of had this tight feeling between your shoulder blades, that, *Where are they? How are they surviving? Is everybody all right?*"[35]

Adversity struck the squadron again at the end of January 1944, when a jeep in which flight nurse Lieutenants Mildred Wallace, Mary Allen, and Dorothy Booth were riding overturned. Wallace, who had arrived as a replacement the previous month, suffered a skull fracture and died

5.1 Dorothy White of 807 MAES
(USAF photo)

shortly after the accident. Allen, the least injured, dislocated her shoulder. Booth, who suffered facial and head lacerations and fractured teeth
and vertebrae, required air evacuation to a hospital in Algiers, but the
plane on which she was traveling on 24 February 1944 crashed, killing
all on board, including the flight nurse for the mission, Lieutenant Elizabeth Howren, who had graduated with Wallace and Booth from the
flight nurse course on 26 November 1943.[36]

The Allies had landed at Anzio in January 1944 and were engaged
in some of the heaviest fighting of the war. Like its sister 802 MAES, the
807 MAES evacuated patients of many nationalities, primarily British,
French, Polish, Italian, and some German prisoners of war.[37] For one
flight nurse of the 807 MAES, a trip from Anzio—one of her first with
American patients—made a lasting impression. All her patients had been
wounded within the previous twenty-four hours, and three of them,
all amputees, were straight from the operating room. "Two boys that

had been through the Sicilian and Italian invasions together. They had stepped on mines and both had lost both feet. These two were directly opposite each other on the plane and were very cheerful—at least they were together still. One boy was shot through the neck and had a tracheotomy tube inserted, along with fractured legs, arms, and many shrapnel wounds." The trip was, in the flight nurse's words, a nightmare—and these were only a small number of almost a thousand patients evacuated that day. "Our boys can really take it," the flight nurse concluded. "Not one complaint of pain or remorse on the trip."[38]

The interior of the aircraft on which the 807 MAES personnel flew sometimes required unusual attention before they could on-load patients comfortably. White once encountered a plane covered with glossy nude photographs. Thinking her patients had enough problems and didn't need any more, she took Band-Aids and "dressed the entire ceiling of the plane," giving her patients a good laugh. They might not have paid much attention to the photographs, White realized, "but they thought the Band-Aids were funny." Another plane had transported a dozen mules to the front line. Lacking a way to hose down the floor, the crew chief was left with only a broom to sweep up the mess. When the patients complained about the terrible odor, White lied, "Well, I can't smell a thing—it's just your imagination." But the patients knew otherwise. "Nurse, you better get your nose checked!" one of them replied.[39]

On another flight, it was the view outside the aircraft that caused White's patients to react. On a nighttime trip from Brie to Malta, she and her patients flew into a bad storm, and Saint Elmo's fire made the plane look like its wings were flaming. Fortunately White knew about the phenomenon, but the patients, who all had mental diagnoses, were convinced the aircraft was on fire and would not take no for an answer. In his excitement, one patient hit White on the chin, knocking her head on the top litter, causing some bruising. She and her enlisted technician subdued him, strapped him into his litter, and calmed him down with conversation.

Then the pilot called White up front to ask if she had ever been to Malta before, because he could not spot it below. She knew by the clock that they should be very close and convinced the pilot to radio Malta to turn on the airfield lights. The airfield came into view immediately, and the pilot prepared to land. But had White not reminded him of the altitude, the plane might have crashed into the sea instead of landing on top of the mountain. "And these patients were all mental patients anyway, so how are you going to tell a patient who is very psychotic and either catatonic or wild? You can't tell them you might have to go swimming tonight," White pointed out. Her calm demeanor and ability to "talk a blue streak when you have to" diffused a stressful situation that could have gotten out of hand.[40]

White was more nervous during a mission in which she had an eight-and-a-half-month-pregnant member of the Polish army as a patient. The weather was rough for the flight, and White kept thinking, "*Hey, what if she goes into labor, what am I going to do?*" The patient was positioned in the middle of the plane, so all the other patients could see what was going on with her. The flight nurse used her one word of Polish—"*ból,*" meaning "pain"—when checking on the patient. The woman apparently remained pain-free during the flight, much to White's relief.[41]

Allied forces landing near Anzio on 22 January 1944 found their way to Rome blocked by German forces that encircled the beachhead. Unable to make any headway against the enemy, Allied troops "were locked in a bloody stalemate" lasting five months.[42] They finally broke out and fought their way north through the Liri Valley and on to Rome, which they liberated on 4 June 1944, two days before the D-Day invasion of Normandy.

That November, the 807 MAES, which had evacuated patients to Naples but had not relocated there because of the rapid progression of Allied fighting, moved instead farther north to Lido di Roma, which the 802 MAES had once called home. The flight nurses' quarters looked beautiful from a distance, but on closer inspection, it was clear the retreating Germans had damaged the electrical system and plumbing, shattered the glass in the windows, and planted mines in the ground surrounding the building. Water brought in for bathing and laundry, and candles for light made the quarters livable until repairs could be made and a generator obtained.[43]

Toward the end of the war, White transported a German POW with a sucking chest wound. Because of the extent of the wound, his breaths gasped out his back. He was "a horrible shade of gray" and needed oxygen, but the plane was not equipped for its use. White discovered that the crew chief had a tank of oxygen and a funnel, and using a rectal tube as the connection, she held the apparatus to the patient's face for three hours to give him some relief. The crew meanwhile radioed ahead for a physician to meet the plane at the airfield. When the British doctor came on board and saw White's "fancy gadget," he said, "I don't believe it—American ingenuity!" The patient survived the flight, thanks to White's ability to improvise.[44]

During the summer months, the squadron was at its busiest, and additional detachments opened to meet air evacuation needs as the army moved forward. In July alone, the 807 MAES evacuated more than thirteen thousand patients—a record for them—bringing the squadron total to more than thirty-seven thousand.[45] Lieutenant Edith Belden was struck by the wounded patients' positive spirits, exemplified by one particular soldier she evacuated during the Italian campaign: "He was the 'smilingest' boy of the 18 litter patients on the airplane as I climbed aboard, and he was apparently eager for this, his first plane ride. Having heard stories of things that go on at the places where these boys have been wounded, I wondered how it was possible for any of them to have anything that even resembled a cheerful look." The grinning patient, who spoke broken English, offered to help Belden as she tried to decipher diagnoses from medical tags written in French. Her smiling patient, she learned, had lost a leg in battle. "It was not easy to turn and face him with a smile that could match his own. How do they do it? I wonder."[46]

In August 1944, the Allies invaded southern France. The 807 MAES moved its detachments in France four times to keep pace with the advancing Allied units and evacuated more than seventeen hundred patients from France to Italy.[47] In anticipation of heavy casualties, the 819 MAES arrived from England to support the 802 and 807 MAES, but the number of patients needing evacuation by air actually fell during that month. The 819 MAES learned the problems of ground forces firsthand as they accompanied them in the invasion, promoting better cooperation between air and ground units.[48] Like their colleagues in the 802

MAES, the flight nurses of the 807 MAES were preparing to rotate back to the United States if they had enough points or to travel to the Pacific to augment air evacuation units on that front. Word that war with the Japanese was winding down caused a welcome change in plans—the entire squadron was now homeward bound.

★ ★ ★ 06

Flight Nurses
behind Enemy Lines

Elsie Ott made her first air evacuation flight before earning her wings at Bowman Field. A year later, another mission in which flight nurses participated—this one seemingly routine—made a different kind of history. While Ott's flight occurred before she had been trained as a flight nurse, several members of the 807 MAES barely had started applying their flight nurse training before unusual circumstances cut their overseas flying careers short.

When thirteen of the twenty-five flight nurses assigned to the 807 MAES boarded a C-53 transport plane in Catania, Sicily, for the ninety-minute flight to Bari, Italy, around eight o'clock in the morning on 8 November 1943, it was just another day in what was shaping up to be a busy tour of overseas duty. The 807 MAES was tasked with providing air evacuation support for British troops on the eastern, Adriatic side of the Italian peninsula by establishing forward detachments from which air evacuation teams operated to transport patients to medical facilities behind the front lines of combat.[1] Because of bad weather, plans to position flight nurses and enlisted technicians at two of these forward locations—Bari and Grottaglie, Italy—had been delayed. Once the weather cleared, military authorities thus decided to transport a larger-than-usual number of flight nurses and enlisted technicians to these destinations.[2] The flight nurses, twelve 807 MAES enlisted technicians, and one enlisted technician from the 802 MAES were simply passengers this trip, on their way to another duty location, and they must have been eager to be on their way to the airfields closer to the fighting and to the patients needing their nursing skills in flight.[3]

Although it was raining and storms were predicted at the destination, trip planners determined that the mission would be completed well in advance of any inclement weather. The flight thus was cleared for departure. Half of the nurses and technicians would deplane at Bari, the first scheduled stop, a distance of about 260 miles; the rest would fly on to Grottaglie.[4] The travelers never made it to either destination, however, and before the day had ended they were putting into practice what they had gleaned from their classes at Bowman Field concerning military tactics and survival in enemy-occupied territory.

A Rough Flight

Perhaps because of faulty weather reporting, once airborne the C-53 encountered severe thunderstorms and flew around aimlessly for several hours. According to one source, the other two planes that had taken off from Catania at the same time returned to the base instead of trying to navigate around the storm; only the C-53 with the medical personnel on board forged ahead. It was "one of the worst flights as far as rough," Agnes Jensen, one of the nurses, remembered. "If we didn't have our seatbelts on, we'd have hit the ceiling or been pitched out. It was really unbelievably rough."[5]

In a string of misfortunes, the flight crew lost radio contact and was unable to land the plane at Bari. Eventually spotting an airfield through a break in the clouds, the pilot made an attempt to land, but the airstrip was held by Nazis, who opened fire—hitting the plane's tail—and sent two fighter planes to intercept the C-53. The American pilot's evasive maneuvers prevented further enemy action, but with his plane now dangerously low on fuel, the pilot was forced to land on a flat spot in the mountains around one o'clock that afternoon, about five hours after take-off from Catania. In preparation for the emergency landing, Jensen wanted to check on the Mae West life vests swinging in the back of the plane but was afraid of creating panic, especially since crew outnumbered the available life vests. So after resigning herself to a fate of either hitting a mountain or running out of gas, she looked at all her colleagues on board, smoothed out some musette bags next to her, loosened her seatbelt, slid down in her seat, and thought, *"What the hell, I'd rather be sleeping."*[6]

The plane bogged down and nosed over on landing, but all its occupants survived. The only casualty was the crew chief, who had not been seated and belted in for the landing and consequently injured his knee and sustained lacerations. The nurses gave him first aid and administered morphine. One of the nurses was hit by a flying object—possibly a flying tool chest or the crew chief's foot—that cut a gash in her cheek and loosened a few teeth.[7]

Only after the flight nurses, technicians, and crewmembers—pilot, copilot, crew chief, and radio operator—left the plane did they learn that they had landed in south-central Albania, occupied by the Nazis. Because a young boy among the armed Albanian partisans surrounding the plane recognized the American aircraft insignia, indicating "friendly forces," the plane's occupants were greeted as friends, not foes.[8]

The Americans' top priority was now to find their way back to Allied territory, an ordeal that took two very long months, even with the assistance of Albanian and later British and American guides. Because the plane's occupants related their experiences to military authorities during official debriefings after arriving in Italy, details of their time in Albania are known. Agnes Jensen Mangerich, one of the flight nurses on board, has written her own account of the journey in *Albanian Escape: The True Story of U.S. Army Nurses behind Enemy Lines*.

On 8 November 1943, when the plane had not landed at either of its intended destinations and a thorough search of the area had not revealed its whereabouts, the War Department declared the aircraft and its occupants missing. This official action was necessary to secure replacements for the missing personnel, who were then dropped from the rolls of their organizations.[9] The Albanian underground sent word to authorities in Italy that the nurses and enlisted technicians were safe and in their country.[10] Colonel Richard Elvins, chief surgeon for the 12th Air Force in Florence, Italy, sent sketchy details of the situation to the army air forces air surgeon, Major General Grant, at the end of November and attached a

6.1 Albania

list of the nurses' names, ranks, and serial numbers. Definite information was not yet available, and what was known was highly secret, but Elvins could tell Grant, "It is expected that they will be returned by secret underground methods in the very near future."[11] By this time, the nurses and enlisted technicians had been in Albania for three weeks.

Albanian Underground

At the urging of the Albanian partisans, immediately after their unexpected arrival somewhere between Elbasan and Berat, the American flight crew and medical personnel quickly removed necessities from the plane—medical supplies, blankets, water, personal belongings, and food in the form of D- and K-rations—and left the site; the Germans were not far away and might have seen or heard the plane come down. The Albanians led the survivors by foot to a farmhouse, which was possibly a partisan hideout, two miles away. Here the entire party slept in one room on a rug-covered floor, with a fireplace providing the only warmth. For breakfast the next day, they were treated to a feast of water buffalo, cornbread, and cheese. The crew returned to the landing site later that morning and set fire to the plane.[12] The morning after that, the partisans took the group to Berat, a two-day walk south. In what would become a pattern, the Albanians held the trail in some places and the Germans controlled it in others. Albanian scouts kept the travelers informed of German activity up ahead. By now, the Americans were becoming accustomed to narrow, rocky paths often mired in mud and slick from rain. Albanian partisans, notified in advance, prepared meals for the Americans along the way and provided donkeys to carry the baggage and transport the injured crew chief.

The residents of Berat, delighted at what they thought was the arrival of an advance invasion party, welcomed the Americans with open arms and boarded them in their homes and in the hotel for three nights. No record was made of where each member of the group was staying. The third morning, the ten Americans staying in the hotel awakened to shouts of alarm—the Germans were shelling the town across the river. Fearing their city might be the next target, the Albanians rounded up the Americans and took them out of town by truck. The Germans bombed Berat that same day. When regrouping for their hasty departure, none of the Americans thought to count heads, and consequently three of the nurses were left behind when the rest of the squadron forged ahead amid the chaos of the impending attack.

The truck proved an unreliable form of transportation and had to be abandoned when the Germans began shelling, then strafing the road and the vehicles traveling out of town. In the confusion of the air attack, the group scattered and started traveling on foot in two directions. Some headed north, and the remainder continued south—just ahead of the Germans, they later learned. The Americans occasionally dodged German bullets along their route. For four days, Albanian partisans led the groups from village to village; they never stayed longer than one night in any village, because of the scanty provisions to feed such a large group of people and because their presence could put the Albanian village at risk for German attack. Food and lodging were always a problem, since villages might have only four or six houses and the Germans had raided the inhabitants' food supplies. Meals usually consisted of cornbread and goat cheese.[13]

At Dobrusha, the northbound travelers, who had since turned south, caught up with their southbound colleagues. Here the Americans, who had heard of a secret British mission somewhere in Albania, sent a handwritten note via an Albanian runner to the British, who were in the country to organize the Albanian partisans against the Germans. The British had been keeping watch on Albania from Cairo since 1940 and had placed a number of officers to help arm and equip the partisans to resist the Italians and Germans.[14] The Americans traveled as one group for the remainder of their time in Albania. While awaiting word from the British, they moved higher and higher into the mountains to avoid the activity of the Ballists, who, unlike the partisans, collaborated with the Germans.

When the Albanian guide learned that the Ballists had moved into a village on the route the travelers had planned to take, the group had to go over, not around, the next mountain. The weather was frigid, and at the top of the mountain the Americans almost perished in a blizzard. In the whiteout conditions, the guides were unsure of the route, and snow covered foot tracks and obscured landmarks, leaving no signs to guide them. With their insufficient footwear, the nurses were slipping and sliding in the snow, and their thin leather gloves offered little protection against the freezing temperature. When the group finally descended into the small village of Terlioria, the Albanians greeted them as heroes for having crossed Mount Tomorrit, one of the highest mountains in the country, after September.[15] Good news awaited the survivors when they reached the village, for the Albanian runner was waiting with a note from "Smith" of the British Special Operations Executive. A week later, at the village of Lovdar the Americans came face to face with Smith, a British captain, who was staying in the nearby village of Krushove.

Unknown to the survivors, during their time in Lovdar another Captain Smith—Lloyd G. Smith, an American intelligence officer assigned to the Office of Strategic Services in Bari, Italy—received orders to proceed to Albania, find out where the American survivors were, contact them, and take them to the Albanian coast for evacuation by sea.[16]

The Brits Take Over

The next day, 1 December, the rejuvenated nurses, technicians, and flight crew traveled with Smith, the British captain, to Krushove. During their hours in Lovdar, the nurses had reveled in the luxury of warm baths, a pleasant supper, beds with feather mattresses, and clean, shampooed hair. Knee- and waist-deep snows impeded progress once back on the trail but did not dampen their spirits as the trekkers put themselves in the capable hands of their British guide. To evade the Germans and the Ballists after their crash, the group had traveled farther and farther east until they were now near the country's border with Greece.

Once they had reached Krushove, Smith gathered up the shoes and boots that could be repaired and submitted a request for GI-issue replacements for those beyond repair. He also requisitioned extra socks and underwear for the travelers. All supplies were airdropped into this mountainous location.[17] In Krushove the group met Gavin "Gary" Duffy, a British lieutenant who, along with Sergeant J. W. "Blondie" Bell, a wireless radio operator, would accompany them to the coast.

On 7 December, the evening before the Americans left on their journey to the coast, the American Smith arrived by boat at Seaview, the coastal cave that served as the base headquarters for the British contingent in Albania.[18] He had not yet received word regarding the location of the nurses and others preparing to leave Krushove.

The group began its cross-country trek on 8 December, passing through villages and hiking over Mount Nermerska into Shepr. Between Shepr and Gjirokastër, the crew spotted a large green field the Italians had once used as an airstrip.[19] It was now late December, and the travelers had hopes of returning to Allied territory in time for the holidays. A few days before Christmas, which was spent at Doksat, the pilots raised the possibility of evacuation by air with Duffy, who opposed the plan, insisting that his orders specified a coastal evacuation by sea.[20]

Despite his reservations, however, Duffy sent a message to Cairo to make arrangements for an aerial evacuation of the Americans, who were still in Doksat. Bad weather delayed implementation of the plan for several days, but on December 28, Duffy finally received a reply from Cairo. An air rescue attempt had been set in motion, and with a break in the weather, planes were scheduled to arrive the next day to pick up the stranded Americans. A signal was arranged: five of the enlisted technicians were to stand at one end of the field with yellow parachute cloths to indicate all was well for landing when the planes flew overhead.[21] Duffy called off the air evacuation, however, believing it was too risky, with Germans occupying Gjirokastër nearby.[22] In their debriefing after returning to Italy, Lieutenants Thrasher and Baggs, the C-53 pilot and copilot, related the outcome: The Germans were on one hill and the Americans on another when the planes arrived and flew around for ten minutes. "The women started crying and the men were on their knees praying. They knew that if they went down on the field they would all have been killed. It was a finishing blow to realize that if the airplanes could land they would be in Allied territory in 40 minutes."[23]

This heartbreaking episode was still vivid in Jensen's mind when she finally returned to Italy. "If I live to be 100 years old I shall never forget nor be able to express my feelings when I saw that swarm of planes sent out by the 15th Air Force just to rescue us," she said.

We were told "planes with escort were coming" but in my wildest dreams I couldn't believe there would be more than a transport with 6 P38's. It was almost sickening to me that we couldn't fill our end of the bargain by signaling them to land after they had gone all out for us. Because of the Germans in the city across the road from the airport we could only lie on that hill above the airport and watch the P38's, 1 Wellington bomber and 2 transports fly low over the field as if they were just begging for the signal to land.[24]

Colleague Lillian Tacina concurred: "To think the U.S. Army put forth so much effort to get us out of enemy territory and we couldn't do our part."[25] The display of power gave flight nurse Lois Watson the incentive to persevere in their journey; after the fliers had risked their lives in the rescue attempt, "we just had to get back to our army."[26]

The planes left, and the Americans resumed their journey to the coast. When they returned to Doksat, the village they had just left, morale was at an all-time low. Two days later, the Americans were once again on the move, but they spent New Year's Day in Albania, not in Italy.

The Final Push

When the fighting eased up, the Americans headed back toward the coast, taking care to avoid enemy detection, and on the road to Kalarat they encountered the American Smith. When air rescue of the American party seemed imminent, Smith had been ordered back to Italy and had only returned to Albania when a message on 30 December instructed him to proceed with the original plan for sea evacuation.[27] He now took over from Duffy to lead the Americans to the coast. From here on, the journey was by night.

Occasionally, they had the luxury of riding in a truck, but most of their traveling was by foot. Mules were brought along to carry the equipment and sick or injured travelers. Although physically fit from their drills and maneuvers at Bowman Field, the squadron members suffered ill effects from their roaming. One enlisted technician developed pneumonia; many individuals had dysentery, with its abdominal cramping and diarrhea;

and others, yellow jaundice. Several of the group had head and body lice. "Really, it's amazing that we girls didn't have more problems, what with never bathing or seldom bathing," Jensen reflected, adding, "And of course we [flight nurses] all stopped menstruating."[28] Thinking that they would not be in Albania very long, early in their journey the nurses had used their medical supplies to treat the Albanian partisans as a goodwill gesture and did not have any supplies left to treat themselves and their colleagues later when they needed them.[29]

One more mountain stood in their way to the coast. After a lengthy climb, they reached the summit; in far less time, the weary travelers descended by whatever means they could. Jensen recalled that final push: "Looking out at the Adriatic, it was a beautiful view, and it was a nice day, and so I slowly kind of slid myself down."[30] Their journey across Albania over at last, the Americans reached Seaview on the southwest coast after daylight on 8 January 1944 for their rendezvous with the boat that would return them to Italy. Situated in a cove, the cave that served as Allied headquarters was well provisioned with a stocked pantry and accommodations for sleeping. After a good meal and a few hours of sleep, the nurses, enlisted technicians, and flight crew were rowed out to a British boat bound for Bari, Italy, around midnight. Ten hours later they were back on Allied soil.

When the repatriated nurses, shown in illustration 6.1, and the rest of the group arrived in Bari, they received a heroes' welcome before being taken to the 26th General Hospital. The first order of business was interrogation—before they could forget any details of their time in Albania, the occupants of the ill-fated C-53 relived their observations and experiences for the benefit of military intelligence officers. Once the debriefings ended, attention turned to medical care. Within a week, most of the group was healthy enough to return to their base in Sicily. One nurse and one enlisted technician had to stay behind for further medical treatment.[31]

Dorothy White, one of the nurses in the 807 MAES in Sicily, recalled the "fantastic" moment when the squadron's nurses knew their missing colleagues had returned. While flight nurses in Catania were eating lunch in their mess hall, the phone rang, and chief nurse Grace

6.1 Flight nurses of 807 MAES on return from Albania, January 1944 (USAF photo)

Stakeman answered it. "Sergeant Brock," she called to the mess sergeant in a loud voice, "we will have thirteen guests for lunch." White continued the story: "And everyone stopped. Forks were in midair, and then we finally stopped, and we looked at each other. That number thirteen gives me chills to this day. And then nobody could eat any more. . . . We didn't know what to do, we were all so eager and excited. Pretty soon we could hear some jeep horns honking, and here they came in, in the jeeps, and I remember just standing there looking at them. I couldn't believe it! There was my roommate for a whole year and a half, walking up, 'Hi, Whitey, what's for lunch?' Just like as nonchalant as could be."[32] But for the three nurses still in Berat, the ordeal was not yet over.

Left in Berat

On the morning of 15 November 1943, when the Americans and many residents of Berat hastened out of the city, Lieutenants Helen Porter, Ava Maness, and Wilma Lytle, who were staying in the home of an Albanian family, did not rush out into the street to join the other members of their group. The nurses had thought Lieutenant Thrasher, the pilot, would send word to them, but when that did not happen, they followed their host's instructions and went downstairs to the section of the basement used as a bomb shelter. They heard but did not see the firing and soon watched through a window as the Germans poured into town. Believing that they would be turned over to the enemy, the flight nurses contemplated whether they should disclose their presence to the Germans now, to protect the household, or wait to see if they were seized.[33] Their host informed them that their colleagues had left town already and told them to remain at the house.

Later in the day, two Germans came to the house and entered the room where the flight nurses were staying. After a brief exchange in which the Germans learned that the women were nurses, they told the hosts that if the flight nurses stayed in the house, they would be all right. The family with whom the nurses were staying were Ballists and had some influential friends among party officials.[34] The next morning, their host reported the nurses' presence to the Ballist officials and received assurance of their safety. The next week, the Ballists sent a patrol to inspect the house. When they found the nurses at home, they responded in a friendly manner and left. Shortly thereafter, to provide both an escape route for the nurses and access to the radio next door, their host opened a passageway in the basement between his house and the adjoining one belonging to his cousin.

When the Ballist commandant visited a few days later and asked the nurses if they needed anything, they replied that their primary interest was in returning to Allied territory. About two weeks after this visit, another man came to see them, asked their names, ranks, and serial numbers, and inquired whether they wanted to send a note to their colleagues through him. Hesitant to express themselves in writing, the nurses sent a note to Lieutenant Thrasher saying they were in good health and being treated very well by the people with whom they were staying. They signed the note "P.M.L.," using the first letters of their last names.[35]

The Ballist commandant returned to the house in early January with a note for the nurses. Dated 27 December, it was not from their colleagues but from Major Kendall, a British officer at Seaview. It read: "Dear P.M.L., received your note to C.B.T. [the pilot] We are expecting the other members of your party soon, and I have asked Mr. Maco [Mecho] to bring you to me. He is trustworthy. We guarantee getting you back to where you came from. Happy New Year. Signed, S.S.K." Their host thought that since the nurses were not suffering physically, they should be content to remain at his home until peace came to the world, but the nurses remembered their military obligation to reunite with their colleagues. Although they did not know who S.S.K. and Mr. Maco [Mecho] were, the nurses sent word that they would be glad to come to S.S.K.[36]

Days turned into weeks, and weeks into months for the nurses who were desperate to rejoin their squadron mates but without the means to do so. Without their knowledge, after returning to Bari with the first group of nurses rescued from Albania, Lloyd Smith recently promoted to major, had received orders to return to Albania to arrange for the safe passage of the remaining three nurses from Berat and, if necessary, to bring them himself to the coast for evacuation. But because officials at Seaview had been told that some prominent Ballists had promised to bring the nurses safely to the base within the next ten days, Major Kendall instructed Smith not to set out for Berat immediately. Around 26 February 1944, when the promise could not be fulfilled, Smith and a wireless radio operator set out to bring the nurses back to Allied territory. A reliable Albanian served as a messenger: Smith wanted to know if the nurses preferred to travel by car—in which case they would need civilian clothes that the messenger would purchase—or have Smith come bring them to the coast by foot.[37]

The Ballist commandant in Berat passed Smith's message along to the nurses, who told him they were willing to walk if necessary. Time must have stood still for the nurses as they awaited further developments in their departure plans. Because the first part of the journey out of Berat would be by car, the nurses offered to make their own clothing for the trip with the help of the women of the household where they were staying. They would be allowed to bring their uniforms with them, however, tied up in small bundles. Since they were without passports, as another preparation for the trip to the coast, the Albanians photographed the women, gave them Albanian names, and stamped each of their new passes with an official seal.[38]

By 10 March, Smith had received no word from his Albanian messenger, who was to return with the nurses. Four days later, he received a message from Cairo telling him to return to Bari without further instructions if the nurses could not be evacuated successfully within thirty days. Smith decided he would start on foot for Berat if he had not seen or heard from the nurses within the week.[39]

On Their Way at Last

On 18 March, the nurses finally were on their way to the coast. Under the care of an Albanian charged with the first stage of their escape, they slipped out of the basement exit of the house next door to where they were staying and into a waiting car. A truckload of Albanian soldiers supposedly being transported to fight the partisans offered the necessary ruse when stopped by German patrols.[40] The trip was not without incident. Along the way, German sentries stopped them, and the occupants encountered frequent mishaps such as flat tires. Once the vehicle was well out of Berat, the nurses and an Albanian guide walked for the rest of the day, spent the night in a shepherd's hut, and resumed their travel by foot the next morning. Late that afternoon, they arrived at a house where two British soldiers were waiting to take Major Smith word of their location. When it got dark, the nurses were taken to a deserted house for their rendezvous with Smith, who arrived that same night.

Shortly after midnight, Smith led the nurses up the mountain so that by daylight they would be out of sight of any Germans, who held roads in the area. The nurses reached the top of the mountain an hour before noon, and about three hours later they, like their colleagues before them, were welcomed at Seaview, where they awaited sea transportation across the Adriatic. The next day, shortly before midnight, Smith and his charges left Albania on an Italian vessel for the two-hour voyage to Otranto, Italy. After their mandatory debriefings, the three nurses went to 26th General Hospital in Bari for medical evaluation. On 27 March

1944, they returned to Catania, where the 807 MAES was still assigned—over four months after what was to have been a routine day of flying.

Courage and Fortitude

Tributes to the nurses following their arrival back in Italy attest to their abilities to endure the hardships of the experience. The pilots of the C-53, Lieutenants Thrasher and Baggs, observed, "During the entire trip the women stood up with the men all the time and did not impede progress. In fact, the women showed a better spirit than the men who were passengers on the plane."[41] James Cruise, the enlisted technician who had developed pneumonia during the journey, was even more complimentary: "Our experience and trip was dam tough and rugged. The thing that impressed me the most during the entire trip was the courage and fortitude of our female members. In my estimation they deserve all the praise in the world. Our American women surely have a great deal of stamina. God bless the Army Nurse Corps."[42]

Jensen said the worst thing about the Albanian experience was what could have happened to them—missed patrols, acute illnesses, broken bones—but she refused to give in to despair. "One thing we wouldn't tolerate from anybody was for them to say, 'If I ever get out of here.' Oh, we jumped all over them! You could say 'when we got out.'" The flight nurse and her companions kept their spirits up by living one day at a time. Youth and a trusting nature were also on their side: "When you're young, nothing can happen to you," she reflected. Yet she felt the need for more assertiveness training: "You're in the military, you're subordinate . . . all the way down. And we were at the bottom of the pile as second lieutenants and always as nurses." Jensen, who was the senior-ranking nurse in the group, deferred to the pilot for any decisions that had to be made concerning the welfare of the group. Since the pilot was in command of the airplane, she thought he of course would know what to do. But he, too, lacked the training and assertiveness required to handle the situation.[43]

Since new squadron members had replaced them during their absence, the returning nurses all received military orders to return to the

United States.[44] Military policy was that "anyone who had crash-landed and escaped from enemy territory could not remain in the same theater of war."[45] Yet another reason why these nurses could not stay in Europe was that if the nurses were captured again, having spent several weeks behind German lines, they might be treated not as prisoners of war but as spies.[46] Lieutenants Jensen, Maness, and Eugenie Rutkowski were later assigned to the School of Air Evacuation as instructors.[47] As part of the training program for flight nurses, they accompanied flight nurse trainees on actual air evacuation missions within the continental United States. Seven other flight nurses of the Albanian contingent—Lieutenants Gertrude Dawson, Pauleen Kanable, Ann Kopsco, Wilma Lytle, Ann Markowitz, Helen Porter, Elna Schwant, and Lillian Tacina—had the chance to fly again with air evacuation squadrons activated in 1944 and assigned to the ATC with duty stations in Hawaii or the United States.

07

Flight Nursing on the European Front: United Kingdom, France, North Atlantic

While the 802 and 807 MAES were shifting their air evacuation activities forward as the Tunisian, Sicilian, and Italian campaigns liberated the Mediterranean from Axis control, ten MAES were arriving in the United Kingdom in preparation for the invasion of Normandy. The first of these, the 806 MAES, which had been activated at Bowman Field in December 1942, debarked from the SS *Thomas H. Barry* at Liverpool, England, in July 1943 and traveled by train to Newberry.[1] The 806 MAES eventually was joined by nine MAES activated from September through November 1943—the 810 and 811, and the 813 through 819—that sent more than two hundred flight nurses to the United Kingdom between January and April 1944. The MAES traveled to initial duty stations throughout England in Aldermaston, Balderton, Barkston Heath, Bottesford, Cottesmore, Fulbeck, Greenham Common, Spanhoe, and Welford Park. As was the case in the Mediterranean, the MAES assigned in England changed locations as needed, even before relocating in France.

Awaiting D Day

Because these MAES were positioned for an event that had not yet occurred, a major concern was how to keep so many flight nurses and enlisted technicians constructively occupied while their services were not needed on a regular basis for air evacuation of patients. For all the

7.1 Northwest Europe

MAES, the months leading up to D Day were filled with duties both on the ground and in the air. But Denny Nagle of the 815 MAES remembered that the flight nurses "were just kept busy doing nothing, actually. I hate to say that, but it's true."[2]

As the first to arrive in England, the 806 MAES established a pattern of activity that was followed by the other squadrons. During the four months after its arrival at Newberry, the 806 MAES opened and staffed the station sick quarters, presented plane-loading demonstrations and lectures to soldiers in training at the American School Center at Shriven-ham, and participated in its own training similar to that at Bowman Field.[3] A C-47 mock-up at Cottesmore offered the MAES personnel real-istic practice on ditching procedures.

Jenny Boyle, a flight nurse in the 816 MAES, remembered spend-ing most of the time before D Day in calisthenics but also spending a month at a bomber base.[4] To give its flight nurses and enlisted tech-nicians direct experience with combat casualties, each squadron sent them to bomber bases. The flight nurses were at the airfield when the planes departed and when they returned, often with casualties result-ing from these combat missions. The nurses observed and assisted in emergency treatment. They learned about the equipment aboard bomb-ers and how the planes could be configured to accommodate patients if needed. Attendance at lectures, predeparture briefings, and post-mission debriefings taught the flight nurses about airborne combat missions from a different perspective. When not at the airstrip, they helped with sick call and in sick quarters.

The flight nurses of the 818 MAES thought the detached service at bomber bases was valuable both professionally and personally—their enjoyment of the life on such a base had much to do with social as well as airfield activity.[5] A flight surgeon assigned to the 816 MAES was not convinced of the value of the flight nurses' experiences, however. He thought the two weeks spent at bomber bases about a week too long. "The observing of B-24's taking off and landing may have been exciting, the briefing and interrogations must have been interesting, but should it have taken two weeks to see all of this?" He concluded that, given the negligible duties performed, "it was very difficult to find some logical reasoning for the whole matter."[6]

Ethel Carlson's experience supports his views. When she and Mary Taggert, both from the 815 MAES, arrived at Kimbolton, that bomber base experienced no casualties during the flight nurses' month-long stay. Carlson, shown in illustration 7.1, remembered not doing much except playing baseball and smoking cigarettes at the flight line while waiting for the planes to return from missions, then giving the aircrews a shot of whiskey after they had landed, perhaps to relax them before or after

7.1 Ethel Carlson of 815 MAES
(author's collection)

their debriefing. As soon as the flight nurses returned to their own base, Kimbolton began experiencing casualties again.[7]

Soon after arrival at their first duty stations, the MAES personnel were issued bicycles. Because living quarters were often some distance from the airfields, and because buildings at the various stations were widely dispersed, squadron members needed a form of transportation. Bicycles got them where they needed to go, but they also provided an opportunity for healthy recreation. The more enterprising nurses used them not only to get to meals and classes but to explore the English villages and countryside.

The flight nurses began settling in, turning their attention to their new homes away from home. Carlson remembered her first quarters at Welford Park: they expected to pitch tents and instead found themselves in a gorgeous mansion with formal gardens on an acre of land. They couldn't believe it—a great entrance hall, spiral staircase, heads of game on the walls, a marble fireplace. "And this was our own private little barracks," she concluded.[8] Elsewhere in England, flight nurses of the 819 MAES named their less ostentatious quarters in Aldermaston "The Last

Resort," perhaps hinting at a place where they at last could shed their military personas and assume more relaxed, feminine ones. Quarters boasted lounges in which the flight nurses hosted formal receptions and dances, giving them opportunities to don evening dresses. "Our wearing of formals seemed even more appreciated than the punch," wrote chief nurse June Sanders of the 819 MAES about an open house she and her colleagues hosted in April 1944.[9]

In December 1943, the 806 was the first MAES in England to participate in air evacuation when one flight nurse–enlisted technician team was assigned on temporary duty to ATC to fly twelve patients from England to the United States. The 806 squadron history identified the mission as the first transatlantic air evacuation of patients from Europe, though Robert Futrell cites a November 1943 mission that transported fourteen repatriated American POW casualties from Prestwick, Scotland.[10] Other squadrons also made air evacuation flights before D Day, transporting patients from Meghaberry, Northern Ireland, to England; within England; from England to Prestwick or Renfrew, Scotland; and from Prestwick to the United States. This last route was music to the ears of 811 MAES personnel, who were eager to put their training to use in the air.[11] The 810 MAES considered the trips from Northern Ireland to England, which used from two to ten planes daily, practical training flights. After a month they turned the missions over to the 813 MAES.[12]

In May 1944 all flight nurses and enlisted technicians of the 810 MAES were participating in air evacuation flights out of Prestwick when the first tragedy struck their squadron. Lieutenant Elsie Keasey was riding in a jeep with her flight nurse colleague Lieutenant Frances Surgalia when the vehicle was involved in an accident. Keasey was killed; Surgalia apparently suffered only minor injuries, requiring a three-day hospitalization.[13]

Flight nurse Edith Jackson, whose 816 MAES made its first air evacuation flights in April 1944, recalled that flight nursing was hard work and could have its down side. She offered a May 1944 flight from an airfield in England to Prestwick as a prime example of a mission gone awry. The pilots first landed at the wrong airfield before finding the correct one, where crews on-loaded eleven patients who had been waiting for over an hour. By then Jackson was dizzy from the takeoffs and landings, perhaps because, as she groused, although the patients were fed, the flight crew had not had a chance to eat. The trip from England to Scotland was not a long one, but that day's mission lasted over nine hours. Unnecessary waiting due to lack of communication resulted in grumbling, unhappy patients, according to the flight nurse. "What a messy flight it had been," Jackson concluded. She eventually earned an Air Medal and believed she deserved it especially for that flight.[14]

Of particular interest is the difference between Jackson's account and the corresponding entry in the 816 MAES monthly historical report, which read: "On May 5th, Lt. Edith Jackson and Tec 3 Dillinger evacuated eleven patients by plane from the 1st General Hospital, London, England, to Prestwick, Scotland. The flight was uneventful."[15]

Earlier in the war, three 802 MAES flight nurses—Ellen Church, Retha Rodgers, and Jo Sansone—were transferred to England to coordinate air evacuation in that theater, drawing on their experience and expertise in the Mediterranean. Both the 816 and 819 MAES personnel benefitted when Sansone talked with them in April and May 1944, respectively, about the practical aspects of air evacuation and gave them a better understanding of how their work fit into the big picture as the squadrons anticipated their upcoming role in D Day.[16]

D Day and Normandy Invasion

With D Day and the invasion of Normandy came what some flight nurses considered the "real work" for which they had been trained and sent to England.[17] Although they had been restricted to their duty stations in the past, when on 1 June all troop carrier groups and air evacuation squadrons again were restricted to their stations, MAES personnel sensed that this was the real thing and the invasion was imminent. "Mystery, tension, and rumors" abounded as the 819 MAES and its neighboring squadrons awaited word that the invasion had begun.[18] Squadrons implemented their contingency plans, which involved setting up hospital holding tents at airfields for receiving the wounded flight crews returning from France.

On 6 June, D Day, the MAES personnel watched the planes take off from airstrips in Britain headed for the Normandy coast of France as part of Operation Neptune, the assault phase of Operation Overlord. The flight nurses then worked in sick quarters and receiving tents while sweating out the return of planes to their airfields. The MAES personnel spent the next few days watching, waiting, and wondering when they would begin evacuating casualties from France. The 816 was the first MAES in England to participate in air evacuation, when on 10 June flight nurse–enlisted technician teams on three C-47s escorted by fighters flew from Membury into France to pick up patients in Normandy. The medical crews were dressed in the impregnated clothing worn by the combat troops, with helmet. A pistol belt; knife; canteen; mess gear; gas mask; first-aid kit; Mae West; parachute; and an escape kit of food, French currency, compass, and a map of France completed their gear. Theirs were the first planes to make scheduled landings on Omaha Beach after the invasion began. The sight of "miles and miles" of navy vessels—battleships, destroyers, landing craft—on their approach was unforgettable. Battleships and artillery were firing, land mines were exploding, dead German soldiers lined the airstrip, and German prisoners were "everywhere." German forces were about four miles away.[19]

Frances Sandstrom, the flight nurse on the first plane, remembered landing at Sainte Mere Eglise on the newly laid steel-mat airstrip. She saw wrecked gliders littering the countryside and heard land mines exploding. She was told not to leave the plane, because German snipers were in the surrounding woods. "So I didn't," she said. "I just stood there and almost hugged the aircraft until we could take off." Around sundown they went back to the beach to load eighteen patients from the clearing station where they had been brought from the battlefield. Sandstrom then encountered the indomitable spirit of new invasion casualties: "Most of them were badly wounded. They were dirty, right out of the foxholes. Many of them were suffering, but I had not one murmur of complaint from any of them. It was hot and dusty, but they were calm and asked for nothing except water. Each time I gave a man a drink he smiled, or tried to, and thanked me as if I had done something very heroic."[20]

7.2 Grace Dunnam (second from left), Dolly Vinsant (third from left), and colleagues of 806 MAES (USAF photo)

On 11 June, Grace Dunnam, chief nurse of the squadron, was the flight nurse when the 806 MAES made its first authorized air evacuation flight to France, also to Omaha Beach, where she picked up sixteen patients. Recalling the mission, Dunnam remarked that everyone has a few moments in their life when they prove themselves. This was her moment.[21]

The 819 MAES was next to fly into France, when it evacuated invasion casualties back to England on 14 June. Particularly vexing was how they learned that air evacuation into France had begun—from a front-page photograph that the *Stars and Stripes* military newspaper had printed of 816 MAES flight nurses smiling from the doorway of an aircraft in France, holding poppies in their arms. The 819 MAES medical teams were impressed with the efficiency of the air evacuation operations in Normandy and returned from their first mission with high hopes of doing their part in this military campaign. But their expectations were short-lived. Sanders expressed the disappointment of her flight nurses, who felt redundant and specialized almost the entire month in being alerted and un-alerted. "We set the new world records in dressing and undressing," she quipped.[22]

Louise Anthony, a flight nurse with the 816 MAES who made her first trip into Normandy on 15 June, flew over, as did other medical crews, in planes loaded with gasoline for Patton's army. Afterward, as the patients were brought on board the plane now configured for air evacuation, enemy shells were getting close, and an officer told the crew to shut the door and take off. Anthony saw that one of her patients was dying and, realizing he might not survive the flight, tried to find someone to remove him from the plane. But it was too late—the ground crews had left. As soon as they were airborne, Anthony asked the radio operator to call for a doctor to meet the plane. When the patient died over the English Channel, Anthony successfully hid the fact from the other patients: "I did not cover his face, I turned his head, I adjusted his pillow, I checked his pulse, I pulled the blanket back to check his dressings—the same as all the rest of the patients. . . . And so no one knew anything."[23]

The 813 MAES made its first flight into France on 20 June; six flight nurse–enlisted technician teams from the 814 MAES flew on air evacuation missions into France on that same day, returning with 114 patients.[24] By 22 June, when the 818 MAES made its first flight into France, casualties were mounting, and the flight nurses and enlisted technicians traveled across the channel in forty C-47s, returning with 186 patients.[25] The 815 MAES personnel, who watched impatiently as other squadrons made trips across the English Channel, had to wait until 23 June, when they sent fifteen flight nurse–enlisted technician teams on flights into Normandy.[26] The 810 and 817 MAES eventually were alerted for their own missions into France. The 811 MAES did not begin evacuating invasion casualties until early July, by which time the squadron had moved to France; five teams from the 814 MAES joined the 811 on detached service to assist in these missions. They had spent the month of June "busily but happily engaged" in flights from Prestwick back to the United States.[27]

On their flights into France, the 814 and 815 were hampered, as were other MAES, by dry runs when no patients were available for loading during the short time the planes were permitted to remain on the airstrip.[28] These planes thus returned to England empty. Despite problems with communication and inclement weather that prevented flying, morale was high in squadrons such as the 815 MAES, which participated regularly in flights to France. When missions slacked off, morale sagged. The 819 MAES nurses, who had started June anticipating frequent flights, ended the month discontented and disappointed with "only a faint hope that we would someday be enabled to at least partake in our primary mission—Air Evacuation."[29]

For most MAES, the weeks and months immediately following D Day offered the greatest flying opportunities, with flight nurses making two or even three missions daily. From 11 to 30 June, the 806 MAES evacuated 4,440 patients from France to England. July was even busier, with the 806 reporting 6,590 patients flown from France to England.[30] Even for the disillusioned 819 MAES flight nurses, "the unexpected occurred. We started working—and loved it." Having reconciled themselves to sleeping their mornings away, tending to personal matters in the afternoon, and socializing in the evenings, they suddenly found themselves flying daily into Normandy, keeping irregular hours, and evacuating newly wounded patients.[31]

Writing tongue-in-cheek, Phoebe La Munyan downplayed the near misses encountered by her 819 MAES flight nurse colleagues on trips from England into Normandy, but in reality the flights were filled with dangers: "Our trips were comparatively uneventful as far as enemy hazards were concerned. [Lois] Roy's ship was fired upon by snipers—but not hit; [Wilma] Janek's tangled with either a barrage line or a land mine and lost a wing; [Margaret "Betty"] Rice hit Air Evac Strip #1 just in time for an air raid; [Margaret] Murphy's plane skidded sideways and blew a tire while landing with a full load of patients; One of [Stasia] Pejko's prepared for a crash landing which luckily failed to be necessitated. However no one was hurt and all were happy."[32] Jenny Boyle of the 816 MAES summed up the prevailing attitude of many colleagues when she said, "There were a lot of things about it that weren't all that great, but we always said that any landing you walked away from was a good one."[33]

The planes transported back from France patients who needed more definitive or extended treatment or lengthy rehabilitation were air-evacuated from Prestwick to the United States. On a flight from England to Prestwick on 27 July 1944, when the plane on which they were traveling crashed en route, Lieutenant Mary Jackley and an enlisted technician, both members of the 813 MAES, lost their lives, as did their thirteen patients and the flight crew. Although exact conditions could not be ascertained, the accident leading to their deaths was thought to be weather related. Jackley was the fifth flight nurse in the 26 November 1943 Bowman Field graduating class to lose her life during World War II.[34]

August was the busiest month yet for air evacuation after D Day, with the 806 MAES returning 9,012 patients from France to England, bringing that squadron's total to 20,142. For the 810 MAES, August was the highlight of their overseas tour and the first month its members sincerely believed they, like their 819 MAES colleagues, were doing the work for which they had been trained.[35]

During the summer months, once the assault phase of Operation Overlord had ended, the invasion of France was progressing, and it was safe to do so, some MAES began relocating in whole or in part to France, sometimes for only a couple of weeks, to Dreux, Le Mans, Marseilles, Metz, Mourmelon, Orleans, Pouilly, Villacoublay, and Le Bourget and Orly airports near Paris. From these sites, they flew air evacuation missions within France, from France to England, and from France to the United States. Flights from the Continent flew first to the Azores before flying on to the United States via either Newfoundland or Bermuda. Although the flight nurses and enlisted technicians typically flew only as far as the Azores, they occasionally continued with the mission all the way to the States.

Air evacuation of patients continued at a rapid pace through the fall of 1944. In September, the 813 MAES evacuated just over seven thousand patients, more than in all other months combined.[36] On 27 September, flight nurse Reba Whittle and enlisted technician Jonathan L. Hill of the 813 MAES were en route to France to pick up patients when their C-47 strayed into German airspace, encountered anti-aircraft fire, and crashed when attempting to land. Germans took the crewmembers, Whittle and Hill among them, prisoner. Whittle's story is the subject of the next chapter.

Like the 813, in September 1944 the 815 MAES shattered its previous record of patients evacuated. October was the busiest air evacuation month since arrival overseas for the 817 MAES. By December 1944, the 813 MAES had evacuated more than twenty-five thousand patients and set a new monthly record of 8,470 patients flown. Most of its squadron members each had fifty air evacuation missions to their credit.[37]

The 817 MAES had reason to be proud of one of its own, flight nurse Ann Krueger, for her heroic action when evacuating twenty-seven wounded soldiers on a C-47 from France back to England on 30 December 1944. Because of bad weather at the destination, as he reached the English Channel, the pilot was ordered to return to France. The radio failed and fuel ran low; then when poor visibility prevented the pilot from locating an airfield, he decided to crash-land. When the pilot informed Krueger of the situation, she controlled her own nerves and reassured her anxious patients as she prepared them for the impending crash. They followed Krueger's every move with their eyes as she calmly went about her work. After checking their safety belts carefully, she led them in song. Krueger, who had neither a safety belt nor a seat of her own, stayed with her patients. Immediately after the plane crashed, it caught on fire. Krueger quickly evacuated all the patients from the plane, which was in danger of exploding. She then checked them for physical injury and mental stress and made contact with the nearest hospital where they could be taken. Krueger's outstanding work on the mission earned her the Soldier's Medal.[38]

Much of the air evacuation activity in the fall of 1944 involved transporting patients from Scotland or France back to the United States, though MAES continued to evacuate patients within Europe. As hospital beds in England filled with casualties from France, increasing numbers of flight nurses and enlisted technicians were allocated to ATC to provide medical teams for transatlantic air evacuation from the United Kingdom, or later France, back to the United States.

Transatlantic Air Evacuation

As a result of global air evacuation requirements, beginning in 1944, ATC expanded its air evacuation capability. Until that time, air transport had been considered only an adjunct to primary transport by sea. Until May 1944, military planners did not consider the overall wartime patient load in Europe heavy enough to merit expanding transatlantic air evacuation. But in preparation for the D-Day invasion of Normandy, that changed when hospitals in Europe needed to clear their beds of patients whose hospitalizations were expected to exceed 180 days. The 830 MAES, which had been activated in November 1944 with headquarters at Gravelly Point, Virginia, had thirty-eight flights, each composed of a flight surgeon, six flight nurse–enlisted technician teams, and two enlisted support personnel, all attached to ATC. The 822 and 829 MAES, also assigned to ATC, were disbanded in December 1944 and incorporated into the 830 MAES; these nine flights then were assigned to air evacuation duty in Europe. By year's end, the 830 MAES had forty flights. To accommodate air evacuation needs on the European front, the number rose to fifty-six by April 1945 and to seventy-eight by that July.[39]

In 1944 the 9th Troop Carrier Command in Europe, in whose planes the MAES flew their air evacuation missions, agreed to lend ATC the 816 MAES in July, then the 806 and 819 MAES in August for transatlantic air evacuation duty at Prestwick. Although the Troop Carrier Command welcomed the use of its underutilized MAES for those flights, it was willing only to loan them, not transfer them permanently to ATC.[40] In October, the 816 MAES moved from Prestwick to France, first to Le Mans, then to Orleans, before moving the next month to Istres to assist in the air evacuation of patients from the Belfort Gap region. In December, the 816 moved back to Orleans to evacuate patients from France and Belgium to Orly and to Prestwick.[41]

Transatlantic flights departed only from Prestwick until Paris was liberated on 25 August 1944, after which flights departed from Orly Airfield near Paris as well. Depending on the seasonal weather, air evacuation missions made intermediate stops primarily in the Azores and Newfoundland—though Iceland and Labrador also provided facilities for transiting air evacuation flights—before terminating in New York.

An alternate route took patients from the Azores through Bermuda and into Miami. In September 1944, flights from the 822 and 829 MAES stationed at Lajes Field in the Azores and at Harmon Field in Newfoundland relieved the medical crews on board air evacuation flights from Prestwick and Orly and flew with the patients to New York. The air evacuation crews shuttled between their bases and the next stations. Teams that left Prestwick or Orly moved to the top of the list for the next leg of an air evacuation trip after a twenty-four-hour crew rest, giving flight nurses and enlisted technicians an opportunity to proceed on to New York, from where, after sufficient crew rest, they returned to their home bases.[42] Because of the time it took for their personnel to return to Europe after a transatlantic air evacuation mission, more than one squadron flew these routes. Often, a primary MAES on detached service to ATC was augmented by flight nurse–enlisted technician teams from other MAES for the first leg of the mission.

The flights from Prestwick to the United States and back were not without danger for patients and crew alike and could be a long, hard grind, with many seriously ill patients requiring considerable nursing care.[43] Blanche Solomon, a flight nurse with first the 822 MAES, then the 830 MAES, was stationed at Harmon Field between May and September 1944, then at Lajes Field, and finally at Orly Field, June through October 1945. Much of her flying was between the Azores and Newfoundland. On one flight, she had at least three blind patients——two in litter tiers and one whose litter was on the floor of the plane. This last one concerned her most: he had lost his eyes as a result of combat wounds, and Solomon had to irrigate his eye sockets fairly frequently. On an earlier leg, the wheels on the plane's landing gear had not rolled properly, but the plane had been taken up and tested without the patients on board, and everything seemed to be working fine. Yet there was still a chance that the wheels would not roll when they landed. Solomon informed the patients about the situation and told the blind patients in the litter tiers that she would yell a warning just before the plane hit the ground so they could hold onto their litters. When she told the patient on the floor, she almost wept when he said, "Lieutenant, when you leave me, tell me you're going so I'm not left talking to myself, because the nurse in the hospital did that, and I was talking for the longest time." As they were getting ready to land, Solomon yelled, "Okay, hang on tight, and you'll know when you're rolling." She sat on the floor next to the blind patient, because he was scared. "The wheels rolled," Solomon said. "We had no problem, and we all breathed a sigh of relief."[44]

On 25 July 1944, Lieutenant Catherine Price of the 817 MAES, on detached service with the 816 MAES, was lost along with her enlisted technician and eighteen litter patients when the aircraft in which they were traveling was reported missing en route to Newfoundland. The last communication with the flight crew occurred about two hundred miles off the southern tip of Greenland. After a month of searching for the missing aircraft and waiting for word from or about its crewmembers, all hope of finding survivors was abandoned. Alice Fraser, a close friend, wrote "The Lost Mercy Plane" in Price's memory. Two of the poem's six stanzas illustrate the tone of the tribute:

> One of the stars in our service flag
> Has turned from blue to gold;
> A nurse's cap has been laid aside
> God has given her a crown to hold.
> . . . .
> And the boys on board that mercy plane,
> Had faith in her gentle hand.
> But why it had to be Catherine
> We may never understand.[45]

Lieutenant Vivianna Cronin, a member of the 818 MAES, was killed shortly after midnight on 28 August 1944, when, returning to Prestwick from a transatlantic air evacuation mission to the United States, the C-54 in which she was traveling as a passenger crashed. The weather was bad, and, apparently, when trying to see the lights on the airfield, the pilot brought his plane in too low and struck a radio tower about a mile outside of Prestwick. The plane burst into flames on contact, and all aboard were killed instantly.[46]

The Final Year of the War

The Germans launched their last major offensive against the Allies in the densely forested Ardennes Mountains region of Belgium in December 1944. Known as the Battle of the Bulge from the way the incursion into Allied lines was depicted in English-speaking newspapers, the German advance caught the Allied forces by surprise at a time Allied aircraft could not attack because of heavy cloud cover. The weather eventually cleared, and, despite supply problems, the Allies prevailed, stopping the German advance in January 1945. But this bloodiest of battles took an enormous toll in soldiers killed and wounded.

Some MAES, whose air evacuation missions had tapered off during the fall months, suddenly found their workloads increased through the spring of 1945 as they evacuated casualties from Belgium to France and on to England or the United States. A new policy implemented during the Battle of the Bulge had authorized air evacuation to the United States for patients whose expected length of hospitalization overseas would be more than 120 days, thus increasing the number of ATC flights needed.[47] The previous policy had kept patients overseas much longer.

The 811 MAES, which, because of poor weather, experienced an all-time low in number of patients evacuated in January, had its busiest month in squadron history that March, when it transported 12,480 patients in thirty-one days. April and May were busy as well. The 815 MAES, which had moved to Orly in February 1945 to transport patients back to the United States, experienced its most active month. The squadron remained in France through March, augmented by teams from the 814, 816, and 817 MAES, for a total of 149 assigned and attached personnel. The 816 MAES achieved its highest number of patients evacuated in April, with 8,725 transported. The 817 MAES, which felt underutilized in January 1945, evacuated 14,860 patients out of Germany in April, following the breakthrough from the Rhine.[48]

Three flight nurses assigned in Europe were killed in aircraft accidents during the final year of the war. Lieutenant Jean Herko of the 814 MAES assigned in England was killed on 2 February 1945 in an aircraft crash while on a routine flight to Italy; she was the sixth flight nurse death from the class that graduated on 26 November 1943.[49]

Two flight nurses lost their lives on the same day in 1945 when on air evacuation missions in Germany. On the morning of 13 April, the C-47 on which Lieutenant Christine Gasvoda of the 817 MAES was traveling in an eighteen-plane formation was en route to Hildesheim, Germany, to deliver a load of gasoline and pick up patients for air evacuation to France. The overcast skies and dense fog required that the pilot fly on instruments alone. Seeing an opening in the fog, he descended, but the fog closed in again and the plane struck trees, flipped over, and crashed twelve miles northeast of Paderborn, Germany. The sole surviving crewmember sought help in a nearby village. All others on board were pronounced dead. Although some crewmembers on other planes in the formation saw black smoke, no trace of the downed aircraft was found.[50]

Lieutenant Wilma "Dolly" Vinsant, shown in illustration 7.2, was killed in an aircraft accident that same day. Assigned with the 806 MAES, Vinsant, who apparently had flown her allotted number of combat missions, allegedly talked her commander into letting her fly one more. One of three planes in formation that had delivered gasoline to an airstrip in Germany, Vinsant's was on its way to another airstrip to pick up a load of patients for air evacuation when it encountered a low cloud ceiling. Attempting to fly below the clouds, the plane formation approached hilly terrain requiring an increase in altitude. Two planes were successful; the third, on which Vinsant was flying, struck trees, crashed near Mülhausen, and was totally demolished.[51]

Frances Sandstrom, a flight nurse with the 816 MAES, had her life saved by a conscious decision to miss a flight, when the plane on which she probably should have flown crashed, killing all on board. She had made it all the way to New York on a flight with patients from Prestwick and was waiting to return to Scotland. After the flight and medical crews had been in New York for forty-eight hours, they were required to report to the base and add their names to a list for a return flight. They then called in every four hours to check space available on the next flight. Captain Fissell, the flight surgeon who had been on Sandstrom's flight, told her about a plane with space on it that she should, by policy, take back to Scotland. For some reason that she afterward forgot, she decided to take her chances on a later flight. "And do you know, when that plane landed in Prestwick, it crashed, and they were all killed. And Fissell was on it," Sandstrom explained. She considered herself lucky to have missed the flight and was in shock for a while, trying not to dwell on it too much. But then she thought, *Oh, I'd better be a good girl. Somebody's been awful good to me.*"[52]

While other squadrons were setting new records for number of patients evacuated, the 819 MAES flight nurses were grousing about their assignment in Prestwick. With three complete squadrons available for air evacuation missions beginning in September 1944, the workload was light. When the 816 MAES had left for France in October and the 806 MAES was rumored to be on its way soon, La Munyan turned to the squadron history as an "outlet for a thousand woes which make the best souls rile," namely, delayed movement orders for the 819 MAES.[53] "Thirty days has November'—and THAT was ENOUGH. Our three months sentence with ATC is finally completed—or should be," wrote Sanders the next month.[54] The situation had not improved by December, and Sanders' parody, ""Twas the night before Christmas' in the ETO," with its prayers "in hopes that our orders soon would be here" brought no results. As the holidays approached, with too much time on the flight nurses' hands, their gripes intensified when holiday packages and mail failed to reach them. When the most wished-for gift—transfer orders—still did not materialize, La Munyan picked up her pen again to indulge in some self-pity that the squadron's transfer orders had been "well ignored": "Our Mail cannot find us; We're parked upon shelves, / We surely feel sorry for—namely—ourselves."[55] Orders finally arrived in February 1945, sending the 819 MAES to Greenham Common and from there to France in April, which proved to be the squadron's busiest month, when it evacuated 12,354 patients from Germany and France to England.[56]

May marked the end of hostilities in Europe. But V-E Day on 8 May did not end the need for air evacuation of casualties. The War Department wanted to move as many patients from Europe as possible before military resources redeployed, so in that month the evacuation policy was changed to transport to the United States those whose hospitalization would exceed sixty days. The new policy gave all medical crews flying with ATC a chance to return regularly to the United States. To accommodate the number of patients requiring air evacuation, in May 1945 nine flights of the 830 MAES were divided between Prestwick and Orly airfields for ATC transatlantic evacuation missions. The 810, 814, and 815 MAES were assigned to ATC, disbanded, and reformed as twelve numbered flights of the 830 MAES and were divided evenly among Prestwick, Orly, and Naples.[57]

In May, the 811 MAES evacuated 8,276 patients. The 806 MAES, located in Pouilly, topped that number the same month, when it transported 8,300 patients in 353 planes, with flight nurses and enlisted technicians flying separately to provide the in-flight medical care. The number of patients needing air evacuation remained high throughout the summer. The 817 MAES moved in May from Toul, in northeastern France, where some of their patients had been liberated from German prisons, to Orly to participate in ATC transatlantic air evacuation of patients. The 819 MAES, still in France, at Mourmelon, that month flew daily air evacuation missions, though the numbers of patients were decreasing. In June, the 806 MAES evacuated 6,788 patients, and in July the 7,617 patients transported included the first air evacuation from Berlin.[58] In August 1945, air evacuation out of Prestwick ceased and MAES moved to Orly, from where all air evacuation to the States now originated.[59]

As summer arrived, many of the MAES were preparing to board ships at a French port, from where they would redeploy to the Pacific for continued air evacuation duties. Word of Japan's imminent surrender caused a change in plans, and the ten MAES found themselves headed for home instead.

08

Flight Nurse Prisoner of War

The flight nurses of the 807 MAES were not the only ones to wind up on the ground behind enemy lines. Not quite a year after their unexpected crash landing in Albania, a flight nurse on duty with the 813 MAES in England was aboard a plane traveling to pick up patients on the Continent for air evacuation when it was forced down in Germany after encountering enemy flak.

Flight Nurse Captured by Germans

When on 26 November 1943 Brigadier General Grant challenged the graduating class of flight nurses, "And so you must go beyond your training—beyond the line of duty when called upon—cheerfully, willingly, gloriously," he could not have anticipated that one of the nurses in his audience would put his words to the test as a prisoner of war.[1] Surely, this was furthermost from her mind when Lieutenant Reba Whittle heard the air surgeon deliver the inspiring speech that launched her class into their work as air evacuation nurses.

After receiving her diploma from the Medical and Surgical Memorial Hospital School of Nursing in San Antonio, Texas, in 1941, Whittle entered the United States Army, with assignments at Kirkland Air Base, New Mexico, and Mather Field, California, before arriving at Bowman Field for flight nurse training. The day of her graduation, she became among the first nurses assigned to the 813 MAES. The squadron, activated the previous month, was one of several destined for duty in Europe in preparation for D Day and the invasion of Normandy. In January 1944, the 813 MAES arrived overseas, where it participated in air evacuation missions within the United Kingdom as well as in flights returning sick and wounded soldiers from Prestwick, Scotland, to the United States. After the invasion of Normandy, the 813 MAES evacuated patients from the battlefronts on the Continent back to the United Kingdom. When Whittle had been flying less than nine months but had forty missions to her credit, one of these trips became her worst nightmare.

On 27 September 1944, Whittle and enlisted technician Jonathan L. Hill were traveling on a C-47 to an airstrip in France where they would pick up twenty-four litter patients for evacuation back to England. Also on board were the pilot, copilot, crew chief, and a passenger. Once over the Continent, the pilot strayed off course, likely a result of his own navigational error, and entered enemy airspace over Germany. Up to this point, the flight had been routine, and Whittle had been making plans for a trip to London on her day off, starting the next day. Her diary, which she kept from that day until the end of November, describes her experience.[2]

Whittle was sleeping soundly in the back of the plane when she was "suddenly awakened by terrific sounds of guns and cracklings of the plane as if it had gone into bits." She had no idea what was happening but noticed that Hill was wounded in the leg and was bleeding. The noise had gotten worse, and Whittle saw the plane's left engine "blazing away." She did not expect to land in one piece: "My prayers were used and quick."

According to accident reports, the plane had been hit by German antiaircraft fire near Aachen, Germany, where it was seen feathered and smoking at treetop level before, in attempting to land, it crashed and burst into flames.[3] Whittle began to scream and cry; Hill consoled her. Hours seemed to pass before the plane suddenly hit the ground, still blazing, and Whittle landed head first in the navigator's compartment. When she noticed other crewmembers crawling out the top hatch, she

8.1 Reba Whittle of 813 MAES after plane crash (USAF photo)

followed them. The pilot, who appeared badly wounded, was the last one to leave the plane; the passenger never made it out.

Soldiers appeared immediately. Whittle thought they might be British, but they were German, and she thought, "We've had it chum." Whittle thought first of her fiancé, Lieutenant Colonel Stanley W. Tobiason, a pilot stationed in England, who would be waiting for her to return that evening. Her next thought was how "thankful and grateful" she was to be alive. She eventually got word to Tobiason that she was alive and well by writing civilian friends who passed her message along to him.[4]

Both Whittle and Hill were injured in the crash. Whittle, shown in illustration 8.1, received a concussion and a severe laceration on her forehead; later that day she developed back and head pain and dizziness. Hill apparently injured his left arm and his leg. The Germans bandaged the injured crewmembers and marched them away on what would be a long trek with several stopping points. "The surprised look on their faces when they saw a woman was amazing," Whittle recalled. The sound of firing was "terrific," and she thought it was headed her way. Her training at Bowman Field came to mind, and Whittle "really wanted to hug the ground." But the German soldiers only laughed at her and motioned that the firing was above her head.

The Americans were taken first to a small village, where their captors had a discussion with an officer, then on to a small town about a mile away, where they were taken to a cellar. Here, a physician checked their injuries and applied fresh bandages to wounds, and the Americans had to give up their personal belongings. Then they were on their way again, this time to a brick house about two or three miles away. The journey was a slow one because of Hill's wounded leg. Along the way, a German soldier yanked Whittle's air corps patch off her uniform and threw it down, saying something in German that she could not understand.

At the house, the Americans stood before several German officers in an office before being pushed outside to sit on the ground dressed only in their flight uniforms, without overcoats or jackets. When a truck came along, the German officers motioned for them to get in it. They rode to a larger village and were put in a barn, where they laid on the floor. Soon a German officer arrived and interrogated the crewmembers one by one. A guard gave Whittle and the others some pears, "which tasted very good, as we had nothing to eat all day." After some time the German officer took them into the kitchen of the house, where they ate black bread and butter and drank some black German coffee. Whittle thought it "heavenly" to have something to eat and to feel a little bit warm again. More German officers arrived and looked at the passes that had already been collected from the Americans. Each German glared at Whittle, seemed startled to see an American female, and called her "Schwester," which was German for "nurse." She mused, "Don't know how monkeys feel in the zoo with so many people looking at them but thought I must know by now."

Prisoner of War

Whittle barely had time for the cup of soup offered her before the group was herded onto a bus for a forty-minute ride to a "huge" prison with a high metal fence and a guard at the gate. After appearing before German officers in an office, the Americans were taken upstairs and locked into two dirty rooms, one for Whittle and the other for the men. Whittle was so frightened of being in a room by herself that she pulled her mattress into the room where the male crewmembers were. Few of them slept that night. First came the interrogator "asking usual questions." Then an air raid alarm sounded, and the German said, "Well to [sic] bad—you know you might be bombed by your own people." Throughout the night, Whittle heard continuous tapping, which awakened her each time she dozed. She couldn't help but wonder with horror what might happen next.

The next morning, after a breakfast of cold black German coffee, black bread, and margarine, the Americans rode in yet another truck through several villages, where people gaped at them and did a double-take when they saw a woman. "Guess many have wondered just what I was," Whittle reflected. Their next stop was a German hospital, where a physician shook his head and told Whittle, "To [sic] bad having a woman as you are the first one and no one knows exactly what to do." The Americans were fed before the truck took them to Koln.

At Koln Whittle again wound up in a room by herself. Again, she did not want to be alone, and for the first time, she "let down and cried. They couldn't figure out what was wrong with me." She asked the Germans to let her enlisted technician stay with her and felt much better when he arrived, but she could not stop crying for "quite awhile."

The next day, the crewmembers were taken into yet another office for questioning by yet another group of officers. The Germans asked Whittle more questions, said what a pity it was for them to have an American nurse, and tried to assure her that she would be released "very shortly." The shock of the experience had caught up with her; she was upset and had trouble holding back her tears. When the Germans saw her crying, they thought someone must have been "brutal" to her and asked her about it. "Then they asked me if I had had enough of it," Whittle wrote in her diary. "So I said, 'Yes enough black bread and cold coffee.'"

After the questioning, the crew had to turn over the rest of their effects. Another meal, and another leg of their journey followed, this time by train to Frankfurt, a stopping point for all POWs. There, Whittle was separated from the other crewmembers and taken to a room about eight feet by eight feet. "Well that was a cell and I was locked in proper," Whittle said. It was "extremely depressing," and the more she thought about being in a cell and wondered what might happen next, the more terrified she became and started crying again. She "felt more like scream-ing and a perfect wonder I didn't."

The place was dirty but warm. Here again, German officers told Whittle "how sorry they were to have a nurse as a POW as they had no facilities at all." They said she would go to a hospital nearby, about a fifteen-minute walk. She wrote: "Arrived through locked gates of course and into a large area which was very beautiful"—Whittle recalled "a nice lawn, flowers and very nice looking buildings under those huge trees." She was taken into a small hall, where she was given "coffee, black bread as usual and butter. It did taste good."

By now, not even a bath, the kindness of a German nurse, and a Red Cross kit with men's shorts, socks, and sundry items could console Whittle, who again began crying hysterically. But her situation definitely had improved with a comfortable room, flowers, fruit, even bobby pins, and daily walks.

Hospital Duty

On 6 October, Whittle was taken to Obermassfeld, a British and American hospital, for a day but was soon on the road again, this time to the hospital at Meiningen, which she described on her arrival as "a very large building which used to be an old concert hall. A few barracks scattered in the yard behind the barbed wire. Many fellows out in the yard." She had a comfortable room, water for daily ablutions, a weekly bath, and walks with a guard several times a week; but she was the only woman in a hospital of five hundred men. This was a rehabilitation hospital, and Whittle worked in the massage room. She apparently got along well with the men. They invited her to their private messes for evening tea, and some of them even wrote her into a song, sung to the tune of "John Brown's Body":

> We also have a Lady Nurse, who come[s] from Texas Way,
> She strokes your hand, and pats your cheek, and smoothes
>   your cares away,
> But when she looks into your eyes—O-Boy!—it's just OK
> In Meiningen Lazarett.[5]

The American, British, and Canadian Red Cross sent food parcels, and Whittle obtained GI clothing from the Red Cross as well. British fliers gave her the silk lining from their flying boots, with which she made underwear.[6] Whittle's diary reflects that all the men did what they could to make her more comfortable and happy, giving her a shirt, some hankies, perfume, little whatnots, even lipstick. "Was too bad I didn't get out of the plane with my jacket," Whittle said, "as I even had nail polish in my pocket." With the gift by a German officer's wife of a few more bobby pins and some curlers, Whittle took great pride in her hair.

But time passed all too slowly. "My mornings were OK as I worked," she wrote, "but afternoons and evening sometimes seemed like days. Tried reading as they had a fair size library but my mind just couldn't stay on a book. Tried drawing, painting, embroidery, knitting, making little animals." After about four weeks, men from a Swiss delegation talked with Whittle, and she had high hopes for repatriation. Her case was unique, though, they explained.

Whittle's diary ended without explanation before she at last was repatriated in January 1945. As part of a prisoner exchange, she left Stalag Luft IX on 25 January, accompanied by members of the German Red Cross. She traveled in a boxcar with other prisoners—most of them ill—and went first to Switzerland, where she was the overnight guest of a Swiss couple. She must have enjoyed the luxury of her first hot bath in months. The next day, she was repatriated with 109 other American prisoners of war.

A Quiet Repatriation

Whittle initially was presumed missing in action when the 813 MAES received word that the plane in which she was flying had been shot down by the enemy. Results of an investigation furnished to the squadron about six weeks later indicated she had been killed in action. By December 1944, the squadron knew she had survived the airplane crash, had been a POW in Germany, and had been repatriated to the United States through neutral sources. An informative cable from the War Department notified Whittle's parents of the news and of her imminent return home. A telegram from President Roosevelt to Whittle, obviously sent to the other POWs as well, was more upbeat in tone: "As your Commander in Chief, I take pride in your past achievements and express the thanks of a grateful Nation for your services in combat and your steadfastness while a prisoner of war. May God grant each of you happiness and an early return to health."[7]

After Whittle arrived in the United States in February 1945, the army put her through the usual physical examinations and security debriefings. She also signed a nondisclosure certificate, which read in part, "I realize that publicity concerning my experiences, by word of mouth or otherwise, will endanger the lives of many persons and therefore it is my duty to take all possible precautions to prevent it."[8] Details about her experience as a POW had been classified as secret military information.

Whittle received the Purple Heart, Air Medal, and promotion to first lieutenant in short succession after her return home in 1945. She also was hospitalized for a full medical assessment and treatment of injuries sustained during the aircraft crash and resulting time spent in the German prison camp.

Ethel Carlson, who had been sent from Europe back to the United States because of a kidney problem, met Whittle when the two were roommates at the Miami Beach Rest and Rehabilitation Center in March 1945, following their stateside hospitalizations. Carlson recalled that Whittle "looked absolutely terrible!" Her hair was bristly where it had been shaved to treat her head wound, and her eyes were "starey," perhaps referring to the "thousand-yard stare" characteristic of combat stress. "She was thin. She looked frightened," Carlson continued. "She looked like, well, she looked like she had been treated badly, although the Germans treated her all right except that they wouldn't give her any special considerations as a nurse until later."[9]

Eventually the medical board found Whittle capable of limited military duty, followed by full duty by the end of that year. She was suspended indefinitely from flying status, however. Assigned as a ward nurse at Hamilton Field, California, in June 1945, she wed Tobiason at the end of the summer. She left the military by choice in January 1946.

Mary Frank has compared Whittle's imprisonment with that of the army and navy nurses imprisoned by the Japanese in the Philippines in 1942: "The nurses in the Philippines endured combat conditions for up to four months and suffered the indignity of formal surrender. Lieutenant Whittle, on the other hand, flew from the relative safety of England literally into harm's way. While she did not resist, she did not formally surrender; rather, she was captured."[10]

The nurses interned at Santo Tomas in Manila could draw strength from their numbers, which had an important positive psychological effect. Whittle was the only woman imprisoned in her group and was separated from the rest of her flight crew as well; she thus endured her experience in relative isolation. After their four years of captivity by the Japanese, the nurses in the Philippines were liberated and returned home to a heroes welcome covered by the media. A month earlier, Whittle's return home in a prisoner exchange after four months as a POW in a

German camp went essentially unnoticed in the press, even after the terms of the certificate of nondisclosure were no longer binding.[11]

One article did appear in the *New York Herald Tribune* on 4 March 1945, however, in which Whittle was quoted as saying, "I'm sure I was the greatest nuisance the Germans ever had. Apparently they'd never taken a woman prisoner before, and they didn't have any facilities for keeping me. I kept quoting the Geneva Convention to them—the part about proper segregation of the sexes among prisoners of war—and the more I quoted the more confused they got. I'll always think they repatriated me in desperation."[12] Whittle's story, as well as those of Agnes Jensen and her colleagues who trekked through Albania, add to the lore of flight nurse history, augmented by the experiences of other flight nurses whose assignments were perhaps at times less spectacular but no less important to the conduct of the war.

09

Flight Nursing on the Pacific Front: Pacific Islands

When the Japanese bombed Pearl Harbor in December 1941, civilian nurse Elizabeth Pukas still had six months left on her contract with the Army Corps of Engineers in Antigua, where they were building the airfield that became Coolidge Field. As soon as she returned to her former job in New York City, the Red Cross recruited her for military service. She agreed to join, with the stipulation that she be assigned as a flight nurse. But the military was too slow in granting her request, the impatient Pukas thought. "There is a big, big war going on, and it's going on in the Pacific," she told her chief nurse. When Pukas entered the army, she was asked where she would want to be sent overseas. She replied, "Definitely not Europe, but the Pacific."[1] Pukas eventually got her wish; she graduated from the flight nurse course on 2 July 1943, became chief nurse of the 812 MAES, and traveled with her squadron to Hickam Field, Hawaii, just before Christmas in 1943.

The war in the Pacific was big geographically as well as militarily. The Pacific front included the Southwest Pacific and Central Pacific areas, China-Burma-India (CBI), and Alaska. Of the MAES serving on the Pacific front, three—the 801, 804, and 820—arrived for initial assignments in the Southwest Pacific. The 809 and 812 served first in the Central Pacific. Four other MAES—the 828 through 831—were assigned to ATC for air evacuation of patients from the Pacific region back to the United States.

By the time the first MAES arrived in the Pacific, the Japanese had invaded the Philippines, Malaysia, New Guinea, the Solomon Islands, and the Dutch East Indies (now Indonesia). Their plan to occupy Midway Island, an important refueling stop for the Allies, had been thwarted by American code breakers, leading to an Allied victory. When the 801 MAES arrived at New Caledonia in February 1943, the Japanese had recently conceded Guadalcanal in the Solomon Islands, with its airstrip later named Henderson Field, to the Allies after fierce fighting. The 804 MAES debarked at Brisbane, Australia, four months later, traveling to Port Moresby, New Guinea, for its first assignment, and in March 1944 the 820 MAES arrived in Milne Bay, New Guinea, for duty at Port Moresby. In some parts of New Guinea, fighting continued until the war ended.

Just as the flight nurses assigned to Europe began their work in North Africa, Sicily, and England and advanced through France with flights into Germany as the Continent was liberated from Axis control, the flight nurses sent to the Pacific began their assignments on islands already secured by Allied forces before island-hopping across the ocean following the military as it forged its path toward the Philippines and, ultimately, the mainland of Japan. And just as was the case in Europe, the various MAES worked together, sharing resources and even living quarters, when the military situation and air evacuation needs dictated such an arrangement.

MAES in the Southwest Pacific

The 801 MAES set up its first camp at Tontouta, New Caledonia, near Nouméa, with detachments in more forward locations on other islands. The MAES, minus its flight nurses, flew into Guadalcanal to evacuate patients on a southward route to New Caledonia and New Hebrides. It did not operate as a separate unit but rather as part of the South Pacific Combat Air Transport Command (SCAT), a combined services organization largely under marine control with a navy commander, whose medical department was tasked to provide medical care to personnel on duty at various bases. The 801 MAES was the only air evacuation unit in SCAT, and because it did not have control over its own work, it could not, by its own assessment, offer the most efficient services of which it was capable.[2] Particularly galling to 801 MAES personnel was their difficulty obtaining permission for the flight nurses to fly into Guadalcanal, a trip they were not allowed to make until 1 March 1943. The nurses still could not remain overnight, however, until adequate quarters had been built for their use.[3]

Air evacuation in the Southwest Pacific had many problems to overcome before the system operated effectively. Dry runs, for example, were all too common. Medical personnel flew on all planes into Guadalcanal, but only half of those planes were used to evacuate patients, because of a priority system that assigned lower points to patients than to other passengers, such as combat crews returning from rest leaves. Additionally, when planes with flight nurses were available, SCAT personnel often gave preference to enlisted technicians rather than use flight nurses

9.1 Helena Ilic (left), Lee Holtz (third from left), and colleagues of 801 MAES in front of Burlap Flats flight nurse quarters on Biak (author's collection)

as medical attendants. In August 1943, flight nurses made more than a hundred flights into Guadalcanal but evacuated patients on only thirty-seven of them. The MAES evacuated about 12,745 patients between the first of March, when the squadron was fully operational with flight nurses, until the end of June 1943, but only 3,864 of these patients were attended by flight nurses.[4] Yet another reason for a lower-than-expected patient count was a tendency to transport patients by hospital ship, even when adequate planes and medical crews were available.[5]

The 801 MAES historian complained about the underuse of the flight nurses in his squadron. With adequate emergency quarters and toilet facilities, he saw no reason they could not fly into any forward area where the seriously wounded soldiers needed a nurse's professional skills and abilities. Medical crews should not, however, be subjected to unnecessary risks, he continued, whether from needless trips when no patients were forthcoming or from inadequate security and air cover at advanced areas.[6] Flying was hazardous, and in their first six months squadron members had already been subjected to bombings and attacks while airborne and narrowly missed crash landings due to engine fires, engine failures, and low fuel in bad weather.[7]

One such flight occurred on 27 April 1943, when Lieutenant Dorothy Shikoski was returning from an air evacuation mission as a passenger on a C-47 transporting a sixteen-hundred-pound airplane engine as cargo. When bad weather prevented the plane from landing at Tontouta, its destination, the pilot was forced to make a water landing. He instructed passengers and crew to remain aft of the cargo engine in case it shifted forward on impact with the water, but one crewmember disregarded the instructions. Shikoski jeopardized her own safety as she rushed forward to instruct him to move to the rear of the plane. The plane hit the water before she could reach him. Both Shikoski and the crewmember were pinned in when the engine lurched forward. The crewmember was killed. The crew freed Shikoski, and, despite back and leg injuries, she helped load the life rafts with medical supplies, rations, and water and helped evacuate the other passengers before the plane sank. She became the second army nurse recipient of the Air Medal in recognition of her heroic action.[8]

When the 804 MAES disembarked in Brisbane, Australia, in June 1943, the squadron's flight nurses encountered restrictions similar to those imposed on their 801 MAES colleagues concerning air evacuation flights into forward areas, in part because their squadron, like the 801 MAES, was not yet under control of the army air forces. The squadron idled at Camp Doomben, a former Brisbane racetrack covered with tents, for two and half months before moving to their first station at Port Moresby, New Guinea, with detachments at more forward locations. Even then, only the male members of the squadron were permitted to fly air evacuation missions north of a line between Port Moresby and Dobodura. It was, as an unnamed 804 flight surgeon complained, "impossible to capitalize on the expert training of our flight nurses where they were most urgently needed." In October 1943 the flight nurses were split between Townsville, Australia, and Port Moresby, New Guinea, but by the end of the month the unit at Townsville had moved to Dobodura. The squadron with its flight nurses moved from Dobodura to Port Moresby in December.[9] When the flight nurses of the 820 MAES arrived in Port Moresby in March 1944, they worked with their 804 MAES colleagues already flying air evacuation missions from that location. When the flight nurses, like the rest of the 804 MAES, finally were placed under control of the 5th Air Force, they were permitted to fly out of Nadzab, where they landed "happy and excited, prepared to do the work they had wanted for so long."[9]

"The Flight Nurses were constantly begging to be sent to our most forward installations," wrote the 804 MAES historian.[10] But flying remained dangerous. On 6 March 1944, Lieutenant Gerda Mulack and an enlisted technician were on a routine mission from Nadzab to Saidor in New Guinea to pick up patients for air evacuation. The plane stopped at Finschhafen to on-load cargo and then took off in formation with a number of airplanes. The formation soon ran into bad weather and searched for a hole in the clouds leading to clearer skies. Spotting an opening, the flight leader led his formation through the clouds on a flight path about two hundred feet above the ocean. The pilot of the plane in which Mulack was traveling radioed the flight leader for permission to turn back to Finschhafen. This was the last communication with the plane, which was not seen or heard from after permission was granted. An extensive search by plane and by boat between Finschhafen and Saidor failed to spot evidence of the plane or its crew.[11] A kind letter of condolence that Lieutenant Colonel Gordon Young of the Australian medical corps wrote to the 804 MAES commander revealed the Allied troops' high regard for Mulack and her flight nurse colleagues: "It is not too much to say that every Australian soldier, who was carried in a plane manned by one of these nurses, will cherish a memory of their efficiency, and the kindness and careful attention which was characteristic of them. This admiration and respect is heightened by the knowledge of the risks which are accepted daily by these gallant women."[12]

Chief nurse Lieutenant Mary Kerr's description of the 804 MAES flight nurses' duties in the Pacific typifies the standard nursing care provided on flights in other squadrons as well. The flight nurse observed the pulse, respiration, and color of each patient, paying special attention to early postoperative cases. Patients with mental diagnoses also required the flight nurse's attention; she checked that they were restrained properly and sedated adequately before take-off. Once airborne, the flight nurse administered oxygen to patients with respiratory distress and could insert rectal tubes to relieve distension in patients with abdominal injuries.[13] Flight surgeons of the 801 MAES considered the prompt and proper use of pain medication, plasma, and oxygen the three most important in-flight nursing medical procedures.[14]

Patients with headaches and various types of minor malaise received aspirin or aspirin with codeine; neosynephrine nose drops relieved patients with sinus discomfort. The flight nurse attempted to allay nervousness and fear of flying simply by chatting with the patients; she might give a mild sedative if the patient's anxiety continued. The medical crew made certain that the plane had an adequate supply of blankets, since at high altitudes the patients were likely to feel cold.[15]

Airsickness was a minor problem, Kerr reported, though without quick action on the part of the medical crew, it could become epidemic. The key was to take care of the situation before other patients noticed and reacted. Over time, the 804 MAES evolved a successful treatment for airsickness by placing the affected individual on a litter or in a reclining position, then administering a sedative and a few breaths of oxygen.[16] Medical teams found that patients who were kept occupied were less likely to become airsick, and for this purpose the Red Cross furnished the planes with ditty bags containing games, playing cards, magazines, and pocket-edition books. In addition, patients were given sandwiches, candy bars, fruit juice, coffee, chewing gum, and cigarettes.[17]

Many of the patients the 804 flight nurses evacuated had psychiatric diagnoses. For example, 13 percent of patients evacuated in July 1944 had mental diagnoses; and 12 percent of patients evacuated in August 1944 had neuropsychiatric problems, most of them of a psychotic nature.[18] Care of these patients in flight was particularly important, because disturbances they might cause could affect the safety of other patients and crew-members. That summer, psychiatric problems had been noted in soldiers who had served a long time in the tropics far from civilization, and their safe transport aboard air evacuation aircraft became a major concern to flight surgeons and flight nurse–enlisted technician teams alike.[19] Using a parachute webbing harness, a flight surgeon of the 801 MAES designed a restraint for use during air evacuation of manic patients transported on litters.[20] As part of a study to evaluate the methods employed in handling those patients, flight nurses of the 804 MAES kept clinical data on more than six hundred patients with mental disorders who were evacuated from Port Moresby to Brisbane over a four-month period.[21] ATC, which flew them from the Pacific back to the United States, limited the number of psychotic patients—"locked litters"—on a plane to five, and the medical crew had to include an additional enlisted technician whenever there was any psychotic patient on board.[22]

Like their 801 MAES colleagues, the flight nurses of the 804 MAES had their share of aircraft accidents. On 10 June 1944, Lieutenant Kathleen Dial, an enlisted technician, and a flight surgeon were on an air evacuation mission with eighteen psychotic patients, fifteen of them on litters, en route to Milne Bay when bad weather prevented their C-47 from landing at its destination. The pilot diverted the plane to Port Moresby, but along the route one of the engines failed, and the plane continued its flight on a single engine. The weather at Port Moresby prevented landing on that airstrip, and with poor visibility and fuel running low, the pilot determined that the aircraft must crash-land. The plane continued to fly for about an hour, during which the medical crew prepared the patients and themselves for the crash. They secured litter patients as well as possible and instructed the ambulatory patients how to get into the crash position, which the medical crew would also assume for impact. The flight surgeon later told how calm Dial and the enlisted technician were as they went about their duties knowing that a crash landing was inevitable.

The plane finally landed on tiny Fisherman's Island, near Brisbane. Three of the patients were injured, but not fatally. The three medical attendants, however, were thrown from the plane and sustained serious injuries requiring eventual air evacuation back to the United States for rehabilitation. Dial suffered multiple contusions and fractures. The accident made squadron officials rethink the adequacy of litter fastenings then in use for take-off and landing and identify squadron personnel's lack of knowledge in crash-landing procedures. The squadron took corrective action in both areas.[23]

The 801 MAES moved its main base of operations from Tontouta to Espiritu Santo in the New Hebrides in October 1943. From here, the original flight nurses of the 801 MAES returned to the United States in April 1944 after having served just over a year overseas. Replacements arrived under the tutelage of chief nurse Lieutenant Lucy Wilson, a veteran of Corregidor who requested flight nurse training after escaping with ten other army nurses and one navy nurse on a submarine in May 1942. While settling into their new home on Guadalcanal, where the full squadron relocated in May 1944, the 801 MAES experienced tragedy, in the death of one of their flight nurses.[24]

Lieutenant Eloise Richardson had a premonition of her death. Helena Ilic, one of the new flight nurses, remembered her saying at a party, "I'm never going to leave here." Ilic replied, "Oh, Eloise, of course we are. We're all going to leave here. One day this war will be over, and we'll all go home." But on the evening of 18 May 1944, the plane in which Richardson was flying on her way to pick up a load of patients departed Bougainville for Guadalcanal and vanished. The weather had been poor in the vicinity of New Georgia, but other planes had gotten through without difficulty. The next day, squadron members—flight nurses among them—went up in planes to search the area where the missing plane might have gone down but saw no trace of wreckage.[25] Richardson was declared missing in action. She was the first nurse from the 801 MAES and the fourth from the 26 November 1943 graduating class killed during the war.

Richardson's death ended her flight nurse colleagues' sense of invincibility against the ravages of war. As Lee Holtz explained, "We never thought that this could happen to us. We had been so lucky, and we just never dwelled on it until it happened." Realizing that they, too, were not immune to death, the flight nurses arranged to have a squadron member notify their parents personally, should they die during the war. "We knew they would be notified officially," said Holtz, "but we thought it would be nice if we wrote to each other's parents." After having a memorial for Richardson, the nurses went about their work again, though not quite as before.[26]

Flight nurses in the Pacific, like their colleagues on the European front, had very little to work with as far as supplies and equipment. Holtz recalled that her squadron had "no equipment, really," and what they did have was of poor quality. "We had bandages and morphine in the pocket, and I told you [about] the pistol under the arm. We had plasma that we could give IV, which we did have a lot of." When one of Holtz's patients started bleeding under a makeshift cast and she had no cast cutters, she had to cut it off with bandage scissors. "It was terrible," she remembered. "I had the navigator come back and try to help me, because, you know, it really got very hard to cut this hard cast off, and yet I could see the red creeping through the cast, and I knew I had to get to it to put pressure on it."[27]

Squadron historians occasionally decried the tendency of some organizations to "push off" onto air evacuation personnel a patient they were unwilling or unable to treat, regardless of the patient's chances of tolerating the flight. Technical Memorandum No. 2, "Air Evacuation," issued by Headquarters 5th Air Force on 11 January 1944 specified which cases were not suitable.[28] The policy was often ignored, however, as Lieutenant Evelyn Ordway of the 801 MAES discovered on a flight from Bougainville when a patient listed as having a fractured cervical vertebra had an extensive wet cast of recent application. The patient did not tolerate the flight well, and Ordway arranged to off-load him at Munda airstrip on New Georgia in the Solomon Islands, where he died in the hospital that night.[29]

The names that the flight nurses gave to their Southwest Pacific quarters—Burlap Flats (801 MAES), shown in illustration 9.1, Bickering Heights (804 MAES)—suggest a good-humored acceptance of their primitive living conditions. Added domestic luxuries, such as curtains, bedspreads, and rugs that could be secured "by methods sometimes orthodox and often more devious," added to the contentment of the nurses, and word apparently spread of their desire for more luxurious accommodations. Flight nurses of the 801 MAES were pleased to discover that "this lust for better homes has been picked up by our well-wishers everywhere and on nearly every island there is now tucked obscurely away, an overnight lodge for flight nurses, invariably bedecked, bedeviled and beguarded."[30] A washing machine was a welcome amenity, its arrival long overdue for personnel of the 804 MAES in New Guinea in January 1944. Flight nurse Dorothy Rice wrote Leora Stroup that the small kitchen in their quarters was the busiest spot in New Guinea "except perhaps our brand new washing machine."[31]

Holtz recalled the efforts of her 801 MAES flight nurse colleagues to make the Christmas holidays memorable by creating little Christmas presents from whatever they could beg, borrow, or steal. Their Christmas tree was very droopy and looked like a weeping willow, but the flight nurses used tin foil from cigarette packages, spoons from the mess hall—anything they could find—to decorate it. "It was a big laugh," Holtz remembered. But an even bigger laugh was the gift she received from the Red Cross—a man's sweater, sent to a woman "sitting on the equator." The gift was "about as useless as anything you could possibly think of," Holtz exclaimed.[32]

As part of the medical support for the return to the Philippines in the fall of 1944, the flight nurses of the 801 MAES from Guadalcanal, 804 MAES from Nadzab, and 820 MAES from Port Moresby found themselves together on the island of Biak. The linking up of these flight nurses from three MAES was not without its humorous moments. As the unit historian for the 804 MAES reported in November 1944, "the 820th nurses arrived bag and *baggage*. Included were a cat and about 3 or 4 dogs. One of these was a Great Dane pup, already the size of a Shetland pony. We looked at him rather dubiously and scanned our [food] ration requests with an anxious eye."[33] The many flight nurses and enlisted technicians from the three squadrons were placed on a single roster to spread the insufficient work around fairly.[34]

On their arrival at Biak, the 820 MAES flight nurses had already participated in two missions connected with the liberation of the Philippines. In the first, on ATC planes they evacuated a group of Americans, all veterans of Bataan and Corregidor, from Hollandia, New Guinea, to Amberly Field on the northeast coast of Australia. The men, who had been prisoners of war, held in Japanese camps in Mindanao, were on a Japanese ship that was torpedoed, but they escaped and an American submarine rescued them. The 804 MAES transported a second group made up of army personnel and Philippine civilians from Owi, a tiny island off the southern coast of Biak, to Brisbane.[35]

MAES in the Central Pacific

Unlike their colleagues in other MAES, members of the 809 MAES traveled to their overseas destination by air, not sea. Officers, including flight nurses, and enlisted men flew from Hamilton Field, California, in five ATC planes to Hickam Field, Hawaii, in November 1943. The 812 MAES arrived at the same location by the more conventional route in December, having sailed from California. The two squadrons pooled their resources, sharing a personnel office and operating jointly to evacuate casualties from the Gilbert and Marshall Islands to Oahu through June 1944.[36]

The flight nurses of both squadrons were housed initially in base quarters at Hickam Field, but, although they were less primitive than those of their colleagues on other islands, these accommodations were not up to the standards of 812 MAES chief nurse Elizabeth Pukas. When she learned that she and her twenty-four flight nurses were to be housed in two three-bedroom houses, she went to the commanding flight surgeon

9.1 The Pacific Islands

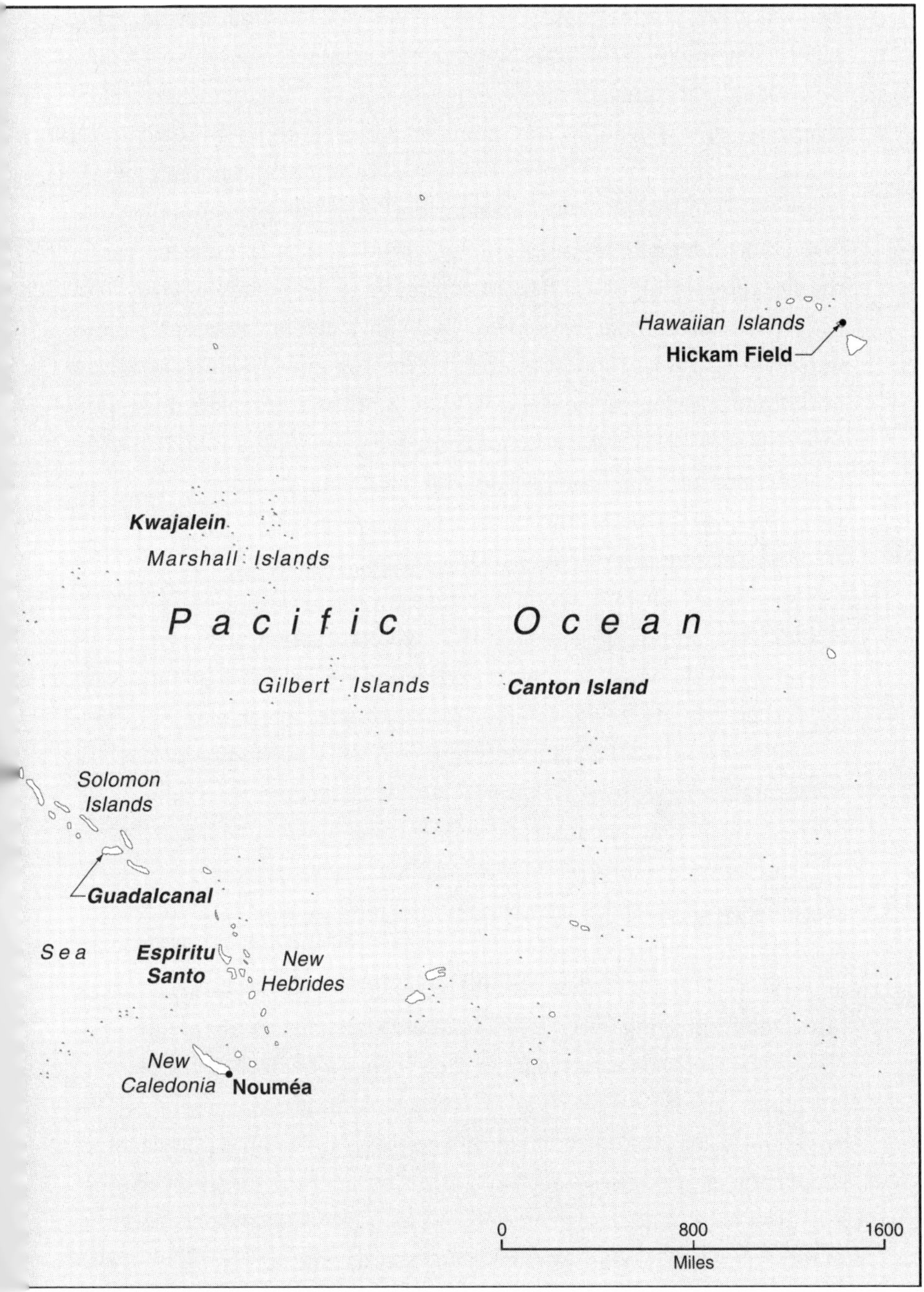

Hawaiian Islands

Hickam Field

Kwajalein

Marshall Islands

P a c i f i c   *O c e a n*

Gilbert Islands   **Canton Island**

Solomon
Islands

Guadalcanal

S e a   **Espiritu
Santo**   New
Hebrides

New
Caledonia   **Nouméa**

0   800   1600

Miles

and requested another house, to make their accommodations more livable. When told that the housing was temporary, since her nurses would be out on flights much of the time, Pukas replied, "Yes, but there will be a number of us having to stay home in between flights to recuperate, to refurbish, to repack. . . . And I'm very sure you would not ask a male counterpart to live in such close quarters." The nurses eventually were given more adequate housing, but not before their chief nurse had taken the situation through the chain of command to headquarters level. "I'm not too forward," Pukas explained, "but I am a chief nurse. . . . My flight nurses are extremely important to me." The amenities of home were also important to Pukas. Once she obtained the third house, she decorated them all with paintings on loan from a local art museum and stocked the kitchens with good foods from the nearby navy commissary. Pukas was, she said, the flight nurses' "surrogate mother."[37]

Shortly after their arrival overseas, flight nurses of the 809 and 812 MAES flew air evacuation missions from Oahu to other Hawaiian islands; six nurses of each squadron were stationed at Canton until the next month, when permission arrived to station them at Tarawa in the Gilbert Islands.[38] Flight nurse Lieutenants Elsie Nolan and Victoria Pavlowski of the 812 MAES made a bit of history as the first two white women known to arrive on Baker Island, when an engine on their plane died en route from Tawara to Hawaii with patients on board.[39]

The flight surgeons of the 801 and 804 MAES provided squadron personnel with didactic instruction on the medical aspects of air evacuation, but flight surgeons of the 809 and 812 MAES carried their training one step further. When the flight nurses of both squadrons were restricted from flying into Kwajalein in the Marshall Islands, resulting in downtime, their squadron leaders took them on bivouac in the Hawaiian mountains for an expected two weeks in May 1944. Flight nurses served as executive officer, mess officer, plans and training officer, and supply officer and filled other key positions under the direction of their squadron commander. Fifteen enlisted men provided support services as mess sergeant, cooks, kitchen help, guards, and drivers. Unlike the bivouacs at Bowman Field, in Hawaii the enlisted men set up the sanitary installations and pitched the tents for the nurses. The nurses also rode most of the way to the campsite and walked only the last two miles. The usual lectures, inspections, calisthenics, and athletics filled their days between meals, which were reported as excellent with plenty of fresh fruit, vegetables, and meat. Movies and wiener roasts with Coca-Cola and beer for purchase filled the evenings.

This was certainly not the standard bivouac protocol, but not all the flight nurses were willing participants. Executive officer Lieutenant Mary Reardon reported that because the flight nurses did not understand the reason for the bivouac, their attitude was "questionable." They had made "a big fuss about it," Sally Jones of the 812 MAES recalled.[40] Many nurses thought they were not learning anything and that the physical activity involved in bivouac could have been accomplished on base. "It must be said, however," Reardon explained, "that many nurses cooperated and tried to do their best to help in conducting the bivouac."[41] All the flight nurses must have been pleased to hear their commander order "Strike Tents" after only one week.[42]

Chief nurse Pukas remembered that she was always the first flight nurse in her squadron to go into an island before air evacuation activities began from that location. While the plane was being converted for patient transport, she did liaison work with the navy in charge of the island to arrange quarters, which were often tents; bathing and laundry facilities; and meals for her nurses. Until these basic needs were met, the flight nurses might fly into an island but did not stay overnight.[43]

As for the care the flight nurses gave their patients, Pukas recalled, the flight surgeons on the ground had left them standard orders regarding decisions about blood, plasma, or medications and more specific orders for particular patients with particular conditions. But in the air, each flight nurse was completely on her own. "Two corpsmen, one flight nurse, thirty-six patients severely wounded. . . . Remember, you're ten thousand feet in the air, ten thousand miles away. There's no one to turn to, and there are extraordinary situations that come up. You do the best you know how, you hope and pray that when you land, that the individual receiving your report will say, 'Fine. I could have done no better.'"[44]

The happy times were when the flight nurses, often out on the islands for days at a time, arrived back at Hickam Field. After making their reports, handing over records, and loading their equipment on a jeep, they arrived at their quarters for at least twenty-four hours, where they could unpack, bathe, wash their hair, relax, and repack. During these times, the flight nurses hosted house parties for which they donned their evening dresses that they, like flight nurses in other areas of the world, had tucked into their footlockers for special occasions.[45]

Jo Nabors of the 812 MAES remembered flying into Canton, Kwajalein, Eniwetok, New Guinea, and Australia. Once her squadron started transporting patients from Tarawa and Saipan, the medical crews were quite busy—"you barely got a load of patients in the plane to take back, then you had to go back down and pick up some more." When the flight nurses were grounded on an island for a few days, the navy would invite them to shipboard dinners. "That was the best thing," Nabors said, remembering the fresh fruit, vegetables, and meat. "We'd sell our soul," they told their commander, "for an invitation to get over there and smell fresh-brewed coffee" after all the C-rations the flight nurses had to endure.[46] Holtz agreed. It did not matter who invited the flight nurses, they always went. "We'd go with anybody to get to eat a meal with the navy. You got to that point."[47]

Of all the patients she transported, Nabors had particular concern for those with psychological problems. Despite working for three months on a mental health ward before her flight nurse assignment, Nabors felt all she really could do was listen to her patients, show compassion, give them hope. Sometimes the patients with minor wounds—the so-called goldbrickers—gave Nabors more problems than the more seriously wounded men. Soldiers in the latter category often were depressed, wondering if they would live, if they could walk again, if their buddies were okay. They looked to the flight nurse to give them encouragement, to show that she cared what happened to them.[48]

MAES with ATC in the Pacific

Beginning in the summer of 1944, the 809 and 812 MAES were attached to ATC, and squadron personnel were distributed over ATC routes in the Pacific. They provided medical crews for air evacuation flights to the

United States as well. In July the majority of patients were flown from Kwajalein to Oahu; in August the patient count increased substantially for the two squadrons, with 2,237 evacuated over a thirty-day period.[49] The next month, the two squadrons combined evacuated 5,657 patients.[50] By November, flight nurses flew from Saipan to Oahu via Kwajalein and Johnston Island, from Guadalcanal to Oahu, and from Oahu to Hamilton Field, California.[51]

With increasing numbers of patients requiring air evacuation from widely separated stations in the Pacific as the Allies moved closer to Japan, additional MAES were needed.[52] Thus, of the ten MAES activated in 1944, half were sent to the Pacific under ATC control to augment the air evacuation work already under way. The 828 MAES, which reached Hickam Field in August 1944, was the first of the additional squadrons to arrive for duty in the Pacific. The 829 MAES followed in October, but both squadrons were disbanded in November, and their personnel was assigned to the 830 MAES, which sent six additional flights to the Pacific in December 1944. The 826 MAES, activated at Bowman Field in May 1944, had been disbanded and its personnel incorporated into the 830 MAES before traveling to Hickam Field. The 831 MAES sent two flights of air evacuation personnel to Guam in January 1945.

Like their colleagues already in the Pacific, the flight nurses of the newly assigned squadrons distinguished themselves in courage and calm thinking when faced with the continued dangers of flying. On 27 September 1944, Lieutenant Mary Hawkins and an enlisted technician, both from the short-lived 828 MAES, were on an air evacuation mission from Los Negros in the Admiralty Islands to Guadalcanal. It was the first flight for most of the twenty-four litter patients aboard the C-47. When their flying time exceeded eight hours, Hawkins asked the pilot for an update and learned that the compasses were not working and radio communications were poor. She informed the enlisted technician, and together they continued with their routine duties. The pilot then entered the cabin and told Hawkins to prepare for a water landing. She announced this to the patients; secured them to their litters, now padded with blankets and clothing; and instructed them how to brace for the impact. The patients took the news calmly, Hawkins wrote, "as if it were going to be an ordinary landing," due no doubt to the composure of the flight nurse.[53] After getting medical and emergency equipment ready for quick use, Hawkins and the technician assumed their crash positions on the floor at either end of the aircraft cabin. The pilots decided it would be safest to crash-land on small Bellona Island in the Solomon Islands. The plane ran into trees, which tore off the left propeller and ripped the left side of the fuselage. A litter pole broke from the impact, severing a patient's trachea and causing profuse hemorrhaging and difficulty breathing. His was the only serious injury. Hawkins directed the removal of all patients from the plane to a nearby clearing. She then gave the critically injured patient morphine, suctioned his throat with an asepto syringe, and used a small rectal tube to administer oxygen from the aircraft walk-around bottle until help arrived.

Meanwhile, the crew had established communication with Guadalcanal, and within an hour planes were circling overhead. Men carried the injured patient to a native hut for the night, where Hawkins and the enlisted technician alternated attendant duties. The next morning, a plane airdropped emergency crash kits containing plasma for the injured patient, and a navy doctor and two pharmacist mates arrived from a waiting destroyer with more plasma. After the patient had been given plasma and glucose, the physician performed a tracheotomy on him. By that afternoon the injured patient, medical crew, and the other survivors of the crash had arrived at the beach, boarded the destroyer, and were on their way to Guadalcanal. Based on this experience, Hawkins recommended that all planes carry at least one unit of plasma, adequate oxygen equipment, and at least one instrument to clamp bleeders on air evacuation flights. Annotations to squadron documents indicate that Hawkins later received the Distinguished Flying Cross and the Bronze Star in recognition of her exceptional performance during this air evacuation mission gone awry.[54]

Allied victories in Saipan, Tinian, and Guam in the summer of 1944 and Peleliu that fall put air force bombers within striking distance of Japan. In October, the Allies landed on the eastern shore of Leyte, north of Mindanao in the Philippines, supported by naval and air bombardment. Landings on the island of Luzon followed, as troops made their way toward Manila amid continued Japanese resistance. The Allies finally secured Manila in March 1945.

The 801, 804, and 820 MAES worked together as they leapfrogged toward the Philippines in the summer and fall of 1944. In October, the 801 MAES sent a detachment minus its flight nurses to Leyte to coordinate air evacuation activities in the Philippines; higher authorities considered flights into Leyte too dangerous for the 801 MAES flight nurses, who remained behind in Biak. The next month, the 820 MAES minus its nurses sent a detachment to the Philippines; the bulk of the squadron embarked by ship to Leyte to relieve the 801 MAES. The 804 MAES was upset to learn that its flight nurses, like those of the 801 and 820 MAES, initially would not be allowed to fly into Leyte, despite quarters prepared for them to remain overnight in Anguar and Peleliu in the Palau Islands. "Why?" flight surgeon Leopold Snyder wondered—surely not danger, since ground force nurses had been on Leyte since a few days after the invasion. Even WACS were on Leyte—perhaps the crowning indignity. Flight nurses on ATC planes flew into Leyte. Flight nurses of the 804 MAES had landed within the sound of gunfire elsewhere at Momote, Tadji, Hollandia, and Wakde. Nor should weather be the deciding factor, he continued, since the 804 MAES nurses had flown through all kinds of weather.[55]

Snyder praised the enlisted technicians, who were doing a splendid job, but added that they were to have been a skilled aid to the flight nurses, not the primary medical attendant on air evacuation flights. He told of a flight nurse in his squadron who had spent twenty-nine days on the ground between flights "and then went up nearby to pick up medical cases which would have done as well if cared for by the crew chief."[56] The sobering fact that a patient who was badly burned had died on a flight between Peleliu and Biak with an 804 MAES enlisted technician as attendant led Snyder to ponder: "Whether he would have lived with a nurse aboard, we can't say. Certainly he would have had a better chance."[56] In December 1944, the 5th Air Force finally gave permission for nurses of the 804 and 820 MAES to fly into Leyte, where the two squadrons established a pool of their flight nurses for air evacuation missions.[57]

In January 1945, 801 MAES nurses made their initial flight into Mindoro, an island southwest of Luzon in the Philippines, and evacuated fifteen patients to Biak; the 804 MAES brought seven flight nurses to Mindoro that same month. The 801 MAES was "busy to the extreme" and enthusiastic about the work of evacuating an average of 115 patients daily, most of them casualties from the battle for Manila or repatriated POWs.[58]

On 15 January 1945, Lieutenant Genevieve Dunleavy of the 820 MAES was on an L-5 Flying Jeep aircraft awaiting a flight from Tacloban to the airstrip at Bayug. Because the flight nurses lived about twenty-five miles from the squadron's main camp, they traveled by air to reach the airstrip, from which they began their missions. A navy transport plane collided with the L-5 as both were taking off. The horizontal stabilizer of the navy plane was sheared off, and the plane crashed and burned, killing all on board. The L-5 had its right landing wheel knocked off, and broken glass in the cabin cut the faces of Dunleavy and the pilot. When the pilot attempted to land on the beach, the plane looped and turned over. Both pilot and flight nurse walked away from the crash with only facial cuts and multiple bruises.[59]

Near the end of the month, a flight nurse on a mission destined for Leyte was lost when her plane disappeared en route. On the morning of 23 January 1945, Lieutenant Thelma La Fave of the 820 MAES and two enlisted technicians had taken off from Peleliu Island on a C-46 to evacuate patients from Tacloban airstrip on Leyte. Weather conditions were apparently good at time of take-off, but the plane never arrived at any airstrip on Leyte. No contact had been made with the plane after take-off. The squadron received no other information on the plane's disappearance. The 804 MAES, with whom the 820 MAES worked closely on air evacuation missions, broke the news that La Fave was considered missing in action.[60]

In February, the 804 MAES noted a busy month, with 3,258 patients evacuated, half with battle wounds; flight nurses had almost six hundred hours of flying time. "This month perhaps more than any other in our experience found us justifying our existence," the squadron historian wrote.[61] On 10 February 1945, flight nurse Lieutenants Victoria Lancaster and Theta Phillips of the 820 MAES were on board a C-47 Jungle Skipper with cargo destined for Clark Field, from where their plane was to fly to Mabalacat to pick up patients for air evacuation. The flight crew was unfamiliar with the area, and Lancaster, who had been to Mabalacat, knew they were lost when the plane was still flying more than an hour past their expected arrival time. Around two o'clock in the afternoon, after flying almost eight hours, with only about half an hour of fuel left, the pilot briefed the cabin occupants on ditching procedures. They immediately began to fill their pockets with medicines and bandages, adjust their canteen belts and get their pistols ready, throw all unnecessary baggage out of the plane, and prepare the four life rafts and other emergency equipment. They then donned Mae Wests and strapped themselves in securely for impact.

When approaching the small island of Batan—not to be confused with Bataan—north of Luzon, the pilot saw a landing strip, but as he approached it, the plane was strafed by the enemy on the ground and by an American P-51 in the air. The pilot of the Jungle Skipper made a speedy getaway and ditched his aircraft in the water on the other side of the island. The P-51 pilot continued strafing and shot one of the life rafts before realizing that the downed plane was likely American. In the eight minutes before the aircraft sank, its occupants got the life rafts out, tied them together, and rowed away from the island. Lancaster and Phillips then bandaged the copilot's toe and another man's finger—the only injuries sustained among the twelve occupants in the life rafts. The ocean changed from smooth to rough and choppy that night, and the survivors were cold, wet, and seasick. The next day, they spotted two PBY Catalinas and two P-51s coming their way. The Catalinas landed and rescued the twelve C-47 survivors as well as a downed fighter pilot who had linked his life raft up with theirs. Lancaster and Phillips bandaged the fighter pilot's leg—a gunshot wound and probable fracture. The Catalinas took the survivors to the Lingayen Gulf, where a small boat and a navy doctor met them for transport to a larger boat. The flight nurses had high praise for their navy hosts. They were "treated wonderfully," they reported, with hot showers, clean clothing, "a drink of American liquor," and lunch served on a white tablecloth—all of which, they said, made them forget what had happened.[62]

Two more flight nurses were lost—one killed in action, the other missing in action—on flights transporting patients between Luzon and Leyte. Lieutenant Martha Black and an enlisted man who helped out on air evacuation missions took off in a C-46 aircraft on 10 March 1945 to bring thirty patients from Mabalacat to Leyte. Around half past four in the evening, Tanauan Tower received a weak emergency message from the plane requesting five ambulances and landing instructions, but tower personnel could not reestablish contact with the flight crew. With the rain and poor visibility at the time, officials speculated that the plane may have drifted off course, run out of gas, and crashed somewhere in Mindanao. Daily air searches over the next two weeks over all possible crash sites revealed no traces of the downed plane. Seven weeks later, its wreckage was found near Cariagara on northern Leyte, where it had been on final approach to the Tanauan airstrip. Squadron members were consoled only with the knowledge that apparently no one had suffered and that death had been instantaneous.[63]

Two days later, on the morning of 12 March 1945, Lieutenant Beatrice Memler and an enlisted technician, who were assigned with the 804 MAES at Fort Stotsenburg on Luzon, departed Hammar strip in Mindoro destined for Tanauan strip on Leyte with twenty-eight patients on board. The C-46 on which they were traveling was never heard from again. Casualty reports suggest bad weather over Leyte as a contributing cause for the aircraft's disappearance. Two operational memoranda issued at Wing level shortly thereafter stipulated that no plane carrying patients would fly in weather calling for instrument flying and that aircraft could carry only the number of patients accommodated by available flotation equipment.[64]

In the spring of 1945, hard-fought battles on the Japanese islands of Iwo Jima and Okinawa resulted in some of the highest casualties of the war. As the last island stepping-stone in the Allied approach to Japan, Okinawa was to be the operations center from which the invasion of the Japanese mainland would be launched. The 820 MAES, which anticipated a move to Luzon, received word to move to Okinawa instead, where it arrived in July 1945; its flight nurses remained on Luzon with the 804 MAES until quarters for them at their new location were ready.[65] The 801 MAES took over all air evacuation in the Philippines.

"We're off! No we're not, yes we are!" wrote an exasperated 804 MAES squadron historian before his squadron finally joined the 820 MAES on Okinawa in August to help evacuate patients from that location to Luzon. He anticipated evacuating Americans liberated from Japanese POW camps, "a task we have all worked for and waited for, for the past twenty seven months."[66] It was to be a short stay before moving on to the Japanese mainland to provide medical crews for intra-island air evacuation missions.[67] Both squadrons moved to Tachikawa, Japan, in September 1945, but a typhoon and continued bad weather suspended air evacuation flights on the mainland.[68] Meanwhile, the 801 MAES's hopes of moving forward from the Philippine Islands to Japan were dashed when the squadron was tasked to assume all air evacuation activities in the Philippines while the 804 and 820 MAES forged ahead.[69]

While the 801, 804, and 820 MAES focused on the Philippines and Okinawa, the 809 and 812 MAES divided their duties between flights farther south in the Pacific and from the Pacific back to the United States. During the summer of 1944, flight nurses of both squadrons transported patients from Saipan back to Oahu and from Kwajalein to Guadalcanal when hospitals on Oahu were overcrowded.

These nurses flew into Leyte and Okinawa as well. A nurse with the 812 MAES, selected to be the squadron's first to fly into Leyte, was sworn to secrecy about the upcoming mission. The situation became awkward when, each time her name reached the top of the duty roster, colleagues noticed that she did not go out on a flight. Realizing that anything could happen on such a mission, she finally told her best friend, adding, "And if anything happens, I want you to send my jewelry to my mother." "You cannot do this," the friend replied dramatically. "Tell them I'll go with you. If you're going to die, I'm going to die with you."[70]

Flight nurse colleague Jo Nabors of the 812 MAES volunteered to be the first flight nurse from her squadron to fly into Okinawa, never thinking hers would be the first of eight names selected from a hat. She flew in the fourth day after the bombing had begun to pick up a load of patients and was petrified, because she could hear the firing and see the devastation from the bombing. When the plane landed and the soldiers saw her, they ran up and crowded around her, asking what she was doing there. "Don't get out of the airplane, you'll get shot," they warned her. Nabors said to the flight surgeon on board, "My God! Get me out of here, because I don't think it's safe here. Even by our boys!" He replied, "You have a gun, don't you? Just use it!" Twenty-four minutes later, the patients were loaded and the flight was on its way. The plane was full of newly wounded patients en route to Guam, many of them double amputees. One patient was blind, and Nabors worried about him the most. Only eighteen years old, he had lied about his age when he enlisted. He did not want to go home, because he was afraid of what his family would say—he had no will to live. "They say nurses are hard," Nabors commented, "but we aren't hard. I cried and cried with that boy." She sensed that he was near death because of his despondency, and indeed he did die, not on her flight, but on his flight out of Guam.[71]

The war on the Pacific front continued through the summer of 1945. Even the Allied firebombing of Japanese cities did not weaken Japanese resolve to continue fighting. Not until after the *Enola Gay* dropped an atomic bomb on Hiroshima on 6 August, followed three days later by a second bomb, which the *Bockscar* dropped on Nagasaki, did Japan surrender to Allied forces, leading to the formal Japanese ceremony of surrender aboard the USS *Missouri* in Tokyo Bay on 2 September 1945.

Three of the flight nurses assigned in the Pacific recalled their reactions to the news that their country had dropped the atomic bombs. For Nabors, learning that the bomb had been dropped was the worst, most frightening, most difficult event of the war. *"How could this ever happen? How could they produce a bomb that would annihilate this many people?"* she thought. She had seen a lot of the war and treated a lot of its casualties and almost crash-landed once on approach to an island without being frightened. "But I was frightened that day," she said. Fear must have shown through her usual calm demeanor during her air evacuation flight that day, for some of her patients asked, "Lieutenant, what's the matter?" It was the first time she had shown her feelings in flight. "Well, you should be happy. The war is over," one of her patients said. "Well, I am happy for that," she replied, "because that means that many less boys are wounded. Our boys can go back home, and it will all be over." But, she asked, what if the bomb had been dropped on

New York or another large American city? "How would you feel if it was your family?" Nabors's heart ached for these victims whom she did not even know.[72]

Hilda Halverson of the 830 MAES was shocked when she heard about the bomb: "Well, I thought of all the burns. It was a terrible thing to [do to] the civilians."[73] Chief nurse Pukas of the 812 MAES drew on her patriotic feelings to justify the act. "This was a mission, it was a decision of my government, of my country. I love it. It was the right thing to do."[74]

As was the case with the flight nurses on the European front, the point system determined when the flight nurses assigned to the Pacific front would return to the United States after V-J Day. Sally Jones of the 812 MAES, who wanted to stay overseas longer to have the privilege of transporting repatriated American POWs from Japan, was not allowed and instead spent her remaining days overseas at Hickam just waiting on orders that would send her back to the States.[75]

Some flight nurses welcomed the end of the war from other strategically important areas of the Pacific front. The defense of Alaska and the CBI fell within the scope of the war in the Pacific, and flight nurses of three MAES were assigned to those remote locations. Their work was no less important than that of their colleagues stationed on islands in the Pacific.

10

Flight Nursing on the Pacific Front: Alaska, China-Burma-India

The war in the Pacific, Alice Hager wrote, fell into two divisions: the "spectacular march up through the Pacific, ending with its fierce impact against the Japanese home islands," and "the bitter and little-known war of the India-Burma and China theaters, for over three years a holding operation," where the Japanese and Chinese had been fighting since the 1930s.[1] A third division might be added, in the defense of the Alaskan Territory against Japanese occupation early in the war and the use of Alaskan airfields to deliver war supplies and ferry planes to the Russian Allies. During the war, three MAES assigned to these areas—the 803 and 821 to the CBI and flights of the 805 to Alaska—provided air evacuation of patients within these lesser-known regions of the Pacific front. The 805 MAES was the first to reach its destination. Eileen Newbeck remembered traveling by train with her flight from Minneapolis to Edmonton, Alberta, Canada, while another flight flew from an airfield near Seattle to one near Anchorage, both arriving in June 1943 just as the Battle of the Aleutians was ending.[2]

MAES in Alaska

In early June 1942, Japanese carrier-based aircraft attacked the port of Dutch Harbor in Amaknak, an island in the Aleutian Islands off Alaska's southwestern coast. A small Japanese force then invaded and occupied the islands of Attu and Kiska. Allied war planners, fearing that the Japanese would use the islands as bases from which to launch attacks against the west coast of the United States, sent American and Canadian troops to expel the Japanese troops. The ensuing battle was fought at the same time as the more newsworthy Battle of Guadalcanal. Because of the remote location, unfavorable weather, and difficult terrain, almost fifteen months passed before Allied soldiers reclaimed the islands. By the summer of 1943, organized Japanese resistance had ceased, and when the Allies invaded Kiska in August, their landing was unopposed—the Japanese soldiers had withdrawn under cover of heavy fog. In the protracted battle, however, soldiers died, were wounded, got sick, and developed occupational ailments of military combat, such as trench foot, and air evacuation was needed to expedite their transport to facilities offering necessary medical services.

But when Newbeck and her flight nurse colleagues of the 805 MAES reported for duty in Edmonton in June 1943, base officials did not know what to do with them, since the nurses were not yet placed on flying status. On a rotating basis, two of them remained in Edmonton, two were sent to Whitehorse in the Yukon Territory, and two went to Fairbanks in central Alaska. They, like flight nurses in England, initially helped out in station hospitals and dispensaries. But, Newbeck recalled, some enterprising officers found an even better use for her training when they sent her and an enlisted technician to the United States with a trainload of patients bound for Iowa. The patients filled one car and part of another, and half of them were what Alaska natives called "bushwacky"—they had been away from civilization too long, out in the bush building the Alaskan Highway. "They looked a little funny," Newbeck said.[3]

The trip, which she later recalled with humor, was no laughing matter. When the train stopped at the various stations, guards had to be posted at each of the train's exits, and Newbeck discovered that no arrangements had been made for food. When the patients were taken to a ward at a military hospital for an overnight stay, the medical staff gave them passes. The patients, who had found the post exchange, returned drunk from beer. The next day when it was time to board the train, the patients were still drunk and so sick that the trainmaster refused to let them board until they had been frisked to remove any bottles of alcohol. Newbeck and her enlisted technician spent the rest of the trip cleaning up after the patients who could not hold their liquor. It was an exhausting, wild and wooly trip, Newbeck concluded. Fortunately, after reporting back to her duty station she began flight nurse duties, thus ending her short assignment as a train nurse.[4]

Flight nurses elsewhere in Alaska got off to a better start. Teams stationed at Adak evacuated patients from that base, Amchitka, and Shemya to the hospital at Fort Richardson, which was adjacent to Anchorage, and on ATC planes to Barnes General Hospital in Portland, Oregon. In its first thirteen months, the flight evacuated 2,518 patients, approximately two-thirds of them within Alaska and the other third to the continental United States. Of all evacuated patients, 20 percent had mental diagnoses; another 25 percent were injured or wounded.[5]

Flying in Alaska was hazardous; Newbeck had been told that because of the terrain, only flights over the Himalayas were more dangerous.[6] In fact, the first flight nurse killed during World War II lost her life in an Alaskan airplane crash. On 27 July 1943, Lieutenant Ruth Gardiner, shown in illustration 10.1, who with Newbeck had graduated from the first flight nurse class and was assigned to the 805 MAES, was en route with an enlisted technician to Unmak Island in the Aleutian chain to pick up a load of patients for air evacuation when their plane crashed near Naknek, a small fishing village at the northeastern end of Bristol Bay, about three hundred miles southwest of Anchorage. "Ruthy," as she was known, was pinned in by cargo, and burns killed her instantly when the plane blew up on impact.[7] Newbeck had heard from a "very reliable source" in Anchorage that the pilot error caused the crash; when he brought the nose of the plane up too fast to clear a rise in the ground, the controls "mushed" and "pancaked in."[8] That is, he likely induced a stall, and with the nose of the aircraft too high, the controls became unresponsive and the plane hit the ground "with little relative forward movement," rather "like a pancake landing back into the skillet after it has been flipped."[9] The members of the 805 MAES must have been comforted to learn that in October 1943, as a tribute to Gardiner, an army general hospital in Chicago was named in her memory.[10]

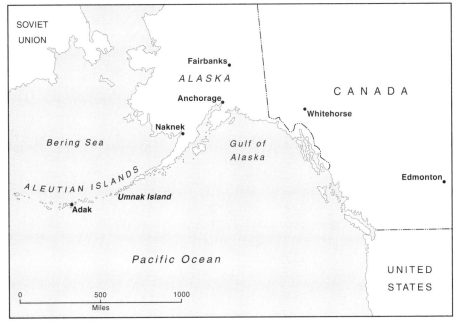

10.1 Alaska and the Aleutian Islands

Most patients the 805 MAES flight nurses evacuated by air were civilians working for the government, not soldiers. Many were engineers who had worked on the Alaskan Highway, begun in March 1942 and completed eight months later, which was constructed to transport supplies by ground, should the Japanese jeopardize Allied air routes. Fractures and burns were common injuries requiring further medical treatment; most of Newbeck's patients, however, had mental diagnoses.[11]

Cold weather was the nemesis of medical crews aboard aircraft in the Alaskan Territory. Although all planes had heaters, not all of these functioned efficiently. Because troop carrier planes were often stripped of their insulation, it was impossible to keep them warm enough for patient comfort, though sleeping bags and blankets helped considerably. ATC planes were insulated and thus much warmer than other aircraft.[12]

The flight nurses and enlisted technicians made flights with patients both within the Alaska region on troop carrier planes and from there back to the United States on ATC planes. Troop carrier pilots flew the C-47 workhorse and the less reliable C-46, which was noted for causing

**10.1 Ruth Gardiner of 805 MAES
(USAF photo)**

trouble. The heater routinely went out on the plane, but Newbeck most remembered another malfunction. On one of her trips, the pilots could not get the landing gear down, so they passed a tin can around, and all the men contributed urine to use as hydraulic fluid. The quick fix worked, and the plane landed safely.[13]

ATC flights were long and tedious. The northwest route extended from Anchorage to Great Falls, Montana, and included stops at Fairbanks, Whitehorse, and Edmonton, all major bases along the route. Miriam Britton wrote to chief nurse Mary Leontine at the School of Air Evacuation about the difficulty keeping her patients entertained on one of her ATC flights from Alaska in August 1943.[14] In February 1944, Newbeck wrote Leora Stroup, Leontine's replacement, about her experiences as a flight nurse in Alaska. With the temperature hovering around zero degrees, Newbeck was wearing "long woolies" underneath her flight suit and parka and was glad for all the warm clothing. She and another flight nurse had recently taken up ice skating and were happily staggering along with members of their Canadian skating club. Work was quiet but offered her a chance to work on projects related to equipment suited for Alaskan air evacuation. For example, she was ready to test a chemically heated jacket designed to keep blood plasma from freezing at minus forty degrees. "My time is spent dashing from Lab. to parachute dept. to dispensary. More fun," she wrote to Stroup.[15]

MAES in China-Burma-India

The flight nurses of the 803 MAES, the first sent to the CBI, shared Newbeck's positive view. While still at Bowman Field, they were known for enjoying what they did "much more than the average," a quality no doubt reinforced when the squadron with its flight nurses began flying duties, as soon as the nurses reached their overseas location.[16]

Until arrival of the 803 MAES, air evacuation within the CBI had been sporadic—about ten patients a week.[17] Large receiving hospitals were few, though Allied soldiers were fighting and becoming sick and wounded in this region of vast jungles and rugged terrain. When World War II began, Japan had already invaded China and set up a puppet government in Manchuria, with the intent of using China's natural resources to further its imperialistic agenda. The Allies joined the Chinese military in its struggle against the Japanese. American, British, Indian, and Chinese troops fought against the Japanese invasion of Burma and India as well. When the Japanese cut off the Burma Road after the fall of Rangoon in March 1942, to close the overland supply route to China, American soldiers and local laborers built the Ledo Road as an alternate route. During the interim, pilots flew supplies over the Hump. The Allies had a vested interest in China, in particular, as a base from which to launch a strategic bombing campaign against Japan. By late 1944, however, the raids were staged from the newly captured Mariana Islands; in November B-29 bombers flying from Saipan bombed Tokyo. But fighting in the region continued throughout the war.

General Grant, the air surgeon, had urged assignment of a medical air evacuation squadron to the region as early as March 1943, but the War Department did not commit until that summer; the 803 MAES arrived in late fall.[18] Their two-month sea voyage from Wilmington, California, in

September 1943 on the USAT *George Washington* to Bombay via Tasmania and from Bombay to Calcutta on the HMS *Nevasa* had been a memorable one, filled with unforgettable sights and the beginnings of lasting friendships. The final leg of the journey was by air from Calcutta to Chabua. Two days later, MAES commander Morris Kaplan and chief nurse Audrey Rogers transported a load of patients to Karachi on their squadron's first air evacuation flight in the CBI.[19] By mid-April 1944, the MAES had evacuated a thousand patients within a week.[20]

The squadron's members spent their first few weeks in India setting up their living space with as many comforts of home as they could buy, build, or rig. Electricity, laundry facilities, and a shower all appeared, thanks to the tireless work of men from the 803 MAES and other friendly squadrons. Once living quarters were in satisfactory condition, the 803 MAES turned its attention to recreational facilities. In March 1944, Kaplan's plan to build a swimming pool eclipsed thoughts of bad-

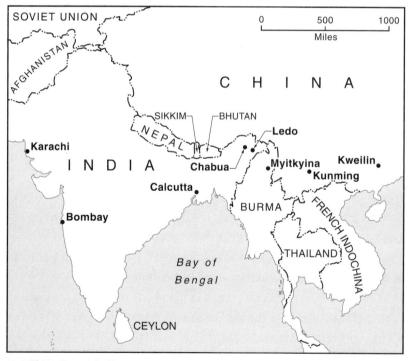

10.2 China-Burma-India

minton, volleyball, Ping-Pong, and a tennis court. Thirty days later, the pool—completed with the generous help of engineers with bulldozer and cement mixer—was the first of its kind in India and the pride of the 803 MAES.[21]

The 803 MAES soon settled into its work, which was divided into valley runs to Calcutta and Karachi, as well as local flights, and combat time earned on flights into Burma. The Karachi flight was the longest; it took four days to cover the two-thousand-mile route.[22] Most patients were battle casualties; many were Chinese soldiers fighting in Burma, followed by patients with psychoneurosis, dysentery, jaundice, and malaria. The squadron was fortunate to have four planes dedicated for air evacuation use, one of which was equipped with individual oxygen valves for patient use when flying over the Hump, at altitudes of sixteen thousand to twenty-two thousand feet.[23] The medical crews transformed their planes into flying hospital wards. Comforters, blankets, sheets, and pillows assured a more comfortable ride for litter patients; seat pads softened the ride for ambulatory patients. Painted peanut and beer cans, hung by wire along the window ledges, became ashtrays. Fruit cans helped in cases of airsickness. Magazines, coffee, sandwiches, and fruit juices obtained from other organizations were added amenities for the patients.[24] Such "luxurious" accommodations were the exception to the rule, however.[25]

In December 1943, one flight of nurses and enlisted technicians was sent to China, where the flight nurses made history as the first American nurses allowed into that country since the war began.[26] Miranda "Randy" Rast, flight leader, went to Kunming, with the other nurses, Jeanette "Tex" Gleason among them, scattered throughout China. In theory, Rast's colleagues would bring patients to Kunming, and she would fly with them over the Hump. In reality, however, Rast recalled, there was not much flying; the flight nurses flew "on demand" and, like other flight nurses in similar situations, helped out in dispensaries when not needed for air evacuation missions. Sometimes lack of supplies, most especially gasoline, grounded the airplanes, or unpredictable weather over the Hump made flying too dangerous.[27]

When Gleason left on an air evacuation mission from her duty station on 17 January 1944, she took her mongrel puppy Murgatroyd along.

Once the last patients were off-loaded in Kunming, Gleason chatted with Rast for a while before departing on her return trip. Rough, stormy skies and ice forming on the wings at high altitude over the mountains plagued the flight. Two hours after takeoff, the pilot, who had to maintain complete radio silence, discovered he was off course. After three hours of trying to correct his position, he was also running dangerously low on fuel. Eventually he had to tell Gleason, the crew chief, the radio operator, and the passenger that they were lost, out of fuel, and would have to bail out. When Gleason jumped, she held Murgatroyd tightly in one arm but had to let go of him when she needed two hands to pull her parachute's rip cord. She landed with a terrific jolt in complete darkness, without serious injury. Remembering her training at Bowman Field, she wrapped herself in her parachute and slept until dawn, when, with bundled-up parachute in hand, she made her way down the mountain, following a stream to a path that led to a Chinese village. Some residents took her to a village with a telephone, from where she called Kweilin, an American base where 803 MAES nurses were assigned, and located the pilot and the crew chief by telephone in another village. The radio operator and the passenger arrived at Gleason's village, and the three of them made their way to the pilot and crew chief, from where they were taken by jeep to Kweilin. Gleason was the first woman to "hit the silk" and become a member of the Caterpillar Club of survivors who have parachuted from a disabled airplane. Kaplan brought Gleason back to Chabua for two weeks of rest leave, after which she returned to her flying duties in China.[28]

Rast made her first return trip over the Hump from China to India in a B-24 in February 1944, after which the trips became frequent. Patient loads swelled in March, as the fighting in Burma escalated. In May, the 803 MAES encountered its heaviest daily patient load: 202 patients.[29] On 18 May, the squadron's first major catastrophe occurred on an air evacuation flight to Myitkyina, Burma, where the Allies had captured the airfield from the Japanese the previous night. The Japanese were strafing the field when the plane with flight nurses Audrey Rogers and Esther Baer, a flight surgeon, and an enlisted technician landed. As they loaded the first patient—a Chinese soldier—shell fragments struck the crew and the patient. The patient was killed instantly, and the crew members who were on the ground or in the doorway of the airplane were wounded. Rogers was hit in the right knee and thigh. Only Baer and the pilot escaped the shrapnel uninjured. Bullets riddled the plane during the attack.

The crew members immediately fled the airstrip for the grass bordering it, from where they assessed and bandaged each other's wounds. After the attack ended, they returned to the plane, which the pilot determined was still airworthy, loaded the rest of the patients, and completed the air evacuation mission as scheduled. After all the patients had been off-loaded at Ledo, the plane, with its wounded crewmembers now on litters and nursed by Baer, returned to Chabua.[30] Kaplan later paid high tribute to her work: "Her calm under that time of stress was the epitome of the reactions of the whole group—and I and all of us were extremely proud."[31] All the wounded crewmembers recovered well. Rogers, the most seriously wounded, was back on duty within three weeks. She, the flight surgeon, and the enlisted technician received Purple Hearts for wounds from enemy action.[32]

Baer later wrote that, odd as it might have seemed, during the danger she was not frightened but rather felt quiet and calm. Afterward, however, was a different story. She recalled that for a week, "I felt like a mound of jello, and kept seeing the Zeroes coming at me in my sleep." The nightmares continued for several nights, and for the first time in her life she was nervous. Her friends kept her busy, which helped, "and before long all was back to normal." But she also remembered how when Major Kaplan decorated her colleagues with their Purple Hearts, she "couldn't help but wish I had gotten just a little piece of shrapnel so I, too, could have a Purple Heart."[33]

The 821 MAES arrived in India in July 1944, following a two-month sea voyage via Australia and joined up with the 803 MAES already working in the CBI. On its arrival in Bombay, one flight of the 821 MAES traveled by air to Calcutta, on to Chabua, and then to Kunming; its arrival permitted the 803 MAES flight nurses assigned in China to rejoin their squadron in India. The other three flights of the 821 MAES arrived in Calcutta by train and traveled onward to Chabua.[34] Both groups had orientation with 803 MAES personnel on their regularly scheduled air evacuation trips. During the fall, the two squadrons shared equally the trips from India and from Burma.[35] In November, the 803 MAES took over full responsibility for air evacuation of India, and the 821 MAES provided air evacuation in Burma, with a planned move to Ledo, India. That same month, the squadron had responsibility for India and China as well, however; the original 803 MAES flight nurses were awaiting orders to return to the United States and the arrival of their replacements.[36]

When the 821 MAES flight nurses arrived in Ledo, in view of the majestic snow-covered Himalayas, in December 1944, they were delighted. While working in conjunction with the 803 MAES, they had yearned for a job of their own. As flight nurse Katherine Hack wrote, "No longer would we have to gratefully accept handouts and crumbs from some other unit. For overnight we found that we were treated differently too. Gone were the 'off at Myitkyina' days. We were given what we had asked for so long. To be allowed to go to the forward areas and bring back our American soldiers."[37]

Not all the patients were American, though, nor were all of them human. On one of the stranger air evacuation missions of the war, a crew from the 821 MAES found itself loading patients onto a plane in which two boats were stacked one inside the other in the cargo space. The crew seated about a dozen Chinese and Indian patients in the inner boat, the litter patient was placed on the floor in the rear of the boat, and the remaining ambulatory patients sat in a row of bucket seats. The trip was otherwise uneventful.[38] On another flight, a dog belonging to an infantry unit came on board with an emergency medical tag and diagnosis—it was being evacuated to Myitkyina for treatment of a swollen leg. The 821 MAES unit historian noted, "His behavior and decorum were excellent. He sat very quietly on a bucket seat all the way."[39]

Writing to Major Ruth Parsons in the office of the air surgeon, chief nurse Frances Barrett of the 821 MAES shared a picturesque glimpse of her flight nurses' working days in the CBI and hinted of other far-from-routine air evacuation missions: "The shopkeeper has his neat little store, the scientist his magnificent laboratory. Our setting is the interior of a C-47. In fact any C-47 that is going our way. For once we leave the comparative comfort and convenience of the hospital ship we are on our own and anything may happen and usually does." Descriptions of the C-47 interiors encountered on air evacuation missions followed, with explanations of how the medical crew improvised to accommodate patients safely in the stripped down interiors of the planes, often devoid even of doors, seats, and metal brackets or web strips for litters.[40]

Barrett then mentioned two missions in which flight nurses of her squadron had transported mental patients. "With them it is the 'little things' that count tremendously," she explained. She gave the example of two Chinese patients who were fussing and bickering with each other. The crew averted open hostilities by putting radio headphones on the head of the belligerent patient and giving him a copy of *Life* magazine. "As luck would have it," she said, "a Chinese musical programme was being broadcast from Chungking and the transformation of the lion into a lamb was remarkable. . . . The situation seemed quite amusing to the other patients."[41]

On another mission, a similarly unconventional idea had a successful outcome for an Indian patient who became restless about an hour into the flight. Because he had lost his medical papers, the medical crew did not know if he had been sedated recently so could not medicate him. Something had to be done, however, because he kept trying to get up from his litter. In desperation, the medical crew members gave the patient a piece of rope about eighteen inches long and some green and silver chewing gum wrappers they had spied on the floor. "For the balance of the trip he was happy and content, for he spent the entire time coiling the rope into various shapes on the floor and minutely examining the gum wrappers. Certainly not standard occupational therapy, but it served the purpose," Barrett reported.[42]

By April 1945, the 821 MAES flight nurses' work was down to "a mere trickle" and required only one plane, the *Miss Nightingale II*.[43] At the end of May, orders arrived sending all the squadron's flight nurses back to the United States.[44] The flight nurses heard the news with mixed emotions: some couldn't get home soon enough, and others who had wanted to stay overseas were sad, even angry about their departure.[45] "So concludes our time together as the 821st Medical Air Evacuation

Squadron," wrote Hack. "Now we are going away, and each on her own way. It has been an experience with capital E, and with deepest regrets do we see ourselves parted from it."[46]

Hack might have been speaking for many of her colleagues on the Pacific front as well as on the European front. Some considered flight nursing a defining life experience, one in which they showed their true mettle. Others found it merely an interlude, just a job to be done because of the war. They had been the face of the new air evacuation system to the soldiers who were their patients, the correspondents who covered wartime air evacuation, and the people back home who followed the events in which their loved ones were involved, especially when news of battle wounds reached them. Their image was on magazine covers, in cartoons, and in newspapers; their voices were heard on the radio.

The flight nurses balanced professional nursing skills with compassion, a military officer's bearing with a feminine appearance. They were aware that their presence had an effect on those with whom they came in contact, and the wise among them used it for the good of their patients, not for their own purposes. Although most lived up to the angelic reputation the media attributed to them, others may have fallen short. Not all squadron members, for example, appreciated the flight nurses. A look at coworkers' perceptions as well as the media's portrayal of these women helps put the flight nurse role in perspective.

11

Flight Nurse Image in Mind and Media

T he novelty and the professionalism of the flight nurse may have sold the air evacuation program to the general public, helped in great measure by media portrayals of flight nurses in articles often given catchy titles—"These Angels Fly on Man-Made Wings," "Hell's Angels," "Invasion Heroine: The Flying Nurse," "Angel Footprints."[1] But not all military personnel were impressed with their work; professional jealousy may have been a factor. To some MAES members, who thought flight nurses should not be in their squadrons and filed complaints against them, the angel analogy was obviously poorly chosen. The flight nurse program was not without its naysayers, as statements initially released in 1945 by the office of the air intelligence contact unit and referred to as the "Flight Nurse Problem" in official correspondence indicated.

"Flight Nurse Problem"

In May 1945, a flight surgeon of the 808 MAES, an enlisted technician of the 802 MAES, and seven enlisted technicians of the 830 MAES who were interviewed after their returns from overseas duty were highly critical of using flight nurses in the air evacuation system. The office of the air intelligence contact unit distributed their comments up and down the chain of command for review by staff of the air surgeon's office in Washington, D.C., and the School of Aviation Medicine at Randolph Field, Texas.

The returnees' complaints covered four repeated themes. First, some flight nurses purposely socialized with high-ranking officials to obtain "unnecessary and undeserved" privileges, such as frequent leaves. Captain Joseph Keith, the flight surgeon, gave as a defining example an instance in which higher headquarters had denied a furlough to an enlisted man whose father was critically ill in the United States but granted a U.S. leave a few days later for a nurse for no valid reason and without his approval.[2]

Louise Anthony validated this type of complaint with her story about a flight nurse in the 816 MAES, assigned first in England and then in France, who would "look out for herself" to obtain a date, better work, or a chance for promotion. Blond and attractive, she turned into "a bit of a sourpuss" for days after a French beautician had used too much bleach on her hair. After the war had ended, Anthony learned the cause for the woman's unhappy disposition on that occasion: she had finagled an invitation to a command-level party in England. When word got back to chief nurse Martha Foster in France that this flight nurse was to be sent on timely detached duty to England for seven days, Foster, who couldn't "lose" the orders, managed to have them delayed. As Anthony recalled, the orders arrived the day *after* the party. Foster took them to the flight nurse, who said, "But it's too late now." The chief nurse replied, "I don't know anything about that. Now here are orders, you are going, as far as I'm concerned. Start packing."[3]

Second, their conscientious sister flight nurses were thus overworked when available to cover for the absentee nurses. But even these diligent women proved incompetent in the eyes of flight surgeon Keith when the enlisted technicians assumed "almost the entire burden" of providing patient care in flight.[4] Sometimes the patients were left in the care of a technician without a nurse; however, this was a common occurrence when number of patients needing air evacuation exceeded number of flight nurses available.

Third, as women the flight nurses lacked both the physical strength to lift and carry heavy flight equipment and litters and the mechanical knowledge to mount those litters and perform other minor duties aboard the aircraft. At Bowman Field, they were taught and had to demonstrate their competence in lifting and loading litters. Anthony recalled the bivouac exercise during which the flight nurses had to carry litters weighted with two sixty-pound sandbags some distance and set them down—twice. She believed that repeating this task was unnecessary, causing needless injury; in practice she and other flight nurses never had to load litters on their own. According to Anthony, "you could always find some man to help you take care of whatever it was."[5]

It was commonly accepted that a flight nurse could find some man to help lift litters. Publicity about air evacuation emphasized the supervisory role of the flight nurse during the litter-loading process, as the opening of a presentation prepared by the Bowman Field office of public relations for the 1st Troop Carrier Command illustrates:

> A pretty nurse in Army Air Corps blue stands in the doorway of the big troop carrier plane. She looks trimly feminine in her neat nurse's uniform, but there is an incongruous touch in the steel helmet that shutters her crisp blonde curls. It's her new Easter bonnet—style of 1943. A gas mask is belted firmly around her slim waist. She glances down to where two boys in buck privates' garb are about to lift a litter-borne patient into the doorway of the plane.
>
> "Not that way!" she warns suddenly, sharply. "Here, let me show you!"
>
> Lithely, she jumps down from the plane; the boys give her an earnest attention as she teaches them—the right way.[6]

As the commander of the 801 MAES in the Pacific explained in an official report of his squadron's activities, because of limited cargo space on airplanes it was not always possible to have an enlisted technician accompany each nurse, nor was it necessary. The nurses did not need to do any manual labor when the crew chief or an ambulatory patient was there to help with loading and unloading crews at the various bases.[7] Officials of the 804 MAES went farther in their written plan for organized air evacuation of casualties when they recommended that all air force personnel engaged in air evacuation have training to familiarize them with the loading of litters: "It is evident that such a crew of four (Pilot, Co-pilot, Radio Man, and Crew Chief) plus an Air Evacuation Team (the Nurse superintending), would constitute a satisfactory loading team."[8] Plane-loading demonstrations and lectures the 806 MAES personnel gave at the American School Center at Shrivenham achieved the same purpose on the European front.

And fourth, some flight nurses saw themselves more as air hostesses than as nurses, undermining the professionalism necessary for air evacuation duty and leaving onlookers with the impression that the enlisted personnel could perform the duties required for in-flight care more capably. On some missions, however, the flight nurse's duties *were* more like those of a hostess than a nurse. Bernice Stick, a flight nurse with the 808 MAES, wrote Captain Leontine at the School of Air Evacuation about one such flight en route between the CBI and Miami.[9] Ethel Carlson of the 815 MAES in England recalled a similar experience on a flight from Scotland to Newfoundland with about twenty-four ambulatory patients in a C-54 that resembled an airliner. Her duties consisted mainly of keeping the patients occupied with playing cards and books. She had always wanted to be a stewardess, and when she walked onto that plane and looked around, she said, "I have arrived—I am a stewardess."[10] Both were ATC flights.

The returnees' complaints were not based on such flights, however, but rather on ones for which nursing care was required but the flight nurses either allegedly slept while the enlisted technicians provided the nursing care or spent more time in the cockpit with the flight crew than in the cabin with the patients.[11] "We have always tried to emphasize the fact that our girls are not 'Airline Hostesses' as so many have considered them. Rather they are darned good nurses who try to prevent the occurrence of an emergency in flight; but if one does arise, they are capable of handling it," 804 MAES flight surgeon Leopold Snyder stated in a unit history.[12] Sergeant Brown's statement that "the administering of morphine shots, transfusion of oxygen, as well as generally making the patient more comfortable, is all that is called for" on air evacuation flights downplays the numerous instances—cited in squadron histories, narratives of awards and decorations, and interviews—when a flight nurse's keen intuition and timely actions saved the life of one or more patients.[13] It also minimizes important nursing actions involving serious medical interventions.

Many enlisted technicians, perhaps including those who filed the complaints, had worked as the sole medical attendants on air evacuation aircraft before flight nurses arrived in an area and before flight nurses could fly into the more forward combat zone areas. Like the army medics and navy corpsmen on the ground who moved with the combat troops for whom they provided battlefield first aid and trauma care, the air evacuation technicians were used to working autonomously and may have resented working alongside flight nurses.

Not all flight nurses were criticized, however; the seven technicians collectively admitted that those overworked flight nurses who were "on the ball," stuck to business, and performed their duties to the extent of their abilities were of value. Yet, the less-than-desirable performances of the other flight nurses led the returnees who filed complaints to recommend the removal of all flight nurses from air evacuation duty. The efforts of those nurses, Keith noted, "seemed to be directed mainly toward 'glamorizing' air evacuation rather than toward performance of assigned duties." In support of his own views "on the incompetency and unreliability of flight nurses," Keith found fifteen other flight surgeons who agreed that "if the nurses were replaced with enlisted men, twice the work could be accomplished with half the trouble."[14] One cannot know how many flight surgeons would have been of a different opinion, however, had they been consulted.

Official Response

Reaction to the report about the "Flight Nurse Problem" making its way through official channels was swift and clearly vindicated the flight nurses. Captain Edwin J. McBride, air inspector for the School of Aviation Medicine, who had interviewed three nurses of Captain Keith's 808 MAES flight, was the first to share his findings with the school's commandant. The nurses were very critical of Keith, whom they described as intemperate, never around, and unknowledgeable about administrative details, McBride stated. They had contemplated, but not followed through on, writing a letter to the air surgeon, stating these facts. McBride assigned little value to the criticisms found in the report, because they were vague and not supported by actual facts and dates.[15]

In his reply to the commandant, Major Frederick R. Guilford, chief of the air evacuation department of the School of Aviation Medicine, said he had learned from a member of Keith's flight that Keith "was admittedly unsympathetic toward the air evacuation operation in general and had an antagonistic attitude toward Flight Nurses from the beginning of the operations mentioned in this report." He added that "a certain amount of ill-feeling toward Flight Nurses often exists among air evacuation Medical Technicians and effort on the part of the Technicians to prove that they are capable of replacing Flight Nurses has been noted on many occasions."[16]

Lieutenant Colonel Fratis L. Duff, the assistant commandant of the School of Aviation Medicine, offered the strongest endorsement of flight nurses, with his belief that "there is no comparison between the professional training and professional skill of the Flight Nurse and the Air Evacuation Technician." He found the use of flight nurses "entirely justified in this respect alone." Their worth was reflected in the excellent medical care the sick and wounded soldiers were receiving. Duff then pointed out an underlying motive behind the returnees' report that other reviewers had not yet mentioned: "This entire recommendation seems to be based on the fact that the Flight Nurse is a female. It has very adequately been demonstrated in this war that female personnel can perform efficiently in the Armed Forces both in the continental limits of the United States and in foreign theaters." He drew on history to drive his point home: similar reports were likely submitted when the army first used female nurses and when the Army Nurse Corps was established in 1901, but the criticism proved invalid.[17]

In his reply to the office of the air surgeon, Brigadier General Eugen G. Reinartz, commandant of the School of Aviation Medicine, was "incensed" at the report's "manifest vituperativeness. There were, no doubt, inequities that needed correction but the manner of reporting the same was most irregular and improper." He recommended that the report be given little weight. Keith had laid himself open to penalization for making official statements critical to his superior officers concerning matters of which he knew nothing, Reinartz stated, and he concluded: "The Air Evacuation Nurse has been instituted by the Air Surgeon and is one of his important and outstanding contributions to the war effort. The criticism of this institution is therefore, a criticism of the Air Surgeon and is thoroughly resented."[18]

Reinartz resented the tone of the report, the writers of the report resented the flight nurses, and the flight nurses resented that a flight surgeon and some of the enlisted technicians with whom they worked maligned them. If, in fact, there was a flight nurse problem, it was one identified by the flight nurses themselves and their more supportive commanders—namely, that nurses were not allowed to fly into war zones where and when seriously wounded soldiers most needed their skills. Whether the reason stemmed from difficulty obtaining adequate quarters for women at these locations, as Sergeant Brown suggested almost as an afterthought in his report, by an urge to protect women from injury and possible death, or by the more chauvinistic attitude that women could not handle the stress of such proximity to active fighting, the end result was that periodically during their assignments overseas, the flight nurses had a lot of time on their hands.[19] And an idle flight nurse was an unhappy flight nurse.

This situation was particularly pronounced on the Pacific front, where flight nurses of the 801, 804, and 820 MAES were kept so far behind the front lines where recently wounded soldiers needed evacuation that they had to settle for casualties less in need of their skilled ministrations—and occasionally work in hospitals rather than on planes. The 801 MAES flight surgeons wanted a definite policy giving flight nurses unrestricted access to areas where their skills were needed, believing that otherwise these nurses' training and skill would be "wasted on ambulatory patients being evacuated from the rear areas, who hardly need medical attention at all." Nurses were needed near the fronts, where seriously ill patients awaited air evacuation, although squadron flight surgeons acknowledged that unnecessary risks should not be taken in these advanced areas before adequate security and air coverage had been achieved. "All nurses in this unit desire such duty," the report concluded.[20]

Hinting at the issues Keith and the enlisted technicians raised, the 801 MAES unit historian gave his support to the nurses of the squadron, who had "won the respect and admiration of all" and had not been involved in any "untoward incidents" that might "preclude the presence of women in these areas." The flight nurses had done their duties cheerfully and well, the historian commented, adding that their only complaint was that they had not been given a sufficient number of patients to care for.[21]

In England, flight nurses of the 817 MAES received similar praise from the commanding officer of the troop carrier group to which they initially were assigned. The wording of Colonel Willis Mitchell's letter of appreciation suggests that a spotty reputation might have preceded them to Barkston Heath. The 817 MAES nurses had shown "superior deportment" and had "in every case conducted themselves as officers—both while on duty and during the social functions in which they have taken part at this base." They had been, the colonel concluded, "true soldiers."[22]

Social functions at bases merited comments in more than one unit history to which flight nurses contributed. Nancy Preston and Ada Endres of the 801 MAES on the Pacific islands, an unnamed historian of the 803 MAES in the CBI, and Phoebe La Munyan of the 819 MAES in England shared enough details to show that many flight nurses had more than their work on their minds. As Blanche Solomon, who flew on ATC routes in the North Atlantic with the 830 MAES said, "we worked hard, but I think most of us played hard, too, in our free time."[23]

That the glamor of flight nursing led to resentment among other military personnel is well documented. Flight nurses who were not evacuating patients could be assigned on a temporary basis to medical installations but had to be available at any time for their primary mission. Duty at army station hospitals, however, which may have given the flight nurses something constructive to do during their down time, could fuel ill will in the nurses it was meant to help. According to Robert Futrell, army nurses in the Southwest Pacific made flight nurses of the 804 MAES remove their wings before arriving at their location. Similarly, when they volunteered to serve in an army hospital on Biak when not permitted to go onto the beachhead at Leyte in the Philippines, the hospital refused to let the flight nurses' help unless they first removed their wings.[24]

Army nurses whose work kept them rooted on terra firma day after day may have believed their bitterness toward flight nurses was justified. If earthbound nurses read Dorothy Rice's "Flight to Kiriwagi," reprinted in the *American Journal of Nursing,* they likely focused on the exoticism and glamor of the work without appreciating its associated hazards.[25]

MAES commanders, alert to flight nurses' glamorous socialite image, kept the women grounded in the more mundane responsibilities of military life. In the 801 MAES, compulsory early morning drills and calisthenics, afternoon lectures on military and medical subjects, and Saturday morning inspections reminded the flight nurses that they were not on vacation. Preston and Endres wrote, for example, of "doing our own laundry and performing all the menial chores that go along with light hut-keeping."[26]

Not all ground nurses resented their airborne sisters, however. When flight nurses of the 804 MAES could not make flights past Port Morseby and Dobodura in New Guinea, station hospitals gave them food and lodging. Janet Foome, chief nurse of the 87th Station Hospital in Dobodura waxed poetic about the nurses she had housed and fed temporarily. The nurses at her hospital would be sorry to see the flight nurses leave for their next flying duties, she wrote, but realized that they had important, though not easy, work to do:

> The little gold wings you wear o'er your heart
> Signify to us that you have a hard part
> To do in this job of winning the war
> So here's to you Nurses of the Army Air Corps.[27]

Glamour and Guts

In its effort to ameliorate the grimness of war, the media tended to glamourize the work—and the appearance—of flight nurses. In a cartoon found on the back cover of the 1 September 1942 *Yank* magazine, shown in illustration 11.1, two hospitalized soldiers in hospital beds see their first flight nurse, who happens to be young and pretty. A cartoon in the July 1944 issue of *Air Force* magazine, shown in illustration 11.2, depicts a GI grooming himself while patients watch "Flight Nurse Nelson" at work. She "the pin-up as well as patch-up girl" on her plane.[28]

"I cannot seem to speak of flight nurses without sounding like a blurb for a flock of movie stars," wrote Maxine Davis in a book about

"MUST BE ONE OF THOSE NEW FLIGHT NURSES THAT WERE JUST
TRANSFERRED HERE."   —M/Sgt. Ted Miller

11.1 Ted Miller, "New Flight Nurses" cartoon, *Yank*, 1 September 1942 (author's
collection)

aviation medicine in World War II. "Frankly, I found the Army Air
Force flight nurses tops. They were gay, friendly, loved their jobs and
performed them efficiently, and they were beautiful. I am convinced
the officials of the School of Aviation Medicine measured them, photographed them, and voted on them as for 'Miss America.' They were,
incidentally, healthy, courageous, and stout of heart."[29] Helena Ilic,
shown in illustration 11.3, was just one of the numerous flight nurses
who merited Davis's accolades.

The reference to Miss America brought instantly to readers' minds
the image of an attractive young woman who has risen above her com-

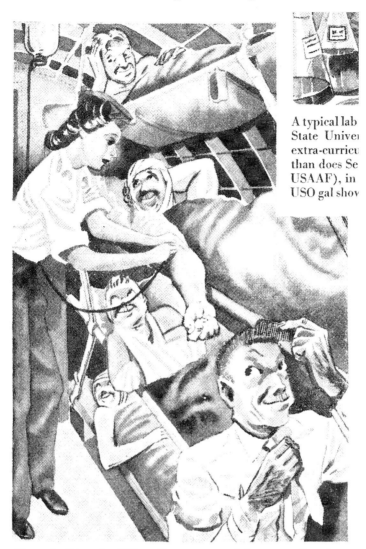

A typical lab
State Univei
extra-curricu
than does Se
USAAF), in
USO gal shov

Since the "Angels of Mercy" were put on flying status there has been a marked improvement in the mental attitude of patients being removed from forward combat areas. A sick man's spirits automatically rise at the touch of a kindly and competent feminine hand. Flight Nurse Nelson is the pin-up as well as patch-up girl of each troop transport she boards these days.

Air Force, July, 1944

11.2 Nurse Nelson cartoon, from [William] T. Lent, "AAF Medics" *Airman*, July 1944 (author's collection)

11.3 Helena Ilic of 801 MAES in Leyte, Philippines, 1944 (author's collection)

petition as the epitome of all that is good in her gender. But because beauty did not necessarily equate to courageous action, correspondents tempered their descriptions with behavior indicative of patriotism and fortitude. And if a photograph of the nurse in uniform could be shown, it reinforced the message. Such was the case in "A Heroine Comes

Home," with its subtitle "Boston Army Nurse Typical of the REAL Miss America," an article about flight nurse Lieutenant Barbara Watts, who served with the 802 MAES and later with the 807 MAES in North Africa and Europe. Watts was, the correspondent said, "typical of the Miss Americas who served so well in the various theaters of war. Thousands, like Lt. Watts, are turning back to civilian life with records that rival those of the men."[30]

Other publications may not have focused as overtly on the flight nurses' femininity, but the message was clear in title and text: the presence of female flight nurses in forward areas and on air evacuation missions had a positive effect on the morale of the troops who might suffer or had already sustained combat wounds or related illnesses. Official military publications also stressed the positive effect on their patients' morale. Because many soldiers were taking their first flights, a young, female nurse calmly going about her duties was a reassuring sight.[31]

The public already had read of the glamour associated with nurses working as airline stewardesses. By association, military flight nurses took on that same glamour in the press, but with an important difference—their well-known image as "angels of mercy" was given a new twist. "These Angels Fly on Man-Made Wings," read the title of an article in the Sunday supplement to the *Louisville Courier-Journal* the week after the first flight nurse graduation. The wings, of course, were airplane wings. Wounded soldiers would "be opening their eyes to a sight both pleasant and welcome, but which is just about the last thing they'd expect to see so near no-man's land"—attractive flight nurses wearing second lieutenants' insignia. Given their article's effusive tone, the authors may have thought it necessary to add, "Because being a flight nurse has glamour appeal, entrance into the school is difficult so as to keep out those who would enter purely through the love for adventure."[32]

The closing caveat was apt. Capitalizing on this love of adventure in *Women in Aviation*, a book written at the end of World War II, Becky Peckham included a chapter about flight nursing, asking: "You girls who crave excitement, how would you like to travel right up within machine-gun range of the enemy in a giant C-47 troop transport filled with grim-faced paratroopers or even commandos, with perhaps a general or two for good measure?" But the author belittled the painstaking and purposeful preparation that made a flight nurse worthy of her wings: "The things that those girls had to pack into their pretty little heads in six weeks of fifty hours each, with classes seven days of every one of those weeks!" Her conclusion was no less damaging to the flight nurse image: "Yes, appointment with the Army Nurse Corp [sic], and assignment to the Army Air Forces offered plenty in the way of excitement. Air Evacuation seemed to be the perfect answer for those girls who 'didn't join the Army Nurse Corps to take care of people with measles.'"[33]

Flight nursing seemed to offer yet another perfect reason nurses might join the army nurse corps. In an article about the new military flight nurse program, a writer for *R.N.* magazine appealed to her readers' personal as well as professional goals. Because the army air corps comprised "the youngest, most vigorous group of men in the service," with the most officers of any branch of the military, marriage opportunities might arise from such stimulating professional and social contacts. "And no sane woman ever completely resisted that challenge!"[34]

Other magazines and newspapers also touted the possibility of finding a husband while working as a flight nurse, but military officials viewed this "side benefit" differently. In the case of flight nurses, Lieutenant Colonel Ralph Stevenson, commandant of the School of Air Evacuation, took a pragmatic view of the situation when he spoke with a reporter. The ideal age of the student flight nurse was twenty-five to thirty-five years old, he said, because younger girls were "apt to be thinking principally of marriage" when work must be their sole object in a six-week course, whereas "the older women look at it squarely from the beginning."[35]

Under the opening "They flew into South Pacific combat zones under the noses of Zeros, crouched long, dark hours in foxholes, sweated out blistering beachhead bombardments and came up with the kind of courage that brought smiles to the faces of the sick and wounded," *Collier's* printed a rare article that downplayed femininity and emphasized brawn over beauty in these flight nurse "Amazons."[36] A photo spread of flight nurses in the Pacific was more balanced in its concise depiction of these women and their work in air evacuation: "They are women with painted fingernails and permanent waves, strictly feminine, but they do a man-sized job."[37]

In some magazine articles, writers alluded to a flight nurse's femininity in an attempt to balance the military persona with the all-American-girl image. A 1945 article in *R.N.* magazine with the misprinted title "Angles Are Well Groomed" offered tips to civilian and military nurses, pointing out, "In uniform you're an angel and always will be. Your patients *want* you to be an angel and, like it or lump it, you can't let them down. Whether your uniform is civilian or military—white, navy, or mud-stained O.D.—it's still your badge of beatitude." The all-American flight nurses might have scoffed at the idea that their uniform rather than their care of wounded combat soldiers earned them that "badge of beatitude." And they surely would have rolled their eyes at the recommended rituals of a daily bath and exercise; twice-daily makeup application; weekly shampoo, wave, manicure, pedicure, and clothes repair; and monthly facial, despite the magazine's apology to military nurses overseas where these "luxury" items were unobtainable. But they knew the importance of good grooming even when regulation uniforms in reasonable sizes were hard to obtain and hair salons were nonexistent. To its credit, *R.N.* then paid tribute "to the nurse who bathes in a helmet or never bathes at all, to the girl who stays on the job despite extreme physical discomfort, whose dungarees and slacks are the greatest symbol of honor the nursing profession has warranted or will deserve in the years to come."[38]

War correspondent Shelley Mydans, who accompanied Victoria Pavlowski of the 812 MAES on an air evacuation mission across the Pacific, headed her article "Young, courageous and pretty, she brings wounded soldiers safely across the Pacific." Mydans described Pavlowski's work, then closed with an appreciation of the flight nurse's dedication to duty, which included a glimpse of her attention to appearance. Throughout the night as Mydans dozed, she would wake and see Pavlowski quietly working. "By dawn her face was pale and her lipstick had worn off. As the patients awoke she straightened their blankets and fed them fruit juice and coffee. She had not rested on the eight-hour trip, but her voice and face still carried the same impassive reassurance and readiness to smile." Just before landing, after strapping the patients in their litters, Pavlowski "went forward to comb her hair and put on make-up.

It is Army regulation that flight nurses look attractive and fresh when they bring their hospital ships in to land."[39]

The correspondent gave a true account of the primping ritual she noticed. Elizabeth Pukas, chief nurse of the 812 MAES, expected her nurses to look "as if they just came out of Elizabeth Arden's salon," with hairdo, makeup, and uniform "absolutely immaculate. . . . She is to be immaculately clean, and as beautiful and as presentable as she has been trained in flight nursing school to be."[40] They did not have to be beautiful, said Jo Nabors, a flight nurse in Pukas's squadron, but they had to be neat and well groomed, look nice, and know how to wear their makeup and hair. "We had to smile. We had to smell nice. You know, that's true. We did," Nabors said.[41] And no matter how long a flight, before landing and picking up patients or offloading them at their destination the flight nurse was expected to "freshen up," reapply her makeup, comb her hair, and, as Pukas said, to "be the most beautiful woman that the wounded are going to rest their eyes on."[42]

The same nurses who might let patients watch them putting their hair up in bobby pins, because it reminded them of sisters and wives, had a serious concern for those patients' emotional and physical welfare. Said Gerda "Gerry" Bouwhuis of the 801 MAES in the Pacific, "I think it is wicked that people write to soldiers and say such things as 'I pray every night you will come home whole.' That makes the soldier worry about how he will be received if he comes back with an arm or a leg missing. It would break your heart to hear them wondering what the folks will say." "Speaking of letters," her colleague Seraphine "Pat" Petrocelli added, "I wish there were some way to put an end to the 'Dear John' letters. They do a lot of harm."[43]

Flight surgeon Snyder of the 804 MAES thought flight nurses deserved even better publicity. When Frances Armin and Josephine Wright brought the first planeload of severely injured men from Nadzab in New Guinea to Los Negros in the Admiralty Islands, once flight nurses finally were allowed to make that trip, the squadron gave the story to the newspapers for wide distribution. "I saw them as they came trudging back to their quarters. Their faces were black, their hair flying. Their steps were weary, but their grins were wide and personally I thought I had never seen them look more attractive," the historian observed.[44]

Snyder was a frequent critic of the type of air evacuation publicity that showed immaculately groomed nurses putting on lipstick. He wanted instead to publicize "the cheerfulness with which our nurses, officers and men face the dirt, misery and true danger of the war as it is being fought in this theater."[45] Hometown press releases prepared by the squadrons were factual in their accounts, but the same could not be said for other stories that appeared in print. Snyder singled out a newspaper article printed about flight nurse Kathleen Dial of the 804 MAES who returned to the United States as a patient, having been injured in a plane crash. "A more untruthful article surely has never been written. The number of missions in which she participated, her total flying time, the story of the crash itself bore but slight resemblance to the truth," he noted.[46] The important work of air evacuation squadrons made good newspaper copy, Snyder continued, but articles that glamorized and exaggerated the truth harmed air evacuation and antagonized outside colleagues, especially hospital nurses. The flight nurses did not seek the publicity, Snyder pointed out; they just wanted to be left alone to do their work.[47]

In England, flight nurses of the 819 MAES, who learned about air evacuation flights into France following D Day from their local military newspaper were not pleased with how they—and by implication their work—were portrayed. They bitterly resented what could be seen as a publicity stunt, given that members of the press accompanied the 816 MAES into France. The flight nurses were photographed picking poppies while the planes sat on the airstrip for more than two hours as fifteen casualties were rounded up for evacuation back to England.[48] The photo op tarnished the flight nurse image, chief nurse June Sanders of the 819 MAES complained. "We knew that our battle for Air Evac had slipped a trifle.—That we had left ourselves open for the ridicule of our ground force sisters—that we would henceforth be referred to in this theater as 'The Poppy Girls.' We have been."[49]

The Associated Press article "Nurses Pick Poppies While Awaiting First Wounded," which appeared in a New Jersey newspaper, reinforced the image. Suella Bernard and Marijean Brown of the 816 MAES, who had been among the flight nurses photographed holding bouquets of the red flowers in the doorway of their C-47 in France, wrote of their experience on the flight, beginning: "We picked poppies in shell-pocked fields of Normandy and brought them back to Britain with the first cargo of wounded to be evacuated from this new European battlefield—two Germans, a French civilian, and two Americans—a Colonel and a G.I."[50]

Both a flight nurse's manner of working and her feminine appearance were of therapeutic value on air evacuation flights, as a photograph caption in *Skyways* magazine suggested: "Air Evacuation nurses and medical technicians work together to remove battle-wounded boys from crowded combat areas. Injured fighters get morale lift from personal care offered by a pretty, competent nurse." Lieutenant Colonel Stevenson, aware of this benefit to soldiers' morale, told the reporter: "A man isn't going to be scared over his first flight if he sees a calm young woman walking around in the plane and looking after him and his buddies. He'd be ashamed to be. Having those nurses along is a terrific morale factor for the boys right from the start, and it does much to keep up the spirit of the boys."[51]

The flight nurses knew the effect they were claimed to have on their patients. Writing for *Cosmopolitan* about being the first white woman to set foot on Baker Island in almost a hundred years, Elsie Nolan of the 812 MAES remarked: "Generals have said that if Flight Nurses couldn't take a temperature or count a pulse they would still be a tremendous asset in this theater of war. It doesn't matter whether or not we're pretty, or that we usually look wretched after a fifteen-hour flight. We're women—white and American."[52]

Fortunately, the lower ranks had a more charitable view of the flight nurse role. A staff sergeant writing for *Brief*, a publication for army air forces personnel, posed the rhetorical questions:

> What kind of a girl is the flight nurse?
> Does she think in terms of capillaries, capsules and traction splints? Is she a spoiled woman who, socially, speaks only to Generals, Colonels and God—in the order named?
> She could be very spoiled. Quite suddenly, she has been transported into a world of men without women.

The author's answer painted a nurse more at the middle of the spectrum:

She has been photographed and whistled at like Hedy Lamarr at a hermit's convention.

In spite of all this she is mostly just an American girl. A pretty good Josie with a fine sense of humor and plenty of guts. She is far less vain than most females . . . military or otherwise.[53]

Although flight nurses of the 801 MAES were outraged "when some soured individual infers that nursing is secondary in our lives here and that we're primarily morale builders," they also had fine senses of humor and could poke fun at themselves and their femininity. Describing themselves and their colleagues "as petty as nice girls are supposed to be," who "recoil at the thought of staying away overnight without lipstick, tooth brush, or clean clothing," Lieutenants Nancy Preston and Ada Endres, writing in "The Feminine Side," presented their "eternal quest" with levity. The flight nurses of their squadron were females "to the very core," and they dreamed of pretty clothes and shoes while dressed in cotton underwear, sensible Girl Scout oxfords, "evil-fitting slacks, and shirts especially designed for Miss America vintage 1916." For flying, they seemed stuck with size 12 G.I. flight suits for the large nurses and size 42 for the small ones, or a "devastating seersucker job, pajama-like in design."[54] Their starched skirts and shirts and rayon hose passed for eveningwear.

With "a stag line that extends ad infinitum," the flight nurses were very popular and treated to so many parties and so much pampering that they occasionally wearied of all the attention. But Preston and Endres admitted that marriage was the ultimate goal. Weariness notwithstanding, "we are to the last one of us good wholesome girls with a bird in the hand and an eye to the future—and there are some few fortunate among us who have the bird by the beak."[55] Writing about flight nurses in the South Pacific, Charlotte Knight, staff writer for *Air Force* magazine, offered another perspective on their social life. A nurse might not fall for the old line about etchings, but she was likely to accept the invitation of a man who had an iron; keeping clothes neat was hard when the nurses' quarters had no electricity.[56]

In a letter to Stroup from New Guinea, Dorothy Rice mentioned the "continuous social whirl if one only had the energy and endurance."[57]

The first few weeks for the 803 MAES flight nurses in India "seemed like a diplomatic convention with the rounds of invitations to dinners, dances, card parties, open houses and teas."[58] They, too, wearied of the constant round of socializing, as Phoebe La Munyan, acting historian of the 819 MAES, whose flight nurses were sent from England to help the 802 and 807 MAES in Italy, reported in 1944. "Parties, Parties, and more Parties!" she exclaimed. "August opened with so many invitations posted on our bulletin board that we could scarcely see what was going on in regards to our primary mission in Italy."[59]

Although one could argue that the press overdid the glamorization of flight nursing, leading to resentment by some of the flight nurses' coworkers, the femininity inherent in such an image served a purpose. Military officials would have found it difficult to discount the feminine image of the flight nurse that sold the air evacuation program during World War II. But to emphasize that image downplayed the professionalism of the flight nurse, the real reason military officials had decided to use female nurses in the program. Thus, they portrayed these women as both glamorous and gutsy. This image helped the sick and wounded soldiers cope with their battle wounds, injuries, and illnesses and, in turn, helped the flight nurses cope with the professional and personal challenges of air evacuation duty in World War II.

12

Challenges of Wartime Flight Nursing

During World War II, female flight nurses first brought their professional nursing skills and compassion to injured and ill soldiers. But with the first use of flight nurses came challenges, both for an environment unaccustomed to the presence of women in its midst and for those women who encountered stresses of war previously known only to male aircrews.

Army nurses were no strangers to the dangers and deprivations of war. They had served overseas in World War I and were serving in World War II as well and had learned how to cope with wartime nursing on the ground. Army and navy nurses assigned to area hospitals experienced the first mass influx of World War II wounded following the attack on Pearl Harbor. When hospital beds, equipment, and supplies ran short, these nurses learned to make do with whatever was on hand. They worked long hours in blackout conditions, triaged patients, assisted in nonstop surgery, and provided ward care for more than twelve hundred soldiers who suffered traumatic amputations, severe burns, and other wounds as a result of the Japanese bombing.

When the Japanese attacked the Philippine Islands later that same day, army and navy nurses staffed hospitals set up in any available space, whether in buildings or out in the open. With patients and hospital personnel, these nurses left Manila for Bataan to escape enemy attacks. The Japanese soon found the new hospitals, however. Around

Easter 1942 they bombed the hospital at "Little Baguio" in Bataan. The nurses survived, though two were wounded; approximately one hundred patients died during the attack, and at least that many were wounded.[1]

In spite of rugged conditions and decreasing food supplies, the nurses soldiered on in their makeshift hospitals and living quarters until ordered to take refuge in the Malinta tunnel, which was equipped with a thousand-bed hospital, on the island of Corregidor. Some of the nurses were taken off Corregidor by seaplane and by submarine before Lieutenant General Jonathan M. Wainwright surrendered the island to the Japanese on 6 May 1942. But sixty-six army and eleven navy nurses in the Philippines and five navy nurses captured in Guam became prisoners of the Japanese; they fought their war in internment camps until American troops liberated them in February 1945.[2]

Army nurses also served elsewhere in the Pacific. They arrived shortly after the American troops at Nouméa in New Caledonia, "the nerve center" of the South Pacific area, in March 1942 to staff field, evacuation, station, and general hospitals in the area. They lived in tents; battled mud and insects; scrounged for furniture while awaiting more permanent housing.[3] Army nurses were among the contingents of medical personnel on the lesser-known islands such as Effete, Kwajalein, and Biak, as well as the better-known Guam, Saipan, and Iwo Jima, all stepping-stones to Japan. Around a hundred army nurses arrived at Santo Tomas Internment Camp in Manila in February 1945 to relieve their newly liberated colleagues who had been working in the camp's hospital.[4]

In North Africa, fifty-seven army nurses of the 48th Surgical Hospital waded onto the beaches with the troops on D Day for Operation Torch. It was the only time a group of female nurses accompanied assault troops on a D-Day invasion. Army nurses traveling and working on HMHS *Newfoundland* in the waters off Salerno, Italy, in 1943 and HMHC *St. David* in the waters off Anzio in 1944 all survived German bombings of those hospital ships.[5] Six army nurses lost their lives when a Japanese kamikaze attacked the hospital ship USS *Comfort* off the coast of Okinawa in 1945.[6]

Army nurses at Anzio, known as Hell's Half Acre, worked in some of the worst combat conditions of the war. German attacks on two frontline hospitals, both under canvas—that is, in tents—on 7 and 8 February 1944 killed five nurses, three of them survivors of the sinking of the *Newfoundland*. Three of the survivors of the latter attack who remained at work in the operating room and postoperative tent were the first army nurses of the war awarded Silver Stars for gallantry.[7]

Hospital compounds often were under canvas, and living and working conditions were primitive. June Wandrey, an army nurse who served in the Mediterranean Theater, recalled: "Water was a very precious commodity. You could really milk the usefulness out of a helmetful of water. First you brushed your teeth, then you washed your hair, your body, and gave your underwear a soak. Depending on the density of the water by then you could throw it out or use it to wash the mud off from your boots." In August 1944, Wandrey, whose frontline hospital was awaiting its role in the invasion of southern France, wrote her sister Betty about an experience markedly different from her own: "Met two flight nurses from my nursing school this week. They really lead a life of luxury, living in a gorgeous apartment in Naples, making frequent trips to USA."[8]

What set flight nurses apart from other army nurses assigned to the European and Pacific fronts was the work that exposed them to the hazards of air travel, the effects of altitude, and the erratic schedules of aircrews. Unlike their colleagues on the ground, flight nurses were at risk for crash landing and water ditching in attacked and disabled aircraft. They worked in an environment of dry air with oxygen content that decreased as they reached higher altitudes. This and vibration and noise from the aircraft engines contributed to the fatigue of flying. And maintenance issues, inclement weather, mandated crew rest requirements, and diverted flights often resulted in irregular work schedules. These airborne stressors were not inherently more dangerous or demanding, only different from those experienced by nurses who worked in the chain of medical evacuation on the ground. Enemy attacks were equally perilous, for example, whether they came from above or from below.

Dorothy Rice's "Flight at 20,000 Feet" submitted to the 804 MAES historical report for August 1944 illustrates many of these stressors. After circling the airfield for over an hour due to heavy airport traffic, a plane with Rice on board landed just after noon on Owi, an island off Biak, northwest of New Guinea, to offload cargo. It took off less than an hour later and was ordered to Wakde, an island off the northern coast of New Guinea, to pick up patients for air evacuation. Because of traffic congestion above the airfield, the pilots decided not to land but to fly to Nadzab in Papua, New Guinea, instead, with no patients on board. An hour into the flight, the weather began to "build up and close in," and the pilots took the plane up to twenty thousand feet to fly over thunderheads. Buffeted about by the turbulent air, the plane dropped repeatedly between one thousand and six thousand feet, then began to shake and vibrate. Ice covered the plane until it descended to eleven thousand feet.

At the high altitude Rice became very sleepy and fought to stay awake, and she even momentarily lost consciousness—all signs of hypoxia from decreased oxygen supply to her body. Her head felt "squeezed" and throbbed with pain. Her body was "fatigued beyond caring," and she felt nauseated and "terribly cold." She made her way to a litter set up just outside the cockpit and grabbed the mask attached to the one oxygen tank on board. This lessened but did not resolve completely her symptoms of hypoxia. The plane finally landed at Port Moresby, Papua, New Guinea, shortly after seven o'clock that evening. After a fitful night's sleep, Rice felt better the next morning but still had a residual headache, fatigue, ear pain, and dulled hearing.[9]

Of many professional and personal challenges, five themes recurred in MAES histories and in interviews with twenty-five former World War II flight nurses: keeping busy, attending to health and hygiene, finding medical resources, conquering fears, and providing patient care. Some trials of wartime nursing were related humorously; others were no laughing matter.

Lack of adequate work to keep them professionally challenged and personally satisfied, whatever the cause, constantly vexed the flight nurses. The situation was ameliorated by a sense of esprit de corps and the knowledge that at least all the squadron's flight nurses shared the same dispiriting predicament. Once the flight nurses began their work in earnest, health and hygiene became an issue: bathroom facilities for the flight nurses, especially at forward airfields, were usually primitive—when they existed at all. Finding humor in an otherwise aggravating dilemma helped the flight nurses make light of a potentially embarrassing state of affairs. Limited medical resources were a problem throughout the war, with a direct impact on patient care. Nurses who were assertive and had learned in their training how to improvise fared far better than those who could not be creative with the assets on hand. Flight nurses' fears never were conquered fully, for their own or their patients' safety. A belief in a higher power or cause, religious or patriotic, was a comfort during dangerous situations in the air and on the ground. Keeping busy, attending to health and hygiene, finding medical resources, and conquering fears were all important in meeting the greatest challenge of wartime flight nursing, the one that offered the greatest satisfaction—providing the best possible care to their patients.

Keeping Busy

Flight nurses had their own ideas of what it meant to keep busy, and these were linked to flying with patients who needed the nursing skills they were trained to provide. Time spent at bomber bases in England, at station hospitals and dispensaries on both the European and Pacific fronts, and in bivouac and training classes on the ground was not, the flight nurses contended, the real purpose for which they had been sent overseas.

Exploring the English countryside on bicycles was not sufficient to keep all 815 MAES nurses entertained while awaiting the flying activities that would begin after D Day. Ethel Carlson remembered that occasionally their boredom got flight nurses into trouble. She was one of some who decided to turn their brown-and-white-seersucker uniform slacks into shorts when the weather got warmer; they "almost got court-martialed for destroying government property."[10]

Some nurses filled their hours of waiting more constructively. Dayrooms in their quarters, when spruced up, offered cozy settings for open houses and parties at which the flight nurses entertained fellow officers. More than one officers' club in Italy benefitted from the flight nurses' knack for turning surplus and discarded lumber, mattresses, and parachutes into furniture, cushions, and curtains with the help of a sewing machine and enlisted men handy with carpenter's tools. Dorothy White of the 807 MAES in Italy organized parenting classes for the new fathers in her squadron to help them understand the growth and development of their new babies back in the United States. Helena Ilic befriended Filipino families from a town in Leyte while stationed in the Philippines and soon was godmother to two babies, one who later became a nurse herself.[11]

Flying—or the lack of it—affected morale. When a squadron was working together and busy doing the work for which it was trained, morale was high. When nurses were separated from the enlisted men because of lack of accommodations or risk perceived at the location of air evacuation activities, morale was low. Such was the case on the European front for the 819 MAES flight nurses transporting patients from Prestwick back to the United States on ATC flights while the squadron's enlisted technicians were flying air evacuation missions in France after D Day. Knitting circles and active social lives did not compensate for the nurses' felt lack of meaningful work—recall, for example, chief nurse June Sanders's mention of her flight nurses' "three month sentence" with ATC in November 1944 (see chapter 7).

Grumbling often occurred when flight nurses were sharing duties with other squadrons. In January 1944, the flight nurses of the 809 and 812 MAES alternated days on the limited number of air evacuation flights within the Hawaiian Islands before their work on outlying islands began. A flight nurse with the 812 MAES remembered that she and her colleagues were "at loose ends quite a bit of the time" but mostly were "a little discouraged that we weren't doing something faster." As she recalled, it took three or four months for them to start flying in earnest. They managed, and even had some fun along the way, however, especially after a big dance party at which many of the flight nurses met boyfriends. "Only we were so impatient to get going with our work," the flight nurse said.[12]

During the fall of 1944, the 819 MAES flight nurses in Prestwick were rotating flights with their colleagues of the 806 and 816 MAES, and by November the 819 MAES nurses felt left behind, with the 816 MAES already in France and the 806 MAES soon to depart. At the same time in the Pacific, flight nurses of the 820 MAES, whose squadron had moved to Leyte in the Philippines in advance of the nurses, joined their colleagues of the

801 and 804 MAES on Biak. With more flight nurses assigned than were needed for air evacuation missions, the scheduler designed a roster that fairly distributed the work. At the same time in the CBI, the flight nurses of the 821 MAES, who initially worked with the 803 MAES, were fussing about having to accept the leftovers from another MAES before their squadron was given its own assignment in Ledo, India (see chapter 10).

Nancy Preston and Ada Endres of the 801 MAES flight nurses on the Pacific front commented, "To be the first girl to land on a newly acquired island is the ardent wish of every member of our crew—and to evacuate the largest number of patients is her sincere hope," wrote flight nurses Nancy Preston and Ada Endres of the 801 MAES on the Pacific Front. Their comment not only suggests the desire to fly as much as possible but hints at rivalry perhaps within squadrons but also well documented between squadrons for the most important air evacuation missions.[13] It was hard on flight nurses in a squadron experiencing a relative lull in activity, for example, to learn that their colleagues from other squadrons were flying into areas where they themselves had not been sent, for whatever reason. "It's the same old story," the commander of the 801 MAES wrote from the Philippines in September 1945. "This squadron has once again been delegated the rear area evacuation duties. Our compatriots in the field of air evacuation in this theater have been assigned the long dreamed of plum of evacuation, that of flying into the Tokyo area."[14]

As part of the program of rest and recreation for August 1945, when "the routine drab evacuation of patients from all the Southern Philippine Islands and Morotai to Leyte continued," enlisted men of the 801 MAES were given three-day passes in Manila. The flight nurses were permitted three-day trips, which their commander expected they would use to pamper themselves with visits to hair salons and shopping, or perhaps to see a boyfriend. "Needless to say all these small liberties pay dividends," the commander pointed out.[15]

Esprit de corps among military colleagues and the support of family members and even patients were key elements in dealing with the challenges of wartime flight nursing. Squadrons had been working together since their days at Bowman Field, and MAES that stayed together throughout the war tended to have higher morale than those in which enlisted men and nurses were sent on different assignments, which often positioned the men in forward areas, leaving the women far removed from the combat zone. The people with whom Jenny Boyle, stationed in Europe with the 816 MAES, worked were "like a family." Flight nursing was "like a little sisterhood," Boyle said. "I mean, we felt in some ways apart from the regular nurses, but we always felt very much a part of each other." Randy Rast's flight nurse colleagues of the 803 MAES in the CBI "seemed more like sisters to me than my own sisters." Clara Morrey, initially stationed in North Africa with the 802 MAES, turned down a chance to accompany a patient back to the United States, because she might not have been assigned to her own squadron on her return from the temporary duty.[16]

Flight nurses praised the work of the enlisted technicians and emphasized the importance of teamwork in providing patient care. "The rapport between the corpsmen and our flight nurses was magnificent," said chief nurse Elizabeth Pukas, whose 812 MAES was stationed in Hawaii. "Oh, it's a team—it was definitely a team," she added.[17] The team extended to flight crews on air evacuation missions, who earned the respect of the flight nurses. The crew chief's help with patient care was invaluable, said Helena Ilic, assigned with the 801 MAES in the Pacific. Her colleague Adele Edmunds, who once was saved from the neck grip of a psychiatric patient by the timely entrance of the crew chief into the cabin of the plane, agreed. Frances Sandstrom of the 816 MAES recalled that the pilots in Europe were also glad to help the flight nurses.[18]

Good leadership contributed to esprit de corps and fostered teamwork. Rast considered Morris Kaplan, 803 MAES flight surgeon, an exceptional commanding officer who saw to unit morale.[19] A flight nurse in the Pacific stated, "I think our chief nurse was good for us. She didn't nag, she didn't pump, she joined us with our laughter, she joined us with our fun, she didn't pick. I think that she had something to do with our being content."[20] Louise Anthony, who flew with the 816 MAES, credited her good assignment in the war at least in part to the quality and fair-mindedness of her chief nurse, who the flight nurses knew would always "go to bat right away" for her nurses.[21]

Grace Dunnam of the 806 MAES in Europe spoke of physicians and commanders who were "right in there with you." As chief nurse of the MAES, she was responsible for seeing that her flight nurses wore their uniforms properly, both on and off duty. She remarked that keeping those girls properly dressed "worried one to death." If someone reported a nurse for uniform infractions, Dunnam felt obligated to talk with the nurse about it, and did. But what she did not hear about, she chose to overlook. For example, she ignored the red nail polish the nurses wore that she believed was good for their morale.[22]

Several flight nurses mentioned family members who could be relied on to send necessities such as casual clothes and underwear and to provide news from home in letters and newspapers to boost their morale. Her family's pride in her sustained Sandstrom overseas. Even the patients whom the nurses evacuated by air were a source of support. Both Dorothy Vancil, who flew with the 805 MAES in Central Africa on Elsie Ott's historic route, and Morrey were struck by how grateful their patients were for everything the flight nurses did for them.[23]

"You never knew a stranger," Rast remarked.[24] Many flight nurses found that the war had its compensation in the people they encountered and with whom they associated on and off duty during their military service. Five of the women interviewed met their husbands during the war. For Eileen Newbeck, it was an added benefit to an already positive experience: "I was so completely happy with what I was doing and the area where I was, which I had always wanted to see. And I went there at the expense of Uncle Sam, which was fortunate for me. . . . And the very best thing in the whole world happened—I met my husband."[25]

But keeping busy with the actual work of air evacuation provided the most positive experiences for flight nurses. As Morrey explained: "The morale of the squadron was always good when we were busy—a sad commentary when you realize that was the time when our soldiers were being killed and injured in great numbers. Somehow we felt that we were helping when we were needed most."[26]

Attending to Health and Hygiene

The primitive conditions in which flight nurses lived and worked placed demands on their hygiene and health. Lack of adequate bathroom facilities was one cause of flight nurses not being allowed to fly into certain airfields. The nurses of the 801 MAES assigned in the Pacific were thus generous in their appraisal of the good people who helped them gain access to these important airfields: "Number one man in our list of 'Nurses Friends' is the man, whoever he is, who finally installed powder rooms at all of our stops."[27]

Flight nurses in Europe were not always as fortunate. White, whose 807 MAES flew into Naples, recalled that the airfield had "absolutely no facilities for women." Consequently, one of the medical officers would pull up to the airplane in a jeep with a sign reading "To the bushes." And that is where he took the flight nurses. They had come prepared, according to White, having stuffed the chest pockets of their Eisenhower uniform jackets with toilet paper and Kotex, which made them appear more buxom than they really were.[28]

The situation was more precarious in the air. "Most airplanes did not have any toilet facilities on board," White explained. "If we were lucky, and you had a long flight, there might be a pail in the back that we had to use. It *is* possible for a nurse with slacks on to aim at the pilot's relief tube. But believe me, it's very difficult, and you have to hope that the plane is going to fly steady while you're there."[29] Sandstrom of the 816 MAES recalled a mission in which, because of fog, a flight that should have lasted approximately ninety minutes lasted about seven hours. Hers was one of thirteen planes destined for England that were evacuating patients from Belgium during the Battle of the Bulge—all of which had to divert to Paris. "The worst part of it was that we had no place to go to the little girls' room," Sandstrom said. "I can remember that was very uncomfortable, to say the least."[30]

Some of the planes had chemical toilets, but some nurses would not use them. As Adele Edmonds of the 801 MAES in the Pacific remembered, they were not enclosed. "It was really just open. . . . Men have a different feeling about things like that. But if you were a woman aboard a plane with all men, you would naturally be a little reluctant to go to the bathroom practically on display."[31] The flight nurses dealt with the lack of bathroom facilities in different ways. Many simply regulated their food and fluid intake. "We just dehydrated ourselves; it took care of that," said Sandstrom.[32]

Nurses occasionally ran out of sanitary napkins, because some locations lacked post exchanges or towns in which to buy more. Chief nurse Lucy Wilson of the 801 MAES recalled flying on a mercy mission to another island in the Pacific to stock up on Kotex for the nurses in her squadron.[33]

While most flight nurses maintained their health during their air evacuation assignments, minor ailments such as diarrhea, constipation, bladder infections, and skin fungus plagued many of them. The flight nurses continued to work despite their discomfort, often to the point of exhaustion. White recalled a time of when she and everyone around her had a type of hepatitis, which they called "golden glitters" because it turned their skin gold; she kept herself going by drinking black coffee.[34]

Irregular hours accounted for much of the indisposition, and dry runs contributed to the accumulated stresses of flight. Food on the ground at destination points was nonexistent or unpalatable, served from a back burner of a stove in the mess hall, by a Red Cross worker, or from a container of C- or K-rations. While most flight nurses learned to sleep deadheading on a flight with no patients, these naps did not compensate for a full night's sleep on the ground. Crew rest varied in length, depending on plane schedules and the number of patients needing air evacuation.

Physical exhaustion was the inevitable result of the hectic pace of flight nursing during the war. Hilda Halverson, whose 826 MAES was incorporated into the 830 MAES for service in the Pacific, remembered that Japanese air raids constantly interrupted her sleep, necessitating trips to the bomb shelter. "Oh, they were tiresome. And the minute you got back, it seemed like you'd get back to sleep, then they'd come again. And you'd think, *Oh, who cares?*" Mental exhaustion—which Halverson described as always being alert, thinking "what you can do for the next person"—was not as easily remedied, though overall good health helped.[35]

Two of the nurses interviewed returned to the United States as patients because of health problems. Carlson had a kidney flare-up; Anthony could not tolerate a back injury she sustained during the flight nurse course when she had to lift a litter with two sixty-pound sandbags on it. She hid the injury as long as she could, because she realized it would disqualify her from flight nursing.[36]

Concern for flight nurses' safety led to some rather embarrassing requirements when the women used bathrooms located away from their living quarters. Usually they stayed in a compound with guards at its gate; latrines were located in the middle of the compound. On Biak, however, the flight nurses all lived in one big Quonset hut and had an outdoor latrine, and at night they had to call for a guard to escort them to it, because of stray Japanese in the area. "I bet he loved his duty during the war," Lee Holtz remarked.[37]

Water for bathing, washing one's clothes, and washing one's hair was limited. For all hygiene needs, the flight nurses' helmets came in handy: "It was a potty, emesis basin, and wash basin," said Alice Krieble assigned to the 818 MAES on the European front.[38] Morrey wrote her mother in 1942 about using her helmet for "everything from taking a sponge bath to washing our clothes." Because the water was so hard at their location, the nurses could not work up soap lather. So Morrey waited for a timely rainfall and caught enough rainwater in five helmets for one wash and one rinse. The soft water felt "luxurious" and made her appreciate something she formerly had taken for granted. "Well, my hair turned out swell, making the other girls envious," Morrey concluded, "so they tried it today—without the rain water—and what a sticky mess they turned out to be!"[39]

Two flight nurses of the 812 MAES remembered that during their stays on one of the Pacific islands they had to resort to a quick shower at a prearranged hour in the men's community shower, a structure surrounded only by wooden walls with the sky overhead. Once when Jo Nabors was showering, she looked up and saw a face. "Well, I screamed, and of course everybody came running in. It was one of the fellows who hadn't seen a white woman for so long. So from then on we wore bathing suits in the shower."[40]

A sense of humor helped keep these annoyances in perspective. Holtz remembered arriving back at her campsite on a Pacific island from flights too late to take a shower, so she just splashed some water on her face from her ever-present helmet. On one occasion, the tent had leaked and all her clothes were wet. "But we hung them all out, and, you know, we just laughed about it. You couldn't get upset about anything, you just couldn't. You couldn't survive that kind of life."[41] A sense of humor also helped flight nurses of the 830 MAES assigned to Harmon Field in Newfoundland resolve the frustrating situation of twenty-five women sharing one bathroom. When the one toilet kept overflowing "accidentally" out into the officers' club, management finally gave them a larger bathroom.[42]

Most of the nurses took the undesirable conditions of wartime living in stride. Vancil, for example, didn't expect to have all the comforts of home. Sally Jones, who was stationed with the 812 MAES in the Pacific, summed up the situation: "How could you have everything plush when there was a war going on? That's ridiculous!"[43]

A policy that sent air evacuation personnel on rest leaves during lulls in the fighting did much to improve both the flight nurses' health and their morale. Sydney was a mecca for flight nurses assigned to the Pacific front. "Would that the Sydney Chamber of Commerce could see the before and after skit that we perform," wrote Preston and Endres, "for it's really an invigorating spectacle to watch our bedraggled, mousy specimens trudging off to Australia to return ten days hence manicured, pedicured, facialled, and curled to the eye-lashes, femmes latules, invariably, we breeze in loaded to the hilt with packages." Black lace negligees, Marabou jackets, and Lana Turner sweaters were popular purchases, even though they could only look pretty hanging in closets when uniforms were the order of the day. "These sprees of self-indulgence are good for us and we attribute much of our congeniality and good spirits to the benefits gained from them," the flight nurses said.[44]

Finding Medical Resources

The flight nurses interviewed displayed an uncanny ability to make do admirably with what was on hand or could be scrounged to augment deficient supplies for patient care. The 807 MAES nurses considered the bulky ninety-five-pound ambulance chest filled with medical supplies that they took on board aircraft unsuitable for their work. Fewer supplies in a smaller medical kit worked just as well and created space to evacuate another patient from the front lines. White, assigned to the 807 MAES, became very adept at procuring supplies for her medical kit from offices and dispensaries she visited. "I used to walk through an office," she said. "They used to be afraid to see me coming, because they didn't know what I was going to leave with." Covers for field telephones that she appropriated on one scouting mission made the perfect medical kit when laced together with shoestrings. The bags quickly caught on with the other flight nurses in her squadron, until "all the field telephones in the area were naked," having been put to medical use.[45]

Wherever she landed in the Pacific, Ilic of the 801 MAES got to know the cooks and made little deals for food that she fed her patients in flight, so that "my men were always well fed." She "scrounged around," Ilic explained. "I was a true-blue. I did what they told us to do—improvise."[46]

Vancil, who flew missions with the 830 MAES in the United States after having served with the 805 MAES in Central Africa, remembered that food was not a concern on her overseas air evacuation missions, but patients complained about the stale sandwiches on stateside flights. Thus, she would stop by the hospital kitchens and request the sandwich fixings in separate containers so that she could make them herself once airborne. "And so I'd spread out a big sheet, and then everybody would come up and, they could have their choice of mayonnaise or mustard or whatever." Years after the war, one of the pilots saw Vancil at an officers club and said, "Here's the girl that made the best sandwiches in the air evac."[47]

Nothing was insurmountable for these women who had been taught to improvise. Nurses training taught White to be frugal: "Well, you never throw things away—you find another use for it, see." Resourcefulness was the most valuable lesson Ilic learned in her nurses training. As she stated, "Ideal situations don't exist in wartime. . . . You don't have all the equipment. . . . And you work with what you have." She fell back on her own ingenuity, making do with what she had and improvising to make up for what she did not have. Brooxie Mowery, a flight nurse with the 816 MAES in Europe, summed up the situation: "So there was a lot of theory, but I think it's true of everything in nursing—theory is fine, but then you have to improvise."[48]

Decisions concerning patient care required discretion and good judgment on the flight nurse's part, since a flight surgeon was seldom on board the airplane, and the nurses did not always fly with an enlisted technician with whom to consult. "With fear and trepidation you made many of these decisions," stated Pukas.[49] When necessary, Ilic relied on her own imagination to decide what to do with each case.[50] For White, who considered her training incidental to what she encountered once on air evacuation duty, the ability to adapt was essential. Some flight nurses, she thought, did not have the courage to act without taking orders from someone else—they needed to be daredevils. "If there's nobody there, somebody's got to do something. So you do something. If it's the wrong thing, well, you're eventually going to find out about it. . . . You gotta tackle the bull by the horns and try."[51]

Several flight nurses mentioned the importance of psychiatric nursing skills when deciding how to deal with patients. Given the limited time, space, asepsis, equipment, and supplies, as well as the circumstances of war, these skills and the ability to communicate effectively with patients were often the most effective recourse. Boyle found that those skills helped her more than any others in understanding the reactions of soldiers on her flights. It was surprising, she remarked, "how much time you can spend without doing anything spectacular, just by being there and helping out and talking with the patients, but you stayed busy for the whole time."[52]

Vancil, who went overseas with thoughts of being another Florence Nightingale, found she was mainly giving moral support to her patients: "If they had something that was going to be a permanent thing, their spirits were low, and a cheery word or a song or even a pat on the back—if you just sat there and held their hand for a while—did more good than all the morphine in the world."[53]

White sometimes saw her patients frightened and in pain but had nothing except pain medication to give them. So she talked with them, reassuring them, but all the while watching their color and assessing their condition. "Someone would be getting excited; you'd stand, you'd hold his hand, you'd talk about any subject in the world to make it easier for them until they could relax." A patient's skin color would change, and White would think, *"Oh, if I had this, if I had that."* Perhaps the soldier had recently had massive abdominal surgery and had a nasogastric tube that showed fresh bleeding, which she knew she could not stop. "You just watched—watched and waited," she said. With only her own will to keep the patient alive, White was afraid if she let go, the patient would die. "So you had the feeling, '*Hold on! Hang on!*' You know, '*Another deep breath*'. . . . And you do your best."[54]

Doing their best for patients was a hallmark of the flight nurses' wartime service. But that standard of care could be difficult to achieve when supplies and equipment were lacking. Sandstrom remembered a close call with a patient who had been hurt in an accident: "But you feel so helpless when your patient's going out and there isn't anything you can do. . . . We had no oxygen on board, no IVs to give him—nothing to help a patient like that. And all I could do was just watch him."[55] Rast spoke for all her flight nurse colleagues when she said simply, "I did the best I could, and then I left it in somebody else's hands."[56]

Conquering Fears

Youth, naïveté, and a trusting nature helped flight nurses endure the dangers of war. Carlson of the 815 MAES remembered flying into France on a cargo plane to pick up patients after D Day. She was napping on top of cargo—probably hand grenades—when the plane lurched, tossing her into the air, which resulted in a bruised side. She was angry at the pilot "for doing something stupid" that made her hurt herself. Even after she found out he was avoiding enemy fire, she blamed him for being in the wrong place at the wrong time. She didn't even think about being shot down.[57] Said Holtz about wartime service, "We never realized the danger of it. That never entered our mind."[58] As White explained, she and her colleagues were young, cocky, and ready to tackle the world. "So there was a war going on," she quipped. "It just kind of got in the way."[59]

"Viewed from a distance, our trips seem uneventful," wrote flight nurses Preston and Endres, "but there is not a one of us who has not tucked away in her never-to-be-forgotten portion of her memory a number of incidents that have added something, be it mild panic, hilarity, pathos, or downright discomfort, which have made most of our working days more than plane-ride days."[60] Flight nurses' funny, pathetic, and uncomfortable situations appear in unit histories and in interviews, but only in interviews did these women reveal fears associated with air evacuation duty.

Flight nurses were often afraid during air evacuation flights, but they kept their fears to themselves to project calmness to their patients. One nurse assigned to the Pacific front never did conquer her fear of flying: "I was petrified of flying. I was scared to death to fly. I was scared on every trip. The smooth trips, which were few and far between, were fine; they didn't bother me. But the minute we started bouncing around, I thought, *How am I going to get these forty patients into life rafts? . . .* I think I prayed harder and longer through those years of flying than I have ever done in my life."[61]

Potential aircraft emergencies were not uncommon on many missions. The possibility of ditching at sea was foremost in many flight nurses' thoughts, since so much of their flying was over water. Jocie French, who flew with the 818 MAES in Europe, wished she had remembered more about her survival training with parachutes. "I kept thinking, *Do I get out of this parachute before we hit the water . . . or do I hit the water with the parachute?*"[62] Solomon of the 830 MAES, on a mission with a planeload of patients during a bad storm, worried particularly about one patient in a body cast. The flight had passed the point of no return, and she wondered what she would do about him should the plane have to ditch at sea. She explained: "We were taught that in case we were going down, and we knew we were going down, and if there was a patient that couldn't be moved into one of the rafts, just to overdose him with morphine." The plane landed safely with just fifteen minutes worth of gas remaining.[63]

Denny Nagle, shown in illustration 12.1, who flew with the 815 MAES in Europe, recalled a flight with a full load of patients during which the plane lost one of its engines. "I was thinking what we were going to do when we go down in that zero [degree] water down there." The flight nurses had been told that a person could survive only twenty minutes in such cold water, she said. "You didn't have a chance. But you'd think, *Can you get them out of here? And what can you do if you do?*"[64]

Flights with patients on board exacted fortitude that at times conflicted with a flight nurse's natural instincts. Nabors recalled a flight into a Pacific island where the harbor was being bombed. "They were shooting at us. . . . I was panicky. And when we landed, and we got

12.1 **Denny Nagle (left) and colleague of 815 MAES on airstrip in Europe (author's collection)**

our load of patients and started back out, I was never so glad to leave an island as I was that day." Despite her panic, she appeared cool and calm to her patients, telling little jokes. When the plane ascended to get out of the range of ack-ack, a patient with an open chest wound began bleeding. Nabors thought, *"Oh, what'll I do, what'll I do?"* She gave him morphine for his pain, administered oxygen, and replugged his wound to stop the bleeding. "Any emergency that comes up, you have to do it. Well, all I could think of was if we were shot down. . . . I was deathly afraid that I would have to ditch first, and then save myself, and then try to save all these boys."[65]

Nabors struggled with the expectation that in the event of an emergency her safety came before that of her patients. She was more valuable than her patients, her commander had said, and unless she and the rest of the crew saved themselves, they would not be able to help the others. "I had to get out of the plane first," Nabors stated. "And that's where I felt that sometimes that it was a little bit difficult to make a decision. How could you make a decision like that?" On one occasion, when her plane lost a propeller, she had to prepare her patients to ditch. The plane landed safely on land, but she had already made up her mind about what she would do. She had planned to shove all her able-bodied patients out the door first, throw a raft down, and then leave the plane herself. As she told her commander afterward, at five-feet-two-inches tall and weighing only 102 pounds, with the water and waves so high in the Pacific, she could never open the raft herself. He replied, "Well, the good Lord has to be looking out for you." Nabors said, "Yes, plus my rosary beads." It was a standing joke—she always had her rosary beads with her.[66]

Faith in one's God, one's colleagues, and oneself all helped the flight nurses through aircraft emergencies. When faced with the possibility that the plane in which she was flying might be shot at by enemy aircraft, chief nurse Pukas in the Pacific placed her faith in the escort planes and her own flight crew. They were qualified to protect her, and she trusted them to do their jobs. "I have no concern or fear, I am there as a flight nurse," Pukas said. "My only concern is this: I have to have complete faith that all is well."[67] Carlson, who flew with dangerous cargo such as hand grenades and gasoline for Patton's army in Europe, reasoned that her chief nurse and her commander would see to it that no harm befell her. "We did what we were told to," she said. "They weren't gonna get us into any trouble."[68]

Faith in one's country in the form of patriotism also sustained nurses during what could be fearful times. The attack on Pearl Harbor and the fear that the United States would be invaded gave Holtz and other flight nurses like her their gung-ho attitude about going to war. "Well, we all wanted to do our part," said Holtz. "I think everybody in the United States felt like that. I don't think there was ever another time in our history that there was such unity as there was during World War II." As Anthony explained, "It was very easy to do. There was no decision to be made. War had been declared. . . . I couldn't have stayed out had I wanted to." Said Sandstrom, "I knew when Pearl Harbor happened that that was what I was going to do. That's when I decided that I was going to do what I could to help." The men all went to war, and the women, too—as nurses, pilots, factory workers. "And everybody went cheerfully, and nobody had to be pushed," Holtz continued.[69]

While they were firm in their convictions to help during the war, they feared more than the specific dangers of war. Said Edmonds of her assignment on the Pacific front with the 801 MAES, "But there were so many crawly things! Lizards and snakes. I don't know how you can prepare yourself for something like that, because I'd always been terrified of them."[70] Holtz, a self-proclaimed coward about such things, remembered their tremendous size. The flight nurses learned to live with the reptiles, because they had no other option. But the snakes were really hard to take, Holtz said: "We could laugh about everything else, but not that."[71] Ilic recalled that the snakes taught her something about herself. She had always been "deathly afraid" of them but realized that she must be a strong person psychologically, because she "didn't go absolutely berserk over those snakes."[72]

Sometimes flight nurses were afraid when they were the only women on an island during an overnight stay. Edmonds remembered wanting to sleep in the plane when she found herself in that situation, but it was against the rules. Nor was she permitted just to sleep in a chair as she requested. Base personnel finally found a place for her in a supply room, but she wouldn't sleep there unless someone else was with her. So the pilot stayed there as well. "They made a big joke out of it, and of course they razzed the pilot unmercifully," she said. "But that was another part of being a woman—being afraid. If you had somebody else with you, it wasn't bad."[73] Nabors brought a load of patients into an island in the Pacific and spent the day sleeping alone in the tent assigned for her crew rest. No one called her when the alarm sounded. She slept through an air raid, and it was much later that she learned that the tents next to hers had been bombed. "It must have been the Lord looking after me. . . . Because when I saw that, I thought—well, that was a frightening experience. That really was."[74]

The flight nurses were more concerned about their patients' fears than about their own. Nabors remembered her patients looking at her during air turbulence, when the plane might drop a thousand feet. Everything in the back of the plane would be bouncing around, because it was difficult to strap some items down securely. Even the patients on litters, who were snugly strapped in, and the patients in seats, with their seatbelts fastened, felt the movement. Nabors checked them all with a smile on her face and a reassuring word, "And there you are, and spread your legs out, because otherwise you'd be flying yourself."[75]

"I think that you owe your patients everything that you possibly can give them. . . . I mean, you owe your patients your best," Ilic remarked about patient care.[76] But when the flight nurses experienced air turbulence, aircraft malfunction, enemy action, or a patient in medical crisis, or when their patients included enemy as well as Allied soldiers, giving one's best could be more of a challenge.

Providing Patient Care

Air evacuation was so new, Sandstrom explained, that the flight nurses had to "play by ear" a number of circumstances involving patient care. "And then when something worked, why then something else would work. And we just did the best we could with what we had and what we could do."[77]

In a dire situation, a flight nurse could tell the pilot that she had a medical emergency on board and ask him to fly lower or land at the next base that had a medical facility. She could request that a physician meet the plane and that the patient be off-loaded as necessary. Anthony exercised that option when her patient died on a cross-Channel flight from France to England (see chapter 7). While the pilots and most physicians respected this course of action, Mowery encountered a

British physician who would not provide the requested medical evaluation when the plane landed at a British base with a medical facility. Mowery rationalized the situation: "I know that when I got a chance, I had a lot to say to myself about what I thought the man [British physician] was. And I'm sure that everyone else would have been very nice. I just happened to pick a stinker."[78]

Certain types of patients were more difficult for the flight nurses to take care of than others. Blind patients, patients whose faces were nearly destroyed, burn patients, and multiple amputees often touched the flight nurses' spirits, requiring unusual fortitude and eliciting intense empathy. Nabors remembered feeling deeply for her patients yet having to give the appearance of "an exterior calm" and to joke with them about things that were not funny, "when deep down inside you're really crying harder than these boys are," but "you couldn't let them know that you felt this way."[79]

Halverson of the 830 MAES recalled that when her plane filled with patients landed at an airfield in the Pacific immediately after an enemy raid, she and her enlisted technician off-loaded the patients as quickly as possible onto the ground soggy from a recent rain. She heard someone say, "Where's the nurse? Is the nurse all right?" She was down in the mud trying to cover a soldier who had a head wound, because she did not want his bandage to get muddy.[80]

Some flight nurses struggled with thoughts of potentially difficult patient care, such as the need to perform and maintain a tracheotomy. When flying in Central Africa, Vancil began to suspect that her colleagues were having a joke at her expense when for the third time she was told, "Well, we're enclosing a tracheotomy set, because this patient may need a tracheotomy." She thought, *This can't be, and if it was going to happen, it will happen, but I'm not going to worry about it.* But she did not know what she would have done in that situation. She had heard of a flight nurse who had to perform a tracheotomy without a kit, using only what she had on hand. "I guess maybe if there was that dire need, I could come up with that extra surge of energy and wisdom and the power to do it. But, ooh!"[81]

Most nurses could remember at least one demanding patient situation that posed a particular challenge in flight. One airsick patient, for example, could set off a chain reaction. "We were always disgusted with the person that threw up first," said Vancil, "because, you know, it's contagious." French remembered getting a soldier with his jaw wired together among a load of patients. The flight surgeon told her to clip the wires if he got sick because of the bad weather. Her stomach began to churn from the thought, until she remembered that the flight nurses did not need a physician's order to administer morphine if they believed it had to be given. So French gave the soldier an eighth of a grain of morphine: "The blessed little fellow slept all the way over, and everybody else on that plane got sick. And I ran out of bags for them to vomit in." She finally found a bucket to pass along, but before the plane reached England, she wished she had given all her patients morphine.[82]

Transporting German and Japanese POWs as patients presented a particular challenge. Some flight nurses refused to take POWs as patients, but others had a more compassionate perspective. Holtz remembered that she might have been the first nurse in the 801 MAES to transport Japanese prisoners as patients: "I felt that they were wounded, and they were patients, and that it was my job to do it, I guess, because I did it. And the patients were very grateful." Patients might be prisoners of war, said Pukas, but that should not affect the care they received from the flight nurse.[83]

Nabors told of a time when American marine patients had their own plans for the three Japanese POWs on board a flight from the Philippines to Guam. Her commander had said that she was responsible for the safety of the POWs and was to use her gun if necessary. "Under no circumstances is anything to happen to those three prisoners. Washington is waiting for them," he warned. Nabors knew that the marines were bitter about the atrocities the Japanese had inflicted on their buddies and would have liked to even the score. "Lieutenant, you're needed up front," they kept telling Nabors. Although they laughed as they said this, Nabors realized they were not joking and took precautions. The unusual appearance of a basket of oranges in the cabin gave the marines an idea.

"Take an orange up to the pilot. The pilot's probably thirsty. He doesn't see oranges very often," they kept telling her.

The flight nurse asked one of the marines, "Now, why do you want me to go up front?" He replied, "We'll take care of your prisoners." Nabors continued: "I knew when he said 'We'll take care of your prisoners' that it wasn't anything good. So I never left the three prisoners' view. I stayed in their view, and I watched them until I landed with those patients." The experience was terrifying: she could empathize with the marines' feelings, yet she bore full responsibility for the safety of the captured prisoners in flight. The flight ended without incident.[84]

Coping with Wartime Nursing

How flight nurses dealt with the challenges of the war depended in large measure on their expectations for and, later, perceptions of its events. All women were volunteers; had they not been comfortable with the thought of wartime service overseas, they could have practiced nursing elsewhere as civilians. Despite the seriousness of war, some of the women interviewed chose to perceive it as an adventure rather than dwell on its dangers. Once they began their air evacuation duties, they maintained their sense of adventure. For Carlson, "it was more adventure than it was danger, really. You didn't think about being hurt or anything like that, not until you found out about some things that happened." For Boyle, flight nursing "had a little more adventure to it than just living in a tent and taking care of people day after day."[85] The flight nurses did not anticipate special treatment during the war—as Mowery put it, they did not expect silk sheets.[86] Boyle knew that D Day was not going to happen just because she had arrived in England—"it was going to happen when they were ready for it."[87]

Viewing their wartime service as an adventure allowed these flight nurses to make the most of the moment, perceive themselves as survivors, and take things as they came. Boyle, for example, did not worry about what she could not do—"about the fact that I didn't have a nice white sheet to put on every litter and that sort of thing. I understood the situation as it was and tried to cope with it as best I could." To Newbeck, acceptance meant the ability to take things as they came and, as she put it, to roll with the punches.[88]

Flight nurses coped with the uncertainty of their wartime experience in different ways. Ilic, who was convinced that she would survive the war, explained, "We lived for the moment, for today, 'cause tomorrow you didn't know where you were going to be. You didn't know whether you were going to be alive." The human spirit adapted to the transitory, temporary nature of the war, Ilic said, but she found the "here today, gone tomorrow" mentality frightening, because it was such an unnatural way to live.[89] Other nurses were more comfortable with the one-day-at-a-time philosophy. "You made very few plans," explained White. "You did not say, 'Next week I'm going to do thus and so,' because next week was too far away."[90] Three nurses admitted during interviews to harboring a fatalistic attitude. What was going to happen—such as an aircraft accident—was going to happen anyway, they reasoned, and they chose not to worry about such an eventuality.

In their lighthearted glimpse of the 801 MAES flight nurses, pundits Preston and Endres commented, "One is not born a flight nurse; I suspect, though, that one must be endowed with a little more than the average share of physical endurance, perseverance and sheer enthusiasm in order to grow to be one."[91] Their measure of the situation for flight nurses on the Pacific front rings true for their colleagues on the European front as well. These women met the challenges of wartime nursing with a commitment reflected admirably in the care they provided to the patients entrusted to them in the air. Interviews revealed two significant tools with which they coped. The first was the prevailing positive attitude shared by the flight nurses about their wartime service. The second was the ingenuity they applied to their work. Both suggest that these flight nurses perceived their role as a challenge, allowing them to feel more confident in their abilities, less emotionally overwhelmed by the exigencies of war, and thus more capable of drawing on available resources. As these women described what it was like to be a flight nurse during World War II, positive feelings of excitement and enthusiasm, indicative of a challenging situation, far outnumbered negative feelings of fear and apprehension, characteristic of a threatening situation.[92]

The flight nurses relied heavily on nursing skills not readily apparent. Good judgment, creativity, resourcefulness, and judicious application of common-sense psychiatric skills—being a good listener, knowing when to talk and what to talk about, providing sensitive reassurance, and giving moral support—marked these nurses' wartime patient care as much as their physical ministrations, which understandably were limited. Their narratives reveal a multitude of coping strategies including reliance on the support of colleagues and friends as well as of family back home, devotion to their country and its war effort, and an ability to find humor in situations that could be perceived as frustrating.

"It would appear, and it's true, that we like our jobs even though we wish ardently for an end to the war," wrote Preston and Endres in an eloquent conclusion to their personal account of flight nursing in the 801 MAES. "The peace of mind which we enjoy even under these circumstances, though, must have some foundation; we attribute our 'esprit de corps' to a great many things: to the fact that we're a well-trained group; to the fact that our work is voluntary; to our good health and hardiness; to the good-will and friendliness and helpfulness which we meet everywhere; but, above all, to the fact that something about all this makes us feel truly like real citizens of the world."[93] Flight nurses in other squadrons would likely concur. Work as a flight nurse in World War II was often life-changing. Friendships formed lasted a lifetime; experiences encountered taught the women about survival in difficult situations. Overseas assignments broadened their horizons and presented challenges that they never would have faced stateside.

Credo

Nearly seventy years have passed since the first army flight nurses embarked upon this special type of nursing duty, but today's flight nurses, now members of the United States Air Force Nurse Corps, can still be found evacuating the sick and wounded wherever Americans are serving their country. Like their predecessors, these women and men face challenges of wartime nursing overseas. The army flight nurses of World War II set the precedent for a unique field of nursing that has continued to the present day, and their experiences offer a valuable lesson on coping with the exigencies of war. Their accomplishments give new meaning to a phrase in the original Flight Nurses Creed, written during World War II: "I will be faithful to my training and to the wisdom handed down to me by those who have gone before me."[94]

EPILOGUE

Prepare for war? We don't prepare for war, we prepare for peace.
And then I got to thinking about it. A lot of time, preparing for peace
is being prepared for war. . . . But to think of a war today, it'd be
hard to anticipate where or how and what type it would be. . . . Now
I think the only thing you can anticipate is what kind of a person
you're going to be yourself.

—ADELE EDMONDS DALY, interview with author

Looking back on her experiences as a flight nurse assigned on the Pacific front in World War II from a perspective of forty years, Adele Edmonds realized that while she might have no control over whether her country went to war, she could control the type of person she would be, should that occur. The war taught Edmonds and the other flight nurses interviewed for this book lessons about themselves that affected their lives long after the war had ended. The women's answers to questions about what they might like to have been different about their time as flight nurses—and what advice they would pass on to their successors—reflect these lessons and still resonate today.

Lucy Wilson, who described herself as a workaholic, would like to have been more people oriented. As chief nurse of the 801 MAES on the Pacific front, she was "the boss," with twenty-four flight nurses under her supervision, and "you didn't brown-nose the boss," she said. "There's a line—you can't get too close," Wilson continued.[1] She was pushing her nurses to "go forward, work harder" with the goal of repatriating the soldiers held in Japanese prison camps, without considering relationships. Loneliness was often the result. Her flight nurses had a different perspective. "We are very good at making her very angry," Nancy Preston and Ada Endres said of Wilson, "and she is even better at putting us properly in our places—which makes for a happy balance all-round."[2]

Ethel Carlson, Jocie French, Frances Sandstrom, and Dorothy White all mentioned the desire to change situations over which they had no control: better coordination of air evacuation activities, thus eliminating dry runs, more medical supplies, including disposables, and more modern equipment. Lee Holtz identified the need for more personal hygiene items.[3]

Other flight nurses would like to have been better prepared for different contingencies of their roles. Hilda Halverson would like to have had more skill in starting IVs, while Edmonds would have liked better preparation in psychiatry.[4] Jo Nabors would like to have been better prepared for both medical and aircraft emergencies. The flight nurse course was fine, she explained, but it had not prepared them for the actual types of patients the flight nurses would encounter. And just practicing an aircraft emergency procedure once did not help, "because when that plane's going down, that's the last thing you think about."[5]

Jenny Boyle reflected, "Well, I wish that we hadn't had to have the war at all. . . . But, I mean, the fact is, there was a war, there have been wars since, and there will be wars in the future."[6] Given this state of affairs, the women who were interviewed offered advice to flight nurses who would follow in their footsteps, to help them cope with the challenges of their wartime work. Flight nurses should be stable people with a good sense of humor, Holtz said. The military was so strict about height and weight and state of health, she said, but it did not always consider the mental angle of flight nursing. Good discipline helped, but "mental compatibility" and "emotional stability" are essential "in a group of nurses that must live and work together under the stress and strain of combat conditions overseas."[7]

Most of the advice that the World War II flight nurses wanted to pass along concerned knowledge, education, and training. Edmonds suggested that if there were another war, the nurses would need to know a lot about psychiatry for their patients and for themselves. Referring to the lizards and snakes that were her nemesis on the Pacific islands, she said, "The unknown is what you're afraid of." Randy Rast agreed. One has less fear when told what to expect. "You adjust better," she explained. "You sort of prepare yourself."[8]

The need for common sense categorized another type of advice. White used the example of dealing with limited supplies. "They would never dream that someone would run out of safety pins, see? Or adhesive tape. But you can, you know? I mean, supposing your whole mess of safety pins rust. What are you going to do then?" In a wartime environment, people needed to use common sense, which often was missing in life, White said.[9] To Agnes Jensen, much of what she did during the war was "a lot of common sense" added to what little training she got. "As they kept saying to us," Jensen remembered, "'We don't know what of this training is going to be any good to you, and whatever it is will have to be sprinkled well with your own good judgment.' And believe me, that was an understatement if ever there was one!"[10]

Eileen Newbeck advised, "Just take each day at a time, and improvise where you have to improvise. Use the brains the good Lord gave you! Because nothing is going to be textbook, period. You're gonna have to improvise on any flight that you go on and use your common sense."[11] "Adaptability" was the keyword for Louise Anthony. "Of course there is the book to be gone by," she admitted, "but the book sort of goes by in wartime a bit." Boyle concurred. "You have to be able to make the most of what you've got and live with it—and don't let it get you down and make you sulky because things aren't just the way you were told they were going to be."[12]

It was good to "go the way the wind blows," to do the best with what you have, Sandstrom said. "So, now we laugh at the days that we didn't have any biffy to go to in the blue room," she said, referring to the airplanes. "We don't laugh because we weren't able to give the kind of patient care that we would like to have given. That isn't a bit funny."[13]

Helena Ilic stressed selflessness and resourcefulness in patient care; Nabors stressed love, compassion, optimism, and a good sense of humor. To Wilson, humor, unity, and good training were the keys to survival still relevant for today's flight nurses. She added her own personal philosophy: "Don't let an incident be a stumbling block, but make it a stepping-stone."[14] As Rast suggested, every situation has some good; flight nurses would be wise to find the good and forget the bad.[15]

Some of the women summed up their advice to nurses contemplating flight duty with one exclamation: "Be a flight nurse!" They recalled their flight nursing experience as very rewarding. Carlson advised, "It would be a great experience for them." "Most certainly learn everything before you go," said French, "but I would still say, 'Go.' I really would."[16]

"It was a great experience. I wouldn't have traded it for anything," concluded Blanche Solomon. "There were some grim times, there were some lousy times, and there were a lot of good times, too. . . . And I think it's the way to go myself." She and French concurred: without question, if they were younger and unmarried and had the chance to repeat their lives, they would be flight nurses all over again.[17]

APPENDIX

Unpublished Flight Nurse Interviews with the Author

Name *	Interview Location	Date
Anonymous	Undisclosed	30 April 1986
Ethel Carlson Cerasale	Satellite Beach, Florida	7 May 1986
Hilda Halverson Chamberlain	Spokane, Washington	21 June 1986
Mary Eileen Newbeck Christian	St. Petersburg, Florida	21 May 1986
Frances Sandstrom Crabtree	Spokane, Washington	21 June 1986
Blanche Solomon Creesy	Cocoa Beach, Florida	23 May 1986
Adele Edmonds Daly	Palo Alto, California	20 June 1986
Louise Anthony de Flon	Cocoa Beach, Florida	23, 24 May 1986
Dorothy White Errair	Cocoa Beach, Florida	24 May 1986
Ivalee (Lee) Holtz	San Antonio, Texas	4 April 1986
Jocie French Huston	San Antonio, Texas	18 June 1986
Lucy Wilson Jopling	San Antonio, Texas	4 April 1986

Name *	Interview Location	Date
Alice Krieble	San Antonio, Texas	3 April 1986
Agnes Jensen Mangerich	Cocoa Beach, Florida	25 May 1986
Dorothy Vancil Morgan	San Antonio, Texas	15 May 1986
Clara Morrey Murphy	San Antonio, Texas	19 April 1986
Josephine (Jo) Malito Nabors	Girard, Ohio	1 May 1986
Denzil (Denny) Nagle	Cocoa Beach, Florida	23 May 1986
Elizabeth Pukas	Walnut Creek, California	9 April 1986
Sara Ann (Sally) Jones Sharp	Winter Park, Florida	21 May 1986
Jenevieve (Jenny) Boyle Silk	Tequesta, Florida	8 May 1986
Helena Ilic Tynan	San Antonio, Texas	26 April 1986
Brooxie Mowery Unick	Satellite Beach, Florida	25 May 1986
Miranda (Randy) Rast Weinrich	Hemet, California	19 June 1986
Grace Dunnam Wichtendahl	San Antonio, Texas	29 March 1986

* Names of flight nurses appearing in the book are those they used during their assignments as flight nurses. Married names, when applicable, appear above.

NOTES

Preface

1. *Official Guide to the Army Air Forces* (New York: Simon and Schuster, 1944), 94.

2. David N. W. Grant, "Five Wartime Achievements of the Army Air Forces Medical Service," speech prepared for International Medical Assembly, Interstate Postgraduate Medical Association of North America, Chicago, 18 Oct. 1944, 21, Air Force Historical Research Agency (hereafter AFHRA) 141.28-91 1943–45.

3. Erling Berquist [Ehrling Bergquist], "Discussion," in David N. W. Grant, "Air Evacuation Activities," *Journal of Aviation Medicine* 18 (Feb.–Dec. 1947): 183.

4. See, for example, Judith Bellafaire, *The Army Nurse Corps: A Commemoration of World War II Service* (Washington, D.C.: United States Army Center of Military History, 1993); and Mary T. Sarnecky, *A History of the U.S. Army Nurse Corps* (Philadelphia: Univ. of Pennsylvania Press, 1999).

5. See, for example, Susan S. Godson, *Serving Proudly: A History of Women in the U.S. Navy* (Annapolis, Md.: Naval Institute Press, 2001); and Doris Sterner, *In and Out of Harm's Way: A History of the Navy Nurse Corps* (Seattle: Peanut Butter Press, 1997).

6. Dorothy White Errair, interview with author; Frances Sandstrom Crabtree, interview with author; Anonymous, interview with author. For full details of these and all flight nurse interviews with the author, see the appendix.

7. David N. W. Grant, "Speech to Seventh Graduation Class, Army Air Forces School of Evacuation, Bowman Field, Louisville, Kentucky," 26 Nov. 1943, 6, AFHRA 141.28U.

Prologue

1. Ethel Carlson Cerasale, interview with author.

2. Ibid.

3. White Errair, interview with author.

4. Carlson Cerasale, interview with author; Ivalee (Lee) Holtz, interview with author; Helena Ilic Tynan, interview with author; Sara Ann (Sally) Jones

Sharp, interview with author; Mary Eileen Newbeck Christian, interview with author; White Errair, interview with author; Josephine (Jo) Malito Nabors, interview with author; Blanche Solomon Creesy, interview with author; Clara Morrey Murphy, interview with author; Jenevieve (Jenny) Boyle Silk, interview with author.

5. Newbeck Christian, interview with author.

6. Ilic Tynan, interview with author; Brooxie Mowery Unick, interview with author.

7. Agnes Jensen Mangerich, interview with author; Solomon Creesy, interview with author; Newbeck Christian, interview with author; Carlson Cerasale, interview with author.

8. Carlson Cerasale, interview with author.

1. Origin of Flight Nursing

1. Berquist [Bergquist], "Discussion," 183.

2. Ibid., 182–83.

3. "Fly Again!" *R.N.* 9 (Dec. 1945): 40; "Nurses Released from Airline Positions," *Trained Nurse and Hospital Review* 108 (Mar. 1942): 207–8; "Discontinued for the Duration," *Trained Nurse and Hospital Review* 108 (Apr. 1942): 268; "War-Time Needs Come First," *American Journal of Nursing* 42 (Apr. 1942): 449–50; "Airline Nurse Stewardesses Released," *American Journal of Nursing* 42 (May 1942): 577–78.

4. Mae M. Link and Hubert A. Coleman, *Medical Support of the Army Air Forces in World War II* (Washington, D.C.: GPO, 1955), 370.

5. Virginia Saunders, "From Chickens to Flying," *Cleveland Plain Dealer,* 16 Dec. 1932.

6. F. W. Emerson, "The Most Recent Emergency Unit of the Los Angeles County Sheriff's Department," *Guardians of Peace and Property,* n.d., 10; M. Aileen Crain, "Lauretta M. Schimmoler," *ANCOA Flashes,* Apr. 1940, 6.

7. Ellen Church, interview with Kenneth Leish, May 1960, in the Oral History Collection of Columbia University, AFHRA K146.34-27.

8. Ellen Church, introduction to Mary F. Murray, *Skygirl: A Career Handbook for the Airline Stewardess* (New York: Duell, Slowan, Pearce, 1951), 13.

9. Church, interview with Leish.

10. Georgia P. Nielsen, *From Sky Girl to Flight Attendant: Women and the Making of a Union* (Ithaca, N.Y.: Industrial and Labor Relations Press, 1982), 7–12; Ellen E. Church, "Nursing Up in the Air," *Public Health Nurse* 23 (Feb. 1931): 74.

11. Aerial Nurse Corps of America, *Regulations Manual* (Burbank, Calif.: Schimmoler, 1940), n.p.; Leora B. Stroup, "A New Service in an Old Cause," *Trained Nurse and Hospital Review* 105 (Sept. 1940): 186.

12. Aerial Nurse Corps, *Regulations Manual,* n.p.; Douglas J. Bintliff, "Aerial Nurse Corps," *Air Trails,* Nov. 1940, 54; Emerson, "Most Recent Emergency Unit," 10; Stroup, "New Service in an Old Cause," 186–87.

13. "The American Nurses Aviation Service, Inc.," *Journal of Aviation Medicine* 2 (1931): 262–63.

14. Ibid.; "The Nurse in Aviation," *Journal of Aviation Medicine* 3 (Mar. 1932): 5; "Constitution and By-Laws of American Nurses Aviation Service, Incorporated," *Journal of Aviation Medicine* 3 (Mar. 1932): 43–52; "The Nurse in Aviation," *Journal of Aviation Medicine* 3 (June 1932): 116–18; "The American Nurses Aviation Service, Inc.," *Journal of Aviation Medicine* 3 (Sept. 1932): 176; "American Nurses Aviation Service, Inc.," *Journal of Aviation Medicine* 4 (Mar. 1933): 19; "Meeting of the American Nurses Aviation Service," *Journal of Aviation Medicine* 4 (June 1933): 68–69.

15. Emerson, "Most Recent Emergency Unit," 10; Leora B. Stroup, "What Is the Aerial Nurse Corps of America?" n.d., unpublished, 2; James Farrer, "Flying Nurses Do without Glamor," *Dayton Sunday Mirror,* 20 Apr. 1941; "Nurses Mobilize for Duties in New Home Defense Service," *Los Angeles Times,* 23 Mar. 1941.

16. Gill Robb Wilson, letter to Mary Beard, 16 Apr. 1940.

17. Lauretta M. Schimmoler, letter to H. A. Coleman, 22 Mar. 1945; Lauretta M. Schimmoler, "The Story of How It All Began: 'And They Said It Wouldn't Be Done,'" unpublished manuscript, n.d., 7, Bucyrus, Ohio, Historical Society.

18. "Relief Wings," brochure, n.d., United States Army Medical Department (hereafter AMEDD).

19. "Relief Wings, Inc.," *Journal of Aviation Medicine* 12 (Sept. 1941): 260; Ruth Nichols, letter to Harriet Fleming, 16 Feb. 1942.

20. Ruth Nichols, letter to Lauretta Schimmoler, 5 Dec. 1941.

21. Nichols, letter to Fleming, 16 Feb. 1942.

22. Aerial Nurse Corps, *Regulations Manual,* 1.

23. Ibid., 4–5, 45, 47–48.

24. "Aerial Nurse Corps," brochure, n.d., 4; "Oath," Aerial Nurse Corps of America, n.d.

25. "Pledge of Allegiance to the United States of America and the Aerial Nurse Corps," Aerial Nurse Corps of America, n.d.

26. Stroup, "What Is the Aerial Nurse Corps of America?" 2; Stroup, "New Service in an Old Cause," 188; Ruth G. Mitchell, "Schedule of Courses and Hours for 3 years," *Aerial Nurse Corps of America Bulletin,* no. 2, n.d.

27. Aerial Nurse Corps, *Regulations Manual,* 2–4; Stroup, "New Service in an Old Cause," 187–88; "Aerial Nurse Corps of America Regulation Uniform," n.d.; Lauretta Schimmoler, "Memorandum: Ordering Regulation Uniforms," Aerial Nurse Corps of America, 28 July 1938; "Official Uniform for Aerial Nurse Corps and Aviation Emergency Corps Members," n.d.

28. "Aerial Nurse Corps," brochure, n.d., 4.

29. "Aerial Nurse Corps," *Trained Nurse and Hospital Review* 107 (Oct. 1941): 281; "Call to Service," *Trained Nurse and Hospital Review* 107 (Oct. 1941): 281; "American Nurses—We Are at War!" *American Journal of Nursing* 42 (Apr. 1942): 354; "Urgent Need for Nurses," *American Journal of Nursing* 44 (Nov. 1944): 1017.

30. "The Meaning of 'Aerial Nurse Corps,'" Aerial Nurse Corps of America memorandum, n.d.

31. Stroup, "New Service in an Old Cause," 184; Stroup, "What Is the Aerial Nurse Corps of America?" 3; "Denver Plans to Have Its Own Unit of Aerial Nursing Corps." *Denver Post,* 31 Jan. 1941.

32. "Sent to Detroit News Announcing the Annual Dance of the Detroit Group," 5 Apr. 1941.

33. Schimmoler, letter to Coleman, 22 Mar. 1945.

34. "A Tribute to Co. C—5th Div. Dayton, Ohio," *ANCOA Flashes* 2 (Dec. 1938): 2.

35. "Leora B. Stroup R.N.," *ANCOA Flashes* 3 (Mar. 1940): 5–6.

36. Jean Pearson, "Detroiter Receives Ideal Job," *Detroit Free Press,* 6 Oct. 1942.

37. "'Flying Nurses' Train Here for Defense," *Detroit Evening Times,* 2 Feb. 1939.

38. Ibid.

39. Margaret Quinn, letter to War Department, Michigan Military Area, 14 Oct. 1940.

40. "Sent to Detroit News," 5 Apr. 1941.

41. John G. Slevin, letter to Leora Stroup, 16 Jan. 1941.

42. H. H. [Henry H.] Arnold, letter to Lauretta M. Schimmoler, 27 Sept. 1937.

43. Arnold, letter to Schimmoler, 20 Oct. 1937.

44. Julia O. Flikke, memo to Malcolm C. Grow, 11 Oct. 1937. Grow's full title was "chief flight surgeon in the office of the chief of the army air corps."

45. "Employment of American National Red Cross," Army Regulation No. 850–75, 30 June 1943 (supersedes Army Regulation 850–75, 30 Aug. 1926), 4–5.

46. *American Red Cross Nursing Service,* abridged ed. (Washington, D.C.: American Red Cross, 1942), 6.

47. Ida F. Butler, letter to Mrs. Maynard L. Carter, 30 Aug. 1937.

48. Ida. F. Butler, letter to Gladyce L. Badger, 3 Sept. 1937.

49. Ibid.

50. Butler, letter to Carter, 17 Sept. 1937.

51. Schimmoler, letter to Coleman, 22 Mar. 1945. The wording resembles that of a letter and its reply recalled in Schimmoler's "How It All Began," 4, in which she asked the army nursing service, "If I were to interest nurses and train them for air duty, would I be rendering my country a service?" and was told, "I don't think nurses will ever fly, and if they do, they will fly in government airplanes and won't need any special training."

52. Butler, letter to Badger, 3 Sept. 1937.

53. Ibid.

54. Butler, letter to Carter, 17 Sept. 1937.

55. Cary T. Grayson, letter to Charles R. Reynolds, 25 Oct. 1937.

56. Reynolds, letter to Grayson, 29 Oct. 1937.

57. Lauretta M. Schimmoler, letter to Julia O. Flikke, 23 Apr. 1938.

58. Flikke, letter to Schimmoler, 29 Apr. 1938.

59. Mary Beard, letter to Mr. Hughes, 31 Mar. 1939.

60. Beard, letter to Hughes, 1 May 1939.

61. Virginia M. Dunbar, letter to Mary Beard, 1 June 1939.

62. Mary Beard, letter to Lauretta M. Schimmoler, 7 July 1939.

63. Ruth G. Mitchell, "The Aerial Nurse Corps of America," speech given at Meeting of Delegates of the California State Nurses Association, San Francisco, 15 Aug. 1939, 4.

64. Mary Beard, "The Aerial Nurse Corps of America, Inc.," 23 Jan. 1940.

65. "Report of the Committee of C.S.N.A. Advisory Council for A.N.C.O.A.," 14 Oct. 1940.

66. Lauretta M. Schimmoler, letter to Ida F. Badger, 28 Oct. 1940; Badger, letter to Schimmoler, 30 Oct. 1940.

67. Gladyce L. Badger, letter to Mary Beard, 30 Oct. 1940.

68. Virginia M. Dunbar, "Notes on meeting of Aerial Nurse Corps, Saturday, May 3, 1941."

69. "Special Committee of the ANA to Confer with the Aerial Nurse Corps of America Report" [16 May 1941].

70. "Sent to Detroit News," 5 Apr. 1941.

71. Leora B. Stroup, "Tentative Reorganization Plans," Aerial Nurse Corps of America, n.d.; Nichols, letter to Fleming, 16 Feb. 1942.

72. John F. Curry, letter to Lauretta M. Schimmoler, 26 Jan. 1942.

73. Nichols, letter to Fleming, 16 Feb. 1942; Lauretta Schimmoler, letter to Leora B. Stroup, 26 June 1942.

74. "American Nurses—We Are at War!" *American Journal of Nursing* 42 (Apr. 1942): 354; "First Reserve Quotas," *American Journal of Nursing* 42 (June. 1942): 614; "Nurses, to the Colors!" *American Journal of Nursing* 42 (Aug. 1942.) 853; and "The Time Is Now!" *American Journal of Nursing* 42 (Aug. 1942): 851–52.

75. Lauretta M. Schimmoler, letter to David N. W. Grant, 24 July 1942, box 279, RG 18, National Archives, Washington, D.C. (hereafter NARA).

76. Grant, letter to Schimmoler, 3 Aug. 1942, box 279, RG 18, NARA.

77. Wood S. Woolford, letter to Victor A. Byrne, 17 July 1942, AFHRA 280.93-5; "History of the School of Air Evacuation," 1 Aug. 1943, 2–4, AFHRA 280.93-3; "History of the School of Air Evacuation," n.d., in "School of Air Evacuation," Army Air Base, Bowman Field, Ky., 9 Dec. 1940–Apr. 1944, Jan. 1944–June 1945, 1–3, AFHRA 280.93-12 v.2; Robert F. Futrell, *Development of Aeromedical Evacuation in the USAF, 1909–1960,* Historical Studies No. 23 (Maxwell AFB, AL: USAF Historical Division, Research Studies Institute, Air University, 1960), 73–74.

78. "Men Nurses and the Armed Services," *American Journal of Nursing* 43 (Dec. 1943): 1066–69.

79. Link and Coleman, *Medical Support,* 367.

80. "Medical History I Troop Carrier Command," 30 Apr. 1942–31 Dec. 1944, 50–52, AFHRA 250.740.

81. Frederick R. Guilford and Burton J. Soboroff, "Air Evacuation: An Historical Review," *Journal of Aviation Medicine* 18 (Dec. 1947): 609; Futrell, *Aeromedical Evacuation,* 78–79; "Medical Air Evacuation Transport Squadron," Table of Organization No. 447, War Department, Washington, D.C., 15 Feb. 1943, AFHRA MED-812-HI.

82. "Nurses for Air Evacuation Service," Memorandum No. W40-10-42, War Department, Adjutant General's Office, 21 Dec. 1942, AFHRA 280.93 (1220-28).

83. "Post Diary," Air Base Headquarters, Bowman Field, Louisville, Ky., Dec. 1940–Aug. 1945, 49, AFHRA 280.93-1.

84. Futrell, *Aeromedical Evacuation,* 80.

85. Clara Morrey Murphy, "Air Evacuation—World War II—African-Europian [*sic*] Theater," First unabridged rough draft of Symposium speech, Nov 12, 1992, 50th Anniversary," AMEDD.

86. "Post Diary," Dec. 1940–Aug. 1945.

87. Schimmoler, letter to Stroup, 17 Jan. 1942.

88. Schimmoler, letter to Coleman, 22 Mar. 1945.

89. Katherine V. Sinks, "Aviatrix Joins Air Wacs," *Glendale (Calif.) News-Press,* 27 July 1944.

90. Dora D. Strother, "The W.A.S.P. Program: An Historical Synopsis," Air Force Museum Research Division, Wright-Patterson AFB, Ohio, Apr. 1972, 11, AFHRA K220.0721-107. The cut-off age was thirty-five.

91. James Rian, *Parachute Nurse,* revised final draft of screenplay, Columbia Pictures, 6 Mar. 1942, 13, Bucyrus, Ohio, Historical Society.

92. Schimmoler, letter to Stroup, 17 Jan. 1942; Schimmoler, letter to Stroup, 5 Mar. 1942; Lida Dolan for Lauretta M. Schimmoler, letter to Leora Stroup, 2 Apr. 1942; Schimmoler, letter to Stroup, 26 June 1942.

93. Schimmoler, letter to Frank, 13 Apr. 1942; Esther Smith, "Ex-Bucyrus Airport Manager Turns to Movies," *Mansfield News-Journal,* 16 Aug. 1942. The recipient may have been F. L. Hopley of Bucyrus, Ohio. "'Parachute Nurse' Timely; 'Halfway to Shanghai' Fair," *Hollywood Reporter* 8 (Sept. 1942): 4, Bucyrus, Ohio, Historical Society.

94. "Parachute Nurses?" *R.N.* 5 (Feb. 1942): 56.

95. Ibid., 56, 58.

96. Schimmoler, "How It All Began," 8.

97. Ibid., 8–9.

98. Ibid., 9.

2. Military Air Evacuation Tries Its Wings

1. Harry G. Armstrong, *Principles and Practice of Aviation Medicine,* 3rd ed. (Baltimore: Williams and Wilkins, 1952), 421; Guilford and Soboroff, "Air Evacuation," 601–2; Link and Coleman, *Medical Support,* 352–61; "History of the School of Air Evacuation," 1 Aug. 1943, 2.

2. Bob E. Nowland, "Operations of the Ferrying Division of the ATC," an AAFSAT Air Room Interview by Brigadier General Bob E. Nowland, [1945], 1–2, AFHRA 248.532-5.

3. Flikke, letter to Schimmoler, 29 Apr. 1938.

4. Oliver La Farge, *The Eagle in the Egg* (Boston: Houghton Mifflin, 1949), 230.

5. Harold F. Funsch, "Graduation Address," Flight Nurse Class 65-B, Brooks Air Force Base, Tex., 2 Apr. 1965, 1.

6. Paul C. Gilliland, "Letter of Information on Air Evacuation by Air Transport Command" to All Wing Surgeons, 3 Mar. 1943.

7. La Farge, *Eagle in the Egg,* 230.

8. Ibid., 229.

9. John D. Gross, "Statement of Military Service of Elsie S. Ott N 722 669," General Services Administration, Army Branch, Military Personnel Records Center, St. Louis, Mo., 20 Dec. 1960.

10. Richard L. Meiling, "Memorandum for: Colonel Walter S. Jensen," [3 Mar. 1943], 1.

11. Ibid.

12. Funsch, "Graduation Address," 4.

13. Ibid., 6.

14. Meiling, "Memorandum," 3.

15. Lois Byrd, "Nurse Here Is First Woman to Win Air Medal," *Louisville Courier-Journal,* 27 Mar. 1943.

16. Elsie [Ott] Mandot, letter to Harold Funsch, 22 Jan. 1965.

17. Gilliland, "Letter of Information on Air Evacuation," 1.

18. Mandot, letter to Funsch, 22 Jan. 1965.

19. Meiling, "Memorandum," 4–5.

20. Ibid., 5.

21. "General Orders, No. 17, War Department, Washington, April 2, 1943," 3.

22. "Nurse Wins Air Medal," *Louisville Times,* 26 Mar. 1943.

23. Mandot, letter to Funsch, 22 Jan. 1965.

24. "G.O. No. 183," Restricted HQ, AAF, India-Burma Sector, China-Burma-India Theater, APO 671, 13 October 1944. . . . "Air Medal (Oak Leaf Cluster) is hereby awarded to 1st Lieutenant ELSIE S. OTT, N-722669, Army Nurse Corps."

25. "The Air Medal," *Army Nurse* 1 (May 1944): 8–9; "Army Nurse Wins Air Medal," *American Journal of Nursing* 43 (May 1943): 443–44; Byrd, "Nurse Here Is First Woman to Win Air Medal" *Louisville Courier-Journal*; "Nurse Wins Air Medal," *Louisville Times,* 26 Mar. 1943.

26. Irving H. Breslauer, letter to Charles H. Franks, 10 Mar. 1961.

27. Harold F. Funsch, letter to Elsie Ott Mandot, 6 Oct. 1967.

28. Philip A. Kalisch and Beatrice J. Kalisch, *The Changing Image of the Nurse* (Menlo Park, Calif: Addison-Wesley, 1987), 102.

29. Philip A. Kalisch and Beatrice J. Kalisch, "When Nurses Were National Heroines: Images of Nursing in American Film, 1942–1945," *Nursing Forum* 20 (Jan. 1981): 23, 28–34.

30. Jeanne Holm, *Women in the Military: An Unfinished Revolution,* rev. ed. (Novato, Calif.: Presidio, 1982), 51–52. See also Sarnecky, *U.S. Army Nurse Corps,* 63–65. For an example of antagonism lingering into World War II, see Theresa Archard, *G.I. Nightingale: The Story of an American Army Nurse* (New York: Norton, 1945), 83–84.

31. Kalisch and Kalisch, *Changing Image,* 104.

32. Ibid., 161.

33. John Ball and Albert Duffy, "The Flight of Elsie Ott" [screenplay manuscript], n.d.

34. Harold F. Funsch, letter to MAFOI (Colonel Garner), 8 Mar. 1968.

35. See Ball and Duffy, "Flight of Elsie Ott."

36. Ibid.

37. Kalisch and Kalisch, *Changing Image,* 230–44.

38. Susan V. Stevens, "Aviation Pioneers: World War II Air Evacuation Nurses," *Image: Journal of Nursing Scholarship* 26 (Summer 1994): 97.

3. Flight Nurse Training

1. "Nurses, to the Colors!" 852.

2. "Army Nurses in the Air," *American Journal of Nursing* 42 (Aug. 1942): 955.

3. "The Army Air Forces Needs Nurses," *American Journal of Nursing* 43 (June 1943): 599.

4. Pearson, "Detroiter Receives Ideal Job."

5. George Arp, letter to Mrs. Elmer [Bertha A.] Stroup, 14 June 1927.

6. Jack La Vriha, "Heads Training of Aviation Nurses," *Cleveland Plain Dealer,* 5 Apr. 1943.

7. Futrell, *Aeromedical Evacuation,* 79; "Annual Report of the 27th AAF Base Unit," AAF School of Aviation Medicine, Randolph Field, Tex., 30 June 1945, 82, AFHRA 287.86-1B; "Medical History I Troop Carrier Command," 52–54. For the remainder of the book, "MAES" rather than "MAETS" is used, for both singular and plural.

8. "Historical Narrative of the 801st Medical Air Evacuation Transport Squadron," 25 May 1942–1 June 1944, 2, AFHRA MED-801-HI.

9. Untitled two-page typed script for NBC *Army Hour* program, n.d., AMEDD.

10. "Bowman Nurses on Army Hour" [photograph] and "Bowman Field Nurses Appear on Army Hour" [article with photograph], *Louisville Times,* 28 December 1942 ; script for NBC "Army Hour," 2, AMEDD.

11. David N. W. Grant, letter with enclosure to Eugen G. Reinartz, 11 Aug. 1942; "Training Program for Nurses and Surgical Technicians of the Medical Department, Army Air Forces, in Air Evacuation," [1942], 1, AFHRA 141.28R.

12. Alice Rogers Hager, "Mercy Takes Wings," *Skyways,* Sept. 1943, 60, 62.

13. Margaret Kernodle, "Army Nurses Sprout Wings," *Cincinnati Enquirer,* 23 Mar. 1943.

14. Carlson Cerasale, interview with author.

15. Newbeck Christian, interview with author.

16. David N. W. Grant, "Graduation of First Class of Air Evacuation Nurses," 18 Feb. 1943, 1, 3, AFHRA 141.28U.

17. "Graduation Exercises, Nurses, 349th Air Evacuation Group, Bowman Field, Kentucky," 18 Feb. 1943 program.

18. Link and Coleman, *Medical Support,* 371.

19. Lois Byrd, "39 Air Evacuation Graduates Face Quick Action," *Louisville Courier-Journal,* 19 Feb. 1943; "Air Evacuation School Awards Diplomas to 39," *Bowman Bomber,* 1 Mar. 1943.

20. Grace Dunnam Wichtendahl, interview with author.

21. "Group History, AAF School of Air Evacuation," [1942–43], 3, AFHRA 280.93-3.

22. "Suggested Activities for Pre-Student Squadron Nurses," n.d., AMEDD.

23. "Three Aerial Nurse Pioneers Reunited at Bowman Field," *Louisville Courier-Journal,* 2 Mar. 1943.

24. "History of the School of Air Evacuation," 1 Aug. 1943, 6–7, AFHRA 280.93-3.

25. "Description by Lt. Col. Ralph T. Stephenson [Stevenson], CO ITCC, Air Evacuation School, Bowman Field, of Air Evacuation," 16 May 1943, 5, 7, AFHRA 280.93 (1220-28-J).

26. "Training Course for Flight Nurses," AAF School of Air Evacuation, Bowman Field, Ky., 16 Aug. 1943, AFHRA 280.93-12.

27. "Bivouac: A Training Project for 349th Air Evacuation Group Nurses," Bowman Field, Ky., AMEDD.

28. G. E. Dunnam and L. B. Stroup, "Student Bivouac, 349th Air Evacuation Group, Bowman Field, Kentucky, March 23/43 to 24/43," AMEDD.

29. Leora Stroup, "Student Assignments for Class in Bivouac Familiarization, prior to Bivouac," Headquarters, 349th Air Evacuation Group, Bowman Field, Ky., AMEDD.

30. June Sanders, "Unit History from Activation to Date: Section III," 819 MAES, in *Squadron History,* Initial Issue, 20 Apr. 1944, 1, AFHRA MED-819-HI.

31. Newbeck Christian, interview with author.

32. "Nurse's Post Graduate Training," group memorandum, Headquarters 349th Aeromedical Evacuation Group, Bowman Field, Ky., 23 Feb. 1943, AMEDD.

33. "Inspection Report, Building No. 262," 20 Mar. 1943, AMEDD.

34. "Policy Governing the Duty Assignment of Flight Nurses" taken from AAF Letter 35-164, 6 Dec. 1944, *Army Nurse* 2 (Jan. 1945): 7.

35. Barney M. Giles, "Special Badge for Flight Nurses," memorandum for the Chief of Staff, 16 July 1943, 211 Nurses, box 388, RG 18, NARA.

36. Link and Coleman, *Medical Support,* 371.

37. J. Duncan Campbell, *Aviation Badges and Insignia of the United States Army, 1913–1946* (Harrisburg, Penn.: Triangle, 1977), 29–30, 76.

38. "Establishment of the Army Air Forces School of Air Evacuation," AG 352 (22 June 1943), War Department, The Adjutant General's Office, Washington, 23 June 1943, AFHRA 280.93-21A; Robert M. Conger, "History of the 'Flight A' Medical Air Evacuation Transport Squadron, 20 April 1943 to 1 June 1944," 805 MAES, 5, AFRHA MED-805-HI.

39. Link and Coleman, *Medical Support,* 372–73.

40. World War II Flight Nurses Association, *The Story of Air Evacuation 1942–1989* (Dallas: Taylor, 1989), 150.

41. R. T. Stevenson, "Promotion of Reserve Nurse, A.N.C. to Assistant Super-intendent," Army Air Forces School of Air Evacuation, Bowman Field, Ky., 29 Sept. 1943; "Special Order No. 324 Extract," War Department, Services of Sup-ply, Office of the Surgeon General, Washington, D.C., 25, 27 Dec. 1943, AMEDD.

42. "Name—Leora B. Stroup, 1st Lt. A.N.C., Title—Instructor, Department of Aviation Medicine and Nursing. Army Nurse Corps representative, Dept. of Training, Army Air Forces School of Air Evacuation, Bowman Field, Kentucky. Duties—," AMEDD.

43. "Duties Pertaining to the Office of the Nurse in the Department of Train-ing," Army Air Forces School of Air Evacuation, Bowman Field, Ky., AMEDD.

44. "Special Orders Number 124 Extract," Army Air Forces School of Air Evac-uation, Bowman Field, Louisville, Ky., 13 June 1944, AMEDD.

45. Russell C. Smith, "Student Nurses—44E Schedule," 2 July 1944 to 8 July 1944, AMEDD.

46. "Swim to Live Program in Full Swing," *Louisville Carrier,* 5 Aug. 1943.

47. "Kicks from Air Nurses: Fliers Learn How to Beat Davey Jones," *Louisville Times,* 29 July 1943; "Swim to Live Program In Full Swing."

48. "Nurses and Curriculum," 803 MAES, AFHRA MED-803-HI.

49. "Training Program for Flight Nurses," Army Air Forces School of Air Evac-uation, Bowman Field, Ky., 16 Aug. 1943, AFHRA 280.93-12.

50. Adele Edmonds Daly, interview with author.

51. "Training Program for Flight Nurses: Department of Military Art and Logis-tics," Army Air Forces School of Air Evacuation, Bowman Field, Ky., 16 Aug. 1943, AFHRA 280.93-12.

52. Dorothy Vancil Morgan, interview with author.

53. Grant, "Speech to Seventh Graduation Class," 5–6.

54. Link and Coleman, *Medical Support,* 378.

55. White Errair, interview with author.

56. "Historical Report for the Month of December 1943," 815 MAES, 3, AFHRA MED-815-HI.

57. Futrell, *Aeromedical Evacuation,* 90.

58. Miriam M. Britton, letter to Mary R. Leontine, 15 Aug. 1943, AFHRA 141.28T (805 MAES).

59. J. Bernice Stick, letter to Mary R. Leontine, 18 Oct. 1943, AFHRA 141.28T (808 MAES).

60. Louise Anthony de Flon, interview with author.

61. "Historical Report for the Month of January 1944," Bowman Field Army Air Base, Louisville, Ky., AFHRA 280.93-17 v.1; "Historical Report for the Month of March 1944," Headquarters, Bowman Field Army Air Base, Louisville, Ky., AFHRA 280.93-19 v.1.

62. [Katherine Hack], "History: Nurses View Point, 20 January 1944–31 Decem-ber 1944," 821 MAES, 2. See also Frances M. Barrett, letter to Major [Ruth] Par-sons, 16 Jan. 1945, AFHRA MED-821-HI.

63. John R. McGraw, "Graduation exercises and review," letter to All Squadrons and AAF School of Air Evacuation, Bowman Field, Ky., 13 Mar. 1944, AFHRA MED-823-HI.

64. "Discontinuance and Reestablishment of AAF School of Air Evacuation," War Department Letter AG 352 (30 Sept. 1944), War Department, Adjutant General's Office, Washington, D.C., 2 Oct. 1944, AFHRA 280.93-20 v.1.

65. Milton Greenberg, "Training of Flight Nurses and Air Evacuation Medical Technicians," *Air Surgeon's Bulletin* 2 (Oct. 1945): 328–29.

66. Robert J. Parks, ed., *Medical Training in World War II* (Washington, D.C.: Office of the Surgeon General, Department of the Army, 1974), 46.

67. Ibid., 145.

68. "Annual Report of the 27th AAF Base Unit," 82–83, 78.

69. Ibid., 79.

70. Kernodle, "Army Nurses Sprout Wings."

71. Futrell, *Aeromedical Evacuation,* 363.

72. "Trumbull Woman Heads Nurses Doing Air Evacuation of Pacific Wounded," *Ohio Nurses Review* 2 (Oct. 1945): 168; "30 Pairs of Eyes Follow Nurse across Ocean," *New York Telegram,* 11 May 1945; John R. McGraw, "Flight Nurse Designation," letter to Commanding Officer 828 MAES, 9 Nov. 1944; "Special Orders No. 25 Extract," Air Transport Command, 1503rd Air Base Unit, Pacific Division, Port of Aerial Embarkation, Hamilton Field, California, 26 Aug. 1944; "Special Orders Number 122 Extract," Headquarters Pacific Division, (1500th Air Base Unit), AAF Air Transport Command, APO #953, 12 Dec. 1944, AMEDD.

73. Parks, *Medical Training in World War II,* 146; Futrell, *Aeromedical Evacuation,* 89.

74. Link and Coleman, *Medical Support,* 378; Parks, *Medical Training in World War II,* 146.

75. Futrell, *Aeromedical Evacuation,* 84.

76. Ruth Y. White, "Army Nurses—in the Air," *American Journal of Nursing* 41 (Apr. 1943): 344.

77. *Official Guide to the Army Air Forces,* 94.

78. "Policy Governing the Duty Assignment of Flight Nurses," 7.

4. From Flight Nurse Graduation to Arrival Overseas

1. Elsie Ott and Georgia Insley, "803rd Lament," 803 MAES, July 1943, AFHRA MED-803-HI.

2. "Medical History I Troop Carrier Command."

3. "Bivouac," 803 MAES, AFHRA MED-803-HI.

4. Jensen Mangerich, interview with author.

5. [Hack], "History: Nurses View Point," 821 MAES, 2.

6. Ibid.; [Hack], enclosure accompanying Barrett, letter to Parsons, 4.

7. Sanders, "Unit History from Activation to Date—Section III," 819 MAES.

8. "Dr. (Major) Morris Kaplan's Personal 'Song of India,'" unpublished manuscript, 1.

9. "Post Graduate Activities," 803 MAES, AFHRA MED-803-HI.

10. Holtz, interview with author.

11. Carlson Cerasale, interview with author.

12. Anthony de Flon, interview with author.

13. Anonymous, interview with author.

14. [Hack], "History: Nurses View Point," 821 MAES, 4.

15. Morrey Murphy, interview with author.

16. "Part II Overseas," in "Historical Narrative of the 801st Medical Air Evacuation Transport Squadron," 25 May 1942–1 June 1944, 4, AFHRA MED-801-HI.

17. Carlson Cerasale, interview with author. Denny Nagle, another 815 MAES flight nurse, remembered the ocean voyage taking over twice that long.

18. "Trip across the Ocean," 803 MAES, AFHRA MED-803-HI.

19. Malito Nabors, interview with author.

20. Guilford and Soboroff, "Air Evacuation," 611; Ralph T. Stevenson, "Air Ambulance Brings Them Back Alive," *Modern Hospital* 2 (Aug. 1943): 53–54.

21. Alberta E. Crowe, "Miss Nightingale II," *Woman Bowler,* Feb. 1945, 5–8, 14; George M. Hellyer, letter to Commanding Officer, 821 Medical Air Evacuation Squadron, 13 May 1945, Subject: Air Evacuation Special Report on Miss Nightingale II, with enclosure "Special Interest Aircraft, C-47B #43–47864," 30 Apr. 1945, AFHRA MED-821-HI.

22. [Mae M. Link], "Aeromedical Evacuation, World War II, Pacific Area," n.d., 37, AFHRA K141.28A-7; [Mae M. Link], "Report of Intratheater Air Evacuation in Pacific Operations during World War II," Surgeon General's Office, Headquarters USAF, n.d., 37. AFHRA 168.7082-574] Guilford and Soboroff, "Air Evacuation," 610.

23. Bellafaire, *Army Nurse Corps,* 14.

24. Hugh M. Crumay, "History of Squadron Activities, 1 February 1945 to 28 February 1945," 820 MAES, 12 Mar. 1945, 138–39, 157, AFHRA MED-820-HI.

25. Guilford and Soboroff, "Air Evacuation," 610.

26. "Emergency Evacuation of Wounded by Glider," in "Historical Report," 816 MAES, June 1945, 90–94, AFHRA MED-816-HI.

27. Suella Bernard Delp, letter to Louise Anthony de Flon, 2 Oct. 1984. See also Sue Bernard Delp, "Glider Pick-up at Remagen by 816th MAES," in World War II Flight Nurses, *Story of Air Evacuation,* 87–88.

28. Martin Wolfe, *Green Light? A Troop Carrier Squadron's War from Normandy to the Rhine* (Washington, D.C.: Center for Air Force History, 1993), 419–20.

29. "Troop Carrier Song—New Guinea," enclosure no. 18 in Leopold J. Snyder, "History of the 804th Medical Air Evacuation Transport Squadron for April, 1944," 27 May 1944, 45, AFHRA MED-804-HI.

30. Wolfe, *Green Light?* 417.

31. Leopold J. Snyder, "History 804th Medical Air Evacuation Squadron, October 1944," 11 Nov. 1944, 7, AFHRA MED-804-HI.

32. Link and Coleman, *Medical Support,* 378–79.

33. Raymond A. Cunningham, "History of Squadron Activities, 1 Jan. 1945 to 31 Jan. 1945," 820 MAES, 6 Feb. 1945, 128, AFHRA MED-820-HI; Hugh M. Crumay, "Quarterly Medical History, 1 Jan. 1945 to 31 March 1945," 820 MAES, 31 Mar. 1945. AFHRA MED-820-HI.

34. "History of the 804th Medical Air Evacuation Transport Squadron through January 1944," 3.

35. Leopold J. Snyder, "History of 804th Medical Air Evacuation Transport Squadron for September, 1944," 31 Oct. 1944, 4–5, AFHRA MED-804-HI.

36. "Historical Report," 816 MAES, June 1945, 99.

37. "803rd Activities for the Month of April 1944," AFHRA MED-803-HI.

38. Malito Nabors, interview with author.

39. Holtz, interview with author.

40. Diane Burke Fessler, *No Time for Fear: Voices of American Military Nurses in World War II* (East Lansing: Michigan State Univ. Press, 1996), 70–71, 112, 115.

41. "Organizations and Operations," in Report of Activities, 801st Medical Air Transport Squadron, [25 Sept. 1943], 19, AFHRA MED-801-HI.

42. Sarnecky, *U.S. Army Nurse Corps,* 256; "History of the Army Nurse Corps: Slide Presentation with Narration," a document of the United States Army Medical Department accessed online at history.amedd.army.mil/ANCWebsite/slpr/ slpr5.html. See the narration between slide 49 and slide 52.

43. "Nurses and Curriculum," 803 MAES.

44. Ray C. Stark, "Air Evacuation: Italian Campaign," *Air Surgeon's Bulletin* 2 (Jan. 1945): 11; "Types of Patients Evacuated," in "Report of Medial Activities," [26 Sept. 1943], 801, MAES, 23.

45. Guilford and Soboroff, "Air Evacuation," 612.

46. Leopold J. Snyder, "Quarterly History, 804th Medical Air Evacuation Squadron, APO 920," 15 Oct. 1944, 7; Snyder, "History of 804th Medical," 31 Oct. 1944, 11–12, AFHRA MED-804-HI.

5. Flight Nursing on the European Front: North Africa, Sicily, Italy

1. Futrell, *Aeromedical Evacuation,* 71–72, 76.

2. Ibid., 131–32, 141, 145.

3. Dorothy Lonergan, "Scott Air Force Base 1942," unpublished manuscript about 802 MAES, n.d., 4, AMEDD. This may have been Assi Ameur, a town in the vicinity of Oran.

4. Frederick G. Holt, "War Diary 802nd Med AET," Feb. 1943, AFHRA 802-MED-HI.

5. Morrey Murphy, interview with author.

6. Ibid.

7. Lonergan, "Scott Air Force Base," 5.

8. Ibid., 6, 7.

9. "Medical History, 802nd Medical Air Evacuation Squadron," 10 Dec. 1942–30 June 1944, 40, AFHRA MED-802-HI.

10. Lonergan, "Scott Air Force Base," 7.

11. Henrietta Richardson, "Flight Nurse," *Air Force* 26 (Dec. 1943): 8.

12. Lonergan, "Scott Air Force Base," 7.

13. Richardson, "Flight Nurse," 8.

14. Fred Rosen, "Flight Nurse," *Trained Nurse and Hospital Review* 115 (July 1945): 22.

15. "Medical History 802nd Medical Air Evacuation Squadron," 10 Dec. 1942–30 June 1944.

16. Lonergan, "Scott Air Force Base," 8.

17. June Wandrey, *Bedpan Commando: The Story of a Combat Nurse during World War II,* 2nd ed. (Elmore, Ohio: Elmore Publishing, 1991), 140.

18. Lonergan, "Scott Air Force Base," 17; Catherine R. Grogan, "802nd (US) Medical Air Evacuation Squadron Unit History," AFHRA MED-802-HI.

19. "Medical History 802nd Medical Air Evacuation Squadron," 10 Dec. 1942–30 June 1944. AFHRA MED-802-HI; Murphy, "Air Evacuation," 4.

20. Murphy, "Air Evacuation," 3; Lonergan, "Scott Air Force Base," 9.

21. Murphy, "Air Evacuation," 3; Lonergan, "Scott Air Force Base," 9–10, 13.

22. Morrey Murphy, interview with author; Lonergan, "Scott Air Force Base," 14.

23. Murphy, "Air Evacuation," 9.

24. Lonergan, "Scott Air Force Base," 9–10.

25. Murphy, "Air Evacuation," 9–10.

26. Grogan, "802nd (US) Medical"; Morrey Murphy, interview with author.

27. Murphy, "Air Evacuation," 4, 9–10; Lonergan, "Scott Air Force Base," 15; Grogan, "802nd"; "802nd Med Air Evac Sq., Outline History, November 1944." AFHRA MED-802-HI; "Biggest Army Hospital Ship to Date Named in Honor of Army Nurse Killed on Duty," *Army Nurse* 2 (June 1945): 3. Seventeen flight nurses were killed during World War II, thirteen of them in aircraft accidents.

28. Murphy, "Air Evacuation," 2.

29. Grace H. Stakeman, "807th (US) Medical Air Evacuation Squadron Unit History," 1943–1944, 42–43, AFHRA MED-807-HI.

30. Ibid., 6.

31. Ibid., 7–8, 10.

32. "Report of Air Evacuation Activities for Period of Sept 4 to Dec 1 [1943]," 807 MAES, AFHRA MED-807-HI.

33. Stakeman, "807th (US) Medical," 23.

34. Ibid., 11.

35. White Errair, interview with author.

36. Stakeman, "807th (US) Medical," 18–19. Six of the flight nurses killed during World War II had graduated from the course on 26 November 1943. Another four flight nurses who died were in the class that graduated on 11 March 1944. The 807 MAES was the squadron with the most flight nurse deaths, having lost three in less than a month in 1943.

37. Ibid., 22.

38. "Stories We Think Worth Mentioning," 807th Med Air Evac Transportation, Year 1944, The Italian Campaign," 2, AFHRA MED-807-HI.

39. White Errair, interview with author.

40. Ibid.

41. Ibid.

42. Evelyn Monahan and Rosemary Neidel-Greenlee, *And If I Perish: Frontline U.S. Army Nurses in World War II* (New York: Knopf, 2003), 277.

43. Stakeman, "807th (US) Medical," 24, 25.

44. White Errair, interview with author.

45. Stakeman, "807th (US) Medical," 26.

46. Edith Belden, "Spirit of the Wounded," in "Stories," 807 MAES, 1.

47. Stakeman, "807th (US) Medical," 27, 30–31.

48. Ibid., 27.

6. Flight Nurses behind Enemy Lines

1. Futrell, *Aeromedical Evacuation,* 187.

2. Stakeman, "807th (US) Medical," 11.

3. "Personnel List," in Twelfth Air Force Escape and Evasion Reports, 1944–1945. AFHRA 650.617; Agnes Jensen Mangerich, "A Balkan Interlude," in World War II Flight Nurses, *Air Evacuation,* 95.

4. Jensen Mangerich, interview with author.

5. Ibid.

6. Ibid.

7. Charles B. Thrasher and James A. Baggs, "Ex-Report," 3–9 Feb. 1944,1; Gertrude G. Dauson [Dawson] and Eugenie H. Rutkowski, "Ex-report," 3–9 Feb. 1944, 1; Robert A. Cranson, Paul G. Allen, Robert E. Owen, and Raymond E. Ebers, "Ex-Report," 3–9 Feb. 1944, 1. All in Twelfth Air Force Escape and Evasion Reports, 1944–45, AFHRA 650.617; Agnes Jensen Mangerich, *Albanian Escape: The True Story of U.S. Army Nurses behind Enemy Lines,* as told to Evelyn M. Monahan and Rosemary L. Neidel (Lexington: Univ. Press of Kentucky, 1999), 24.

8. Dauson [Dawson] and Rutkowski, "Ex-Report," 1.

9. Stakeman, "807th (US) Medical," 11.

10. Futrell, *Aeromedical Evacuation,* 189.

11. Richard E. Elvins, letter to David N. W. Grant, 29 Nov. 1943, AFHRA 141.28T.

12. Thrasher and Baggs, "Ex-Report," 1; Dauson [Dawson] and Rutkowski, "Ex-Report," 1.

13. Thrasher and Baggs, "Ex-Report," 2.

14. James Pettifer, *Albania and Kosovo,* 3rd ed. (New York: Norton, 2001), 84–85.

15. Jensen Mangerich, interview with author.

16. Mangerich, *Albanian Escape,* 99.

17. Ibid., 103–4.

18. Ibid., 118–19.

19. Ibid., 139.

20. Ibid., 143–44.

21. Thrasher and Baggs, "Ex-Report," 1; Mangerich, *Albanian Escape,* 163, 167.

22. Mangerich, *Albanian Escape,* 163.

23. Thrasher and Baggs, "Ex-Report," 4.

24. Agnes A. Jensen, Untitled statement in Fifteenth Air Force "Evaders," [1944], AFHRA 670.614-3.

25. Lillian Tacina, Untitled statement in Fifteenth Air Force "Evaders," [1944], AFHRA 670.614-3.

26. Lois E. Watson, Untitled statement in Fifteenth Air Force "Evaders," [1944], AFHRA 670.614-3.

27. Mangerich, *Albanian Escape,* 169.

28. Jensen Mangerich, interview with author.

29. Thrasher and Baggs, "Ex-Report," 4.

30. Jensen Mangerich, interview with author.

31. Mangerich, *Albanian Escape,* 199–200.

32. White Errair, interview with author.

33. Helen Porter, Ava Ann Maness, and Wilma D. Lytle, "Evaders Statement," 25 Mar. 1944, in Twelfth Air Force Escape and Evasion Reports, 1944–45, 2, AFHRA 650.617.

34. Mangerich, *Albanian Escape,* 207.

35. Porter, Maness, and Lytle, "Evaders Statement," 3.

36. Ibid., 4.

37. Mangerich, *Albanian Escape,* 203, 205.

38. Porter, Maness, and Lytle, "Evaders Statement," 3.

39. Mangerich, *Albanian Escape,* 206.

40. Ibid., 208.

41. Thrasher and Baggs, "Ex-Report," 1.

42. James P. Cruise, "Personal Statement," 13 Jan. 1944, in Twelfth Air Force Escape and Evasion Reports, 1944–45, AFHRA 650.617.

43. Jensen Mangerich, interview with author.

44. Stakeman, "807th (US) Medical," 16–18, 20.

45. Mangerich, *Albanian Escape,* 211.

46. Jensen Mangerich, interview with author.

47. "Annual Report of the 27th AAF Base Unit," 78.

7. Flight Nursing on the European Front: United Kingdom, France, North Atlantic

1. "806th (US) Medical Air Evacuation Squadron: Diary," 17 July 1943–31 Dec. 1945, AFHRA MED-806-HI.

2. Denzil (Denny) Nagle, interview with author.

3. "806th . . . Diary," 17 July 1943–31 Dec. 1945.

4. Boyle Silk, interview with author.

5. Robert R. Smith, "Historical Records: Resume," 818 MAES, 1 May 1944–31 May 1944, 3, AFHRA MED-818-HI.

6. "Historical Report," 816 MAES, June 1945, 28–29.

7. Carlson Cerasale, interview with author.

8. Ibid.

9. Sanders, "Unit History from Activation to Date—Section III," 819 MAES, 3–4.

10. "806th . . . Diary," 17 July 1943–31 December 1945; Futrell, *Aeromedical Evacuation,* 371.

11. "Brief, Running Summary of the Month's Activities: May," 811 MAES, 31 May 1944, AFHRA MED-811-HI.

12. Paul A. Clouse, "810th Med Air Evac T. Sq.," 1 Mar. 1944; August M. Kleeman, "810th Med Air Evac T. Sq.," 1 Apr. 1944, AFHRA MED-810-HI.

13. "History of the 810th Medical Air Evacuation Squadron, 1 May 1944 to 31 May 1944," 3 June 1944, AFHRA MED-810-HI.

14. Edith Jackson, "Report of Evacuation of Patients, Flight A: Evacuation I," [May 1944], unpublished manuscript.

15. "Historical Report," 816 MAES, June 1945, 32.

16. Lonergan, "Scott Air Force Base," 11; "Historical Report," 816 MAES, June 1945, 30; June Sanders, "Unit History for Month of May 1944—Section III," 819 MAES, 1, AFHRA MED-819-HI.

17. "Historical Report for the Month of June 1944," 815 MAES, AFHRA MED-815-HI; Robert R. Smith, "Historical Records: Special Accounts," 818 MAES, 1–30 June 1944, 3–4, AFHRA MED-818-HI.

18. June Sanders, "Unit History for Month of June 1944—Section III," 819 MAES, 1, AFHRA MED-819-HI.

19. "Historical Report," 816 MAES, June 1945, 33–34. Medical crews of the 815 MAES had to return their knives, which were considered a weapon and thus against Geneva Convention. Flight nurses in other MAES were allowed to keep theirs (Carlson Cerasale, interview with author).

20. Sandstrom Crabtree, interview with author.

21. Dunnam Wichtendahl, interview with author.

22. Sanders, "Unit History for Month of June 1944—Section III," 819 MAES, 3.

23. Anthony de Flon, interview with author.

24. "History," 1–30 June 1944, 813 MAES, 2 July 1944, 2, AFHRA MED-813-HI; "Historical Records," Installment V, 1–30 June 1944, 814 MAES, 1 July 1944, 20, AFHRA MED-814-HI,

25. "Historical Records: War Diary," 818 MAES, 1–30 June 1944, 3, AFHRA MED-818-HI.

26. "Historical Report for the Month of June 1944," 815 MAES.

27. "Brief, Running Summary of the Month's Activities: June," 811 MAES, 30 June 1944; "Brief, Running Summary of the Month's Activities," 811 MAES, July 1944, AFHRA MED-811-HI.

28. "Historical Records," 814 MAES, 5 July 1944, 20; "Historical Report for the Month of June 1944," 815 MAES.

29. Sanders, "Unit History for Month of June 1944—Section III," 819 MAES, 2.

30. "806th . . . Diary," 17 July 1943–31 Dec. 1945, AFHRA MED-806-HI.

31. Phoebe H. La Munyan, "Unit History for Month of July 1944—Section III," 819 MAES, 1, AFHRA MED-819-HI.

32. Ibid.

33. Boyle Silk, interview with author.

34. "Unit Historical Report," 813 MAES, 1–31 July 1944, 2.

35. "806th . . . Diary," 17 July 1943–31 Dec. 1945; "History of the 810th Medical Air Evacuation Squadron 1 August 1944 to 31 August 1944: Resume," AFHRA MED-810-HI.

36. "Unit Historical Report," 813 MAES, 1 October 1944–30 November 1944; "Unit Historical Report," 813 MAES, 1–31 Dec. 1944, 1–2, AFHRA MED-813-HI.

37. "Historical Report for the Month of September 1944," 815 MAES, AFHRA MED-815-HI; Oscar A. Miron, "Unit History October 1944: Resume," 817 MAES, AFHRA MED-817-HI; "Unit Historical Report," 813 MAES, 1–31 Dec. 1944, 1–2, AFHRA MED-813-HI.

38. Oscar A. Miron, "Award of Soldier's Medal," 817 MAES, 9 Jan. 1945, AFHRA MED-817-HI.

39. Futrell, *Aeromedical Evacuation,* 375, 358, 360, 363–64.

40. Ibid., 372.

41. "Historical Report," 816 MAES, June 1945, 68–73.

42. Futrell, *Aeromedical Evacuation,* 378, 380.

43. June Sanders, "819th Squadron History for Month of September—Section III," 30 Sept. 1944, AFHRA MED-819-HI.

44. Solomon Creesy, interview with author.

45. Alice Fraser, "The Lost Mercy Plane," 817 MAES, AFHRA MED-817-HI; reprinted in WWII Flight Nurses Association, *Story of Air Evacuation,* 158–59.

46. "Historical Records: Resume," 818 MAES, 1–30 Sept. 1944, 2, AFHRA MED-818-HI.

47. Futrell, *Aeromedical Evacuation,* 387.

48. "Brief, Running Summary of the Month's Activities: March," 811 MAES, 31 Mar. 1945; "Historical Records," Installment XIII, 1–28 Feb. 1945, 814 MAES, 2 Mar. 1945, 37; "Historical Data: Part V—Non-Combat Operations and Air Evacuation," 814 MAES, Mar. 1945, AFHRA MED-814-HI; "Historical Report for the Month of February 1945," 815 MAES; "Historical Data: Part II—Narrative," 815 MAES, Mar. 1945, AFHRA MED-815-HI; "Historical Report," 816 MAES, June 1945, 96; "Historical Data," Apr. 1945, "Part II Narrative," 817 MAES, 9 May 1945, 2.

49. "Historical Records," Installment XIII, 1–28 Feb. 1945, 814 MAES, 2 Mar. 1945, 38.

50. "Part II Narrative," 817 MAES, Apr. 1945; Joseph L. Boucher, "Statement," 100th Troop Carrier Squadron, 441st Troop Carrier Group, Office of the Intelligence Officer, Station A-41, 17 Apr. 1945, AFHRA MED-817-HI.

51. "Historical Data, 806th (US) Medical Air Evacuation Squadron, April 1945," 3 May 1945, 2, AFHRA MED-806-HI.

52. Sandstrom Crabtree, interview with author.

53. P.H.L. [Phoebe H. La Munyan], "Squadron History—Section III: Ode to Squadron Histories," in "Headquarters 819th Medical Air Evacuation Transport Squadron," 31 Oct. 1944, AFHRA MED-819-HI.

54. June Sanders, "819th Squadron History—Section III," 30 Nov. 1944, 1, AFHRA MED-819-HI.

55. P.H.L. [Phoebe H. La Munyan], "Squadron History—Section III," 819 MAES, 31 Dec. 1944, 1, AFHRA MED-819-HI.

56. Emerson C. Kunde, "Part II—Narrative History," 819 MAES, 30 Apr. 1945, AFHRA MED-819-HI.

57. Futrell, *Aeromedical Evacuation,* 387–88, 386-87.

58. "806th . . . Diary," 17 July 1943–31 Dec. 1945.

59. Futrell, *Aeromedical Evacuation,* 389.

8. Flight Nurse Prisoner of War

1. Grant, "Speech to Seventh Graduation Class," 5.

2. Mary E. V. Frank, "The Forgotten POW: Second Lieutenant Reba Z. Whittle, AN," unpublished paper, U.S. Army War College, Carlisle Barracks, Penn., 1 Feb. 1990, 10–26; "Diary of Reba Whittle Tobiason," [1944], typed copy [2001], AFHRA K238.056–16. Whittle's diary differs slightly in some wording and punctuation in each document. I have used the AFHRA document for quotations.

3. "Unit Historical Report, 1 October 1944–30 November 1944," 813 MAES, AFHRA MED-813-HI.

4. "Flight Nurse Tells of Life in German Prison," *New York Herald Tribune,* 4 Mar. 1945.

5. Frank, "Forgotten POW," 22.

6. James D. Straubel, ed., *Air Force Diary: 111 Stories from the Official Journal of the USAAF* (New York: Simon & Schuster, 1947), 121.

7. Cited in Frank, "Forgotten POW," 29.

8. Ibid.

9. Carlson Cerasale, interview with author.

10. Frank, "Forgotten POW," 35–36.

11. Ibid., 35–37.

12. "Flight Nurse Tells of Life in German Prison."

9. Flight Nursing on the Pacific Front: Pacific Islands

1. Elizabeth Pukas, interview with author.

2. "Organizations and Operations," in "Report of Activities," [26 Sept. 1943], 801 MAES, 19; "Personnel," in "Report of Activities," [26 Sept. 1943], 801 MAES, 18, 48.

3. Charles G. Mixter, letter to Air Surgeon, Washington, D.C., Subject: "Report of Activities of the 801st Medical Air Evacuation Transport Squadron," 26 Sept.

1943, AFHRA MED-801-HI; "Organizations and Operations," in "Report of Activities," [26 Sept. 1943], 801 MAES, 17.

4. "Summary of Activities," in "Report of Medical Activities," [26 Sept. 1943], 801 MAES, 30, AFHRA MED-801-HI.

5. "Organizations and Operations," 801 MAES, 17.

6. "Personnel: Flight Nurses," in "Report of Medical Activities," [26 Sept. 1943], 801 MAES, 49; "Recommendations," in "Report of Medical Activities," [26 Sept. 1943], 801 MAES, 61.

7. "Chronological List of Unusual Occurrences," in "Report of Medical Activities," [26 Sept. 1943], 801 MAES, 8.

8. "General Orders No. 139 Extract, 1. Award of the Air Medal," Headquarters USAFISPA, APO #502, 2 June 1943, AFHRA MED-801-HI; "Bowman Trainee First Woman Decorated in South Pacific," *Louisville Courier-Journal,* 22 June 1943.

9. "History of the 804th Medical Air Evacuation Transport Squadron through January 1944," 14, 15–16, 19, 24, 26–27, AFHRA MED-804-HI.

10. "History of the 804th . . . through January, 1944," 27.

11. Leopold J. Snyder, "History of the 804th Medical Air Evacuation Transport Squadron for March 1944," 12 May 1944, AFHRA MED-804-HI.

12. Gordon Young, letter to 804 MAES Commander, 24 June 1944, enclosure no. 9 in Leopold J. Snyder, "History of 804th Medical Air Evacuation Transport Squadron for June, 1944," 12 June 1944, AFHRA MED-804-HI.

13. Mary L. Kerr, "804th Med Air Evac Trans Sqdn: Nursing Care in Flight," 15 Feb. 1944, AFHRA MED-804-HI.

14. "Training," in "Report of Medical Activities," [26 Sept. 1943], 801 MAES, 58.

15. Kerr, "Nursing Care," 804 MAES.

16. Ibid.

17. "Types of Patients Evacuated and the Problems Encountered," in "Report of Medical Activities," [26 Sept. 1943], 801 MAES, 22.

18. Leopold J. Snyder, "Monthly History of the 804th Medical Air Evacuation Transport Squadron for July, 1944," 13 Aug. 1944; Leopold J. Snyder, "History, 804 Medical Air Evacuation Squadron, APO 920, for August, 1944," 28 Oct. 1944, 6, AFHRA MED-804-HI.

19. Futrell, *Aeromedical Evacuation,* 414.

20. Dewitt C. Kissell, "A Restraint for the Air Evacuation of Manic Patients," 801 MAES, 1944, AFHRA MED-801-HI.

21. "Air Evacuation of Psychotics in the South West Pacific," 804 MAES, AFHRA MED-804-HI.

22. Futrell, *Aeromedical Evacuation,* 415.

23. Geoffrey P. Wiedeman, "Casualty Report," 804 MAES, 12 June 1944, AFHRA MED-804-HI; Snyder, "History for June 1944," 804 MAES, 4–5.

24. "Historical Data, 1 April 1944 to 30 April 1944, 801st Medical Air Evacuation Transport Squadron," 27 Apr. 1944; "Historical Data, 1 May 1944 to 31 May 1944," 801 MAES, 2 June 1944, AFHRA MED-801-HI.

25. Ilic Tynan, interview with author; "Historical Data," 801 MAES, 2 June 1944.

26. Holtz, interview with author.

27. Ibid.

28. Technical Memorandum No. 2 "Air Evacuation," 11 Jan. 1944, Headquarters United States Army Services of Supply, Office of the Chief Surgeon, AFHRA MED-801-HI.

29. "Historical Data, 1 September 1944 to 30 September 1944," 801 MAES, 2 Oct. 1944, 3, AFHRA MED-801-HI.

30. Nancy L. Preston and Ada M. S. Endres, "The Feminine Side," Aug. 1944, 2, in "Pictorial History 801st Medical Air Evacuation Transport Squadron, February 1943 to September 1944," AFHRA MED-801-HI.

31. Dorothy Rice, letter to Lenore Stroop [Leora Stroup], 8 Feb. 1944, AMEDD.

32. Holtz, interview with author.

33. Snyder, "History 804th Medical," 11 Nov. 1944, 7.

34. Wilbur A. Smith, "Historical Data: 1 October 1944 to 31 October 1944," 801 MAES, 8 Nov. 1944, 5, AFHRA MED-801-HI.

35. "History of Squadron Activities, 1 October 1944 to 31 October 1944," 820 MAES, 3 Nov. 1944, 68–69, AFHRA MED-820-HI.

36. "Squadron History Month of November 1943," 809 MAES, 2; "Squadron History Month of December 1943," 809 MAES; "Squadron History Month of December 1943," 812 MAES, 2–3, AFHRA MED-809-HI, MED-812-HI.

37. Pukas, interview with author.

38. 'Squadron History Month of January 1944," 809 MAES; "Squadron History Month of February 1944," 809 MAES; "Squadron History Month of January 1944," 812 MAES; "Squadron History Month of February 1944," 812 MAES, AFHRA MED-809-HI, MED-812-HI.

39. Elsie G. Nolan, "Angel Footprints," *Cosmopolitan,* Dec. 1944, 60–61, 167.

40. Jones Sharp, interview with author.

41. "Squadron History Month of May 1944," 812 MAES; Mary F. Reardon, "Report of Activities at Air Evacuation Bivouac Held 15 May 1944 to 22 May 1944," 30 May 1944, AFHRA MED-812 MAES-HI.

42. "Squadron History Month of May 1944," 812 MAES.

43. Pukas, interview with author.

44. Ibid.

45. Ibid.

46. Malito Nabors, interview with author.

47. Holtz, interview with author. The navy's generosity was not limited to flight nurses; ground nurses, too, had occasion to share meals aboard ships in harbor. See, for example, Sally H. Pullman, *Letters Home: Memoirs of One Army Nurse in the Southwest Pacific in World War II* (N.p.: AuthorHouse, 2004), 165–68.

48. Malito Nabors, interview with author.

49. "Squadron History Month of July 1944," 809 MAES, 1; "Squadron History Month of August," 809 MAES, AFHRA MED-809-HI.

50. "Squadron History Month of September 1944," 809 MAES, AFHRA MED-809-HI.

51. "Squadron History Month of November 1944," 809 MAES, AFHRA MED-809-HI.

52. "Squadron History Month of September 1944," 809 MAES.

53. Mary L. Hawkins, "Statement of Mary L. Hawkins, 2nd Lt., ANC (N-737974)," 1, AMEDD.

54. George W. Jones, "Excerpt from Statement of Lt Jones—Pilot of C-47 #236, 29 September 44"; Hawkins, "Statement of Mary L. Hawkins," AMEDD; Kermit H. Anderson, "Recommendation for Award of Distinguished Flying Cross," 29 May 1945; Kermit H. Anderson, "Recommendation for Award of Soldier's Medal" with annotation "given Bronze Star instead," 29 May 1945, AFHRA MED-828-HI; "Man with Throat Cut Saved by Army Nurse," New York Times, 23 Dec. 1944, AMEDD; "A Makeshift Windpipe," Trained Nurse and Hospital Review 114 (Mar. 1945): 197.

55. Snyder, "History 804th Medical," 11 Nov. 1944, 11–14.

56. Ibid., 13; Leopold J. Snyder, "Monthly History, 804th Medical Air Evacuation Squadron, APO 920, For November, 1944," 15 Dec. 1944, 3, AFHRA MED-804-HI; Futrell, Aeromedical Evacuation, 338.

57. Cunningham, "History of Squadron Activities," 820 MAES, 6 Feb. 1945.

58. Paul H. Cronenwett, "Historical Data: 1 February 1945 to 28 February 1945," 801 MAES, 5 Mar. 1945, AFHRA MED-801-HI; Futrell, Aeromedical Evacuation, 341.

59. Cunningham, "History of Squadron Activities," 820 MAES, 6 Feb. 1945.

60. Ibid.

61. Geoffrey P. Wiedeman, "February History, 804th Medical Air Evacuation Squadron, APO 321," 5–6.

62. Theta E. Phillips and Victoria R. Lancaster, "Report on Experiences during Operational Flight on 10 February to Mabalacat," 12 Mar. 1945, 820 MAES, 233, AFHRA MED-820-HI.

63. "Casualty Report: Martha F. Black," 820 MAES, 30 Apr. 1945; "History of Squadron Activities, 1 March 1945 to 31 March 1945," 820 MAES, 9 Apr. 1945, AFHRA MED-820-HI.

64. Wing Memorandum No. 55-6C "Operations: Emergency Equipment," Headquarters 54th Troop Carrier Wing, 8 Jan. 1945; Wing Memorandum No. 55-60 "Operations: Evacuation of Sick and Wounded," Headquarters 54th Troop Carrier Wing, 15 Mar. 1945, enclosures to Leopold J. Snyder, "March History, 804th Medical Air Evacuation Squadron," 7 Apr. 1945, AFHRA MED-804-HI.

65. Howard H. Gradis, "History of Squadron Activities, 1 June 1945 to 30 June 1945," 820 MAES, 10 July 1945, 177; Howard H. Gradis, "History of Squadron Activities, from 1 July 1945 to 31 July 1945," 14 Aug. 1945; and Leopold J. Snyder, "History of Squadron Activities, 1 August 1945 to 31 August 1945," 10 Sept. 1945, AFHRA MED-820-HI.

66. Geoffrey P. Wiedeman, "August History, 804th Medical Air Evacuation Squadron, APO 337," 5 Sept. 1945, 1, 4, AFHRA MED-804-HI.

67. Gradis, "History of Squadron Activities," 820 MAES, 10 Sept. 1945.

68. Futrell, *Aeromedical Evacuation,* 355.

69. Paul H. Cronenwett, "Historical Data: 1 August 1945 to 31 August 1945," 801 MAES, 5 Sept. 1945, AFHRA MED-801-HI.

70. Anonymous, interview with author.

71. Malito Nabors, interview with author.

72. Ibid.

73. Hilda Halverson Chamberlain, interview with author.

74. Pukas, interview with author.

75. Jones Sharp, interview with author.

10. Flight Nursing on the Pacific Front: Alaska, China-Burma-India

1. Alice Rogers Hager, *Wings for the Dragon: The Air War in Asia* (New York: Dodd, Mead, 1945), 1.

2. Newbeck Christian, interview with author; Conger, "History of the 'Flight A' Medical," 805 MAES, 6. Newbeck, who initially was assigned to the 805 MAES, said her six-nurse flight went to Alaska with the 830 MAES in June 1943, but that squadron was not activated until November 1944.

3. Newbeck Christian, interview with author.

4. Ibid.

5. Conger, "History of the 'Flight A' Medical," 805 MAES, 7–10.

6. Newbeck Christian, interview with author.

7. Conger, "History of the 'Flight A' Medical," 805 MAES, 13.

8. Eileen Newbeck, letter to Gladys Entrekin, 22 Aug. 1943, AFHRA 141.28T (805 MAES).

9. Personal communication with Micah Jones, pilot, USAF, 21 June 2010.

10. "General Orders No. 63 Extract: Designation of general hospitals Section II," War Department, Washington, D.C., 1 Oct. 1943, AFHRA MED-805-HI.

11. Newbeck Christian, interview with author.

12. Conger, "History of the 'Flight A' Medical," 805 MAES, 10–11.

13. Newbeck Christian, interview with author.

14. Miriam M. Britton, letter to Mary R. Leontine, 15 Aug. 1943. See chap. 3.

15. Eileen Newbeck, letter to Leora Stroup, 4 Feb. 1944, AFHRA 141.28T (805 MAES).

16. "Dr. (Major) Morris Kaplan's Personal 'Song of India,'" 7.

17. "Extracts from Letter to Col. Stevenson From Air Evacuation Control Officer of CBI. (M. Kaplan). (Also CO of 803rd MAETS)," 25 Apr. 1944, AFHRA 141.28T; Futrell, *Aeromedical Evacuation,* 270.

18. Futrell, *Aeromedical Evacuation,* 268.

19. "Life in India," 803 MAES, AFHRA MED-803-HI; Futrell, *Aeromedical Evacuation,* 269–70.

20. Kaplan, "Extracts from Letter to Col. Stevenson."

21. "803rd Activities of March 1944"; "803rd Activities for the Month of April 1944," AFHRA MED-803-HI.

22. "Life in India," 803 MAES; Kaplan, "Extracts from Letter to Col. Stevenson"; "Flight Schedules," 821 MAES, 1944–1945, AFHRA MED-821-HI.

23. Kaplan, "Extracts from Letter to Col. Stevenson"; "803rd Activities of September, 1944"; "803rd Activities of October, 1944"; "803rd Activities of March 1944."

24. "Life in India," 803 MAES.

25. "821st Medical Air Evacuation Squadron," 1–2, AFHRA MED-821-HI.

26. "Life in India," 803 MAES; "Lieutenant Audrey Rogers," *American Journal of Nursing* 44 (Feb. 1944): 180.

27. Miranda (Randy) Rast Weinrich, interview with author.

28. "Life in India," 803 MAES; "Dr. (Major) Morris Kaplan's Personal 'Song of India,'" 42–45; Hager, *Wings for the Dragon,* 129–32; "803rd Activities of February, 1944."

29. "803rd Activities of February, 1944"; "803rd Activities of March 1944"; "803rd Activities of May, 1944," AFHRA MED-803-HI.

30. "803rd Activities of May 1944"; "Dr. (Major) Morris Kaplan's Personal 'Song of India,'" 34–36; Hager, *Wings for the Dragon,* 132–34.

31. Kaplan, "Dr. (Major) Morris Kaplan's Personal 'Song of India,'" 36.

32. "803rd Activities of August, 1944."

33. Esther Baer Moseley, *Lady Don't Stop Here* (Peachtree, Ga.: N.p., 1988), 81.

34. Futrell, *Aeromedical Evacuation,* 302.

35. "History 20 January 1944–31 December 1944," 821 MAES, 7, AFHRA MED-821-HI; "803rd Activities of September, 1944"; Futrell, *Aeromedical Evacuation,* 297.

36. "History 20 January 1944–31 December 1944," 821 MAES, 9.

37. [Hack], "History: Nurses View Point," 821 MAES, 6.

38. Katherine Hack, "An Incident," 821 MAES, May 1945, AFHRA MED-821-HI.

39. "821st Medical Air Evacuation Squadron," 6.

40. Ibid., 1–2.

41. Ibid., 4–5.

42. Ibid., 5.

43. "Nurses: April, 1945," 821 MAES, 1–2, AFHRA MED-821-HI.

44. Katherine S. Hack, "Nurses: May, 1945," 821 MAES, 3 June 1945, 4, AFHRA MED-821-HI.

45. "History For the month of June 1945," 821 MAES, 4 July 1945, 1, AFHRA MED-821-HI.

46. Hack, "Nurses: May, 1945," 821 MAES, 6.

11. Flight Nurse Image in Mind and Media

1. Ed Edstrom and Joe Creason, "These Angels Fly on Man-Made Wings," *Louisville Courier-Journal Roto Magazine,* 28 Feb. 1943, 6–8; Clive Howard, "Hell's

Angels," *Family Circle*, 13 Oct. 1944, 10–11, 27, 30–31, "Invasion Heroine: The Flying Nurse," *Look*, 11 July 1944, 30, 32, 34; Nolan, "Angel Footprints," 60–61, 167.

2. Joseph M. Keith, "Air Evacuation Operations and the Flight Nurse Problem," part 1, 21 May 1945, AFHRA 142.053N–3.

3. Anthony de Flon, interview with author.

4. Keith, "Air Evacuation Operations."

5. Anthony de Flon, interview with author.

6. Office of Public Relations, Bowman Field, Ky., Untitled document presented by I Troop Carrier Command, AFHRA 280.93.

7. "Organizations and Operations," in "Report of Medical Activities," [26 Sept. 1943], 801 MAES, 16.

8. "Air Evacuation of Casualties," 804 MAES, 10, AFHRA MED-804-HI.

9. Stick, letter to Leontine, 18 Oct. 1943; see chap. 3.

10. Carlson Cerasale, interview with author.

11. Seven Enlisted Medical Technicians, "Air Evacuation Operations and the Flight Nurse Problem," part 2, 21 May 1945, AFHRA 142.053N-3.

12. Snyder, "History of the 804th Medical," 12 May 1944, 11.

13. Maurice A Brown, "Air-Evacuation Nurses," 1 May 1945, AFHRA 142.053N–3.

14. Keith, "Air Evacuation Operations."

15. Edwin J. McBride, "Comments on Air Evacuation Operations and Flight Nurse Problem as described by Captain Joseph M. Keith," 19 July 1945, AFHRA 141.28–36.

16. Frederick R. Guilford, "Analysis of Air Evacuation Report," 13 July 1945, AFHRA 141.281–36.

17. F. L. Duff, "Comment on 'Air Evacuation Operations and the Flight Nurse Problem' Report," 23 July 1945, AFHRA 141.281–36.

18. Eugen G. Reinartz, "To: Commanding General, AAF, Washington 25, DC. ATT: The Air Surgeon," 23 July 1945, AFHRA 141.281–36.

19. Brown, "Air Evacuation Nurses."

20. "Recommendations," in "Report of Medical Activities," [26 Sept. 1943], 801 MAES, 61; "Personnel," in "Report of Medical Activities, [26 Sept. 1943], 801 MAES, 48, 49

21. "Personnel," in "Report of Medical Activities, [26 Sept. 1943], 801 MAES, 49.

22. Willis W. Mitchell, "Letter of Appreciation" to Commanding Officer, 817 MAES, 13 Sept. 1944., AFHRA MED-817-HI.

23. Solomon Creesy, interview with author.

24. Futrell, *Aeromedical Evacuation,* 91.

25. Dorothy M. Rice, "Flight to Kirawagi," *American Journal of Nursing* 45 (Jan. 1945): 10–11; Rice, letter to Stroop [Stroup], 8 Feb. 1944.

26. Preston and Endres, "Feminine Side," 801 MAES, 5.

27. Janet Foome, "Christmas Greetings and Farewell," enclosure no. 17 in Snyder, "History of the 804th," 27 May 1944, 44.

28. Wm. [William] T. Lent, "AAF Medics," *Air Force* 27 (July 1944): 51.

29. Maxine Davis, *Through the Stratosphere: The Human Factor in Aviation* (New York: Macmillan, 1946), 227.

30. Alfred D. Whelton, "A Heroine Comes Home," *Boston Advertiser,* 9 Sept. 1945.

31. M. Robert Halbouty, Attilio D. Puppel, and Charles E. Bybee, "Air Evacuation in the Combat Zone," *Air Surgeon's Bulletin* 2 (Oct. 1945): 337.

32. Edstrom and Creason, "These Angels Fly on Man-Made Wings," 6.

33. Betty Peckham *Women in Aviation* (New York: Nelson, 1945), 11.

34. Jean De Witt, "Flight Nurses," *R.N.* 6 (Mar. 1943): 34.

35. Hager, "Mercy Takes Wings," 60.

36. Marion Porter, "Nurses with Wings," *Collier's* 113 (22 Apr. 1944): 22.

37. R.S. [Roger Sheldon], "Far-East Flight Nurses," and Benn F. Reyes, Paul Wheeler, and Roger Sheldon, "We Fly an 'Air Evac' Mission," *Wing Ding* [91st Photo Reconnaissance Wing, Philippines], 4 June 1945, 5–6.

38. Jean DeWitt, "Angles [*sic*] Are Well Groomed," *R.N.* 8 (Jan. 1945): 34.

39. Shelley Mydans, "Flight Nurse," *Life* 18 (12 Feb. 1945): 58.

40. Pukas, interview with author.

41. Malito Nabors, interview with author.

42. Pukas, interview with author.

43. Porter "Nurses with Wings," 69.

44. Snyder, "History of the 804th Medical," 12 May 1944, 3.

45. Ibid.

46. Snyder, "History of 804th Medical," 28 Oct. 1944, 8; Snyder, "History of 804th Medical," 12 June 1944, 5–6. See "No 'Glamor Girl' Life, Hero Nurse Avers," *Louisville Courier-Journal,* 3 Aug. 1944; and Insert "3-Medal Nurse Back a Casualty," in Howard, "Hell's Angels," 11.

47. Snyder, "History of 804th Medical," 28 Oct. 1944, 8.

48. Futrell, *Aeromedical Evacuation,* 209.

49. Sanders, "Unit History for Month of June 1944—Section III," 819 MAES, 3.

50. Suella Bernard and Marijean Brown, "Nurses Pick Poppies While Awaiting First Wounded," *Newark Call,* 12 June 1944.

51. Hager, "Mercy Takes Wings," 19, 60.

52. Nolan, "Angel Footprints," 167.

53. Joe Whitley, "Flight Nurses Are Women," *Brief* 1 (14 Nov. 1944): 10.

54. Preston and Endres, "Feminine Side," 801 MAES, 4.

55. Ibid.

56. Charlotte Knight, "Flight Nurse," *Air Force* 27 (Oct. 1944): 30, 62; see also Straubel, *Air Force Diary,* 334–39.

57. Rice, letter to Stroop [Stroup], 8 Feb. 1944.

58. "Life in India," 803 MAES.

59. Phoebe La Munyan, "History for the Month of August 1944—Section III," 819 MAES, 31 Aug. 1944, 1, AFHRA MED-819-HI.

12. Challenges of Wartime Flight Nursing

1. Juanita Redmond, *I Served on Bataan* (New York: Lippincott, 1943), 106–12; Barbara Brooks Tomblin, *G.I. Nightingales: The Army Nurse Corps in World War II* (Lexington: University Press of Kentucky, 1996), 27–28.

2. Holm, *Women in the Military,* 45.

3. Tomblin, *G.I. Nightingales,* 39–40, 50.

4. Elizabeth M. Norman, *We Band of Angels: The Untold Story of American Nurses Trapped on Bataan by the Japanese* (New York: Random House, 1999), 277.

5. Monahan, Evelyn and Rosemary Neidel-Greenlee, *And If I Perish: Frontline U.S. Army Nurses in World War II* (New York: Knopf, 2003), 20, 182–95, 241–47.

6. Tomblin, *G.I. Nightingales,* 63.

7. Monahan and Neidel-Greenlee, *And If I Perish,* 147, 261, 269.

8. Wandrey, *Bedpan Commando,* 19, 126.

9. Dorothy Rice, "Flight to 20,000 Feet," Enclosure No. 9 in Leopold J. Snyder, "History, 804 Medical Air Evacuation Squadron, APO 920, for August, 1944," 28 Oct. 1944, 26–29, AFHRA MED-804-HI.

10. Carlson Cerasale, interview with author.

11. White Errair, interview with author; Ilic Tynan, interview with author.

12. Anonymous, interview with author.

13. Preston and Endres, "Feminine Side," 801 MAES, 2–3.

14. Cronenwett, "Historical Data," 801 MAES, 5 Sept. 1945, 4, AFHRA MED-801-HI.

15. Ibid., 3.

16. Boyle Silk, interview with author; Rast Weinrich, interview with author; Morrey Murphy, interview with author.

17. Pukas, interview with author.

18. Ilic Tynan, interview with author; Edmonds Daly, interview with author; Sandstrom Crabtree, interview with author.

19. Rast Weinrich, interview with author.

20. Anonymous, interview with author.

21. Anthony de Flon, interview with author.

22. Dunnam Wichtendahl, interview with author.

23. Sandstrom Crabtree, interview with author; Vancil Morgan, interview with author; Morrey Murphy, interview with author.

24. Rast Weinrich, interview with author.

25. Newbeck Christian, interview with author.

26. Morrey Murphy, interview with author.

27. Preston and Endres, "Feminine Side," 801 MAES, 3.

28. White Errair, interview with author.

29. Ibid.

30. Sandstrom Crabtree, interview with author.

31. Edmonds Daly, interview with author.

32. Sandstrom Crabtree, interview with author.

33. White Errair, interview with author.

34. Halverson Chamberlain, interview with author.

35. Carlson Cerasale, interview with author; Anthony de Flon, interview with author.

36. Lucy Wilson Jopling, interview with author.

37. Holtz, interview with author.

38. Alice Krieble, interview with author.

39. Clara Morrey, letter to Martha Morrey, 28 Feb. 1942.

40. Malito Nabors, interview with author.

41. Holtz, interview with author.

42. Solomon Creesy, interview with author.

43. Vancil Morgan, interview with author; Jones Sharp, interview with author.

44. Preston and Endres, "Feminine Side," 801 MAES, 6.

45. White Errair, interview with author.

46. Ilic Tynan, interview with author.

47. Vancil Morgan, interview with author.

48. White Errair, interview with author; Ilic Tynan, interview with author; Mowery Unick, interview with author.

49. Pukas, interview with author.

50. Ilic Tynan, interview with author.

51. White Errair, interview with author.

52. Boyle Silk, interview with author.

53. Vancil Morgan, interview with author.

54. White Errair, interview with author.

55. Sandstrom Crabtree, interview with author.

56. Rast Weinrich, interview with author.

57. Carlson Cerasale, interview with author.

58. Holtz, interview with author.

59. White Errair, interview with author.

60. Preston and Endres, "Feminine Side," 801 MAES, 3.

61. Anonymous, interview with author.

62. Jocie French Huston, interview with author.

63. Solomon Creesy, interview with author.

64. Nagle, interview with author.

65. Malito Nabors, interview with author.

66. Ibid.

67. Pukas, interview with author.

68. Carlson Cerasale, interview with author.

69. Holtz, interview with author; Anthony de Flon, interview with author; Sandstrom Crabtree, interview with author.

70. Edmonds Daly, interview with author.

71. Holtz, interview with author.

72. Ilic Tynan, interview with author.

73. Edmonds Daly, interview with author.

74. Malito Nabors, interview with author.

75. Ibid.

76. Ilic Tynan, interview with author.

77. Sandstrom Crabtree, interview with author

78. Mowery Unick, interview with author.

79. Malito Nabors, interview with author.

80. Halverson Chamberlain, interview with author.

81. Vancil Morgan, interview with author

82. Ibid.; French Huston, interview with author.

83. Holtz, interview with author; Pukas, interview with author.

84. Malito Nabors, interview with author.

85. Carlson Cerasale, interview with author; Boyle Silk, interview with author.

86. Mowery Unick, interview with author.

87. Boyle Silk, interview with author.

88. Ibid.; Newbeck Christian, interview with author.

89. Ilic Tynan, interview with author.

90. White Errair, interview with author.

91. Preston and Endres, "Feminine Side," 801 MAES, 1.

92. See Richard S. Lazarus and Susan Folkman, *Stress, Appraisal, and Coping* (New York: Springer, 1984).

93. Preston and Endres, "Feminine Side," 801 MAES, 6–7.

94. Grant, "Speech to Seventh Graduation Class," 6.

Epilogue

1. Wilson Jopling, interview with author.

2. Preston and Endres, "Feminine Side," 801 MAES, 6.

3. Carlson Cerasale, interview with author; French Huston, interview with author; Sandstrom Crabtree, interview with author; White Errair, interview with author; Holtz, interview with author.

4. Halverson Chamberlain, interview with author; Edmonds Daly, interview with author.

5. Malito Nabors, interview with author.

6. Boyle Silk, interview with author.

7. Holtz, interview with author.

8. Edmonds Daly, interview with author; Rast Weinrich, interview with author.

9. White Errair, interview with author.

10. Jensen Mangerich, interview with author.

11. Newbeck Christian, interview with author.

12. Anthony de Flon, interview with author; Boyle Silk, interview with author.

13. Sandstrom Crabtree, interview with author.

14. Ilic Tynan, interview with author; Malito Nabors, interview with author; Wilson Jopling, interview with author.

15. Rast Weinrich, interview with author.

16. Carlson Cerasale, interview with author; French Huston, interview with author.

17. Solomon Creesy, interview with author; French Huston, interview with author.

BIBLIOGRAPHY

This list excludes unpublished documents, which may be found in the footnotes.

Books and Manuals

Aerial Nurse Corps of America. *Regulations Manual.* Burbank, Cali.: Schimmoler, 1940.

Ambrose, Stephen E. *D-Day: June 6, 1944.* New York: Simon and Schuster, 1994.

American Red Cross Nursing Service. Abridged ed. Washington, D.C.: American Red Cross, 1942.

Archard, Theresa. *G.I. Nightingale: The Story of an American Army Nurse.* New York: Norton, 1945.

Armstrong, Harry G. *Principles and Practice of Aviation Medicine.* 3rd ed. Baltimore: Williams and Wilkins, 1952.

Aynes, Edith A. *From Nightingale to Eagle: An Army Nurse's History.* Englewood Cliffs, New Jersey: Prentice-Hall, 1973.

Bellafaire, Judith. *The Army Nurse Corps: A Commemoration of World War II Service.* Washington, D.C.: United States Army Center of Military History, 1993.

Berendsen, Dorothy M. *The Way It Was: An Air Force Nurse's Story.* New York: Carlton, 1988.

Brokaw, Tom. *The Greatest Generation.* New York: Random House, 1993.

Campbell, J. Duncan. *Aviation Badges and Insignia of the United States Army, 1913–1946.* Harrisburg, Pennsylvania: Triangle, 1977.

Craven, Wesley F., and James L. Cate, eds. *The Army Air Forces in World War II.* Volume 7, *Services around the World.* Chicago: University of Chicago Press, 1955.

Davis, Maxine. *Through the Stratosphere: The Human Factor in Aviation.* New York: Macmillan, 1946.

D'Este, Carlo. *Decision in Normandy.* New York: Dutton, 1983.

———. *World War II in the Mediterranean, 1942–1945.* Chapel Hill, North Carolina: Algonquin Books, 1990.

Fessler, Diane Burke. *No Time for Fear: Voices of American Military Nurses in World War II.* East Lansing: Michigan State University Press, 1996.

Flikke, Julia O. *Nurses in Action.* New York: Lippincott, 1943.

Futrell, Robert F. *Development of Aeromedical Evacuation in the USAF, 1909–1960.* Historical Studies, No. 23. Maxwell Air Force Base, Alabama: USAF Historical Division, Research Studies Institute, Air University, 1960.

Godson, Susan S. *Serving Proudly: A History of Women in the U.S. Navy.* Annapolis: Naval Institute Press, 2001.

Hager, Alice Rogers. *Wings for the Dragon: The Air War in Asia.* New York: Dodd, Mead, 1945.

Holm, Jeanne. *Women in the Military: An Unfinished Revolution.* Rev. ed. Novato, California: Presidio, 1982.

Holm, Jeanne M., and Judith Bellafaire, eds. *In Defense of a Nation: Servicewomen in World War II.* Washington, D.C.: Military Women's Press, 1998.

Jackson, Kathi. *They Called Them Angels: American Military Nurses of World War II.* Lincoln: University of Nebraska Press, 2006.

Jopling, Lucy Wilson. *Warrior in White.* San Antonio, Texas: Watercress, 1990.

Kalisch, Philip A., and Beatrice J. Kalisch. *The Changing Image of the Nurse.* Menlo Park, Calif.: Addison-Wesley, 1987.

La Farge, Oliver. *The Eagle in the Egg.* Boston: Houghton Mifflin, 1949.

Lazarus, Richard S., and Susan Folkman. *Stress, Appraisal, and Coping.* New York: Springer, 1984.

Link, Mae M. *History of Aeromedical Evacuation in the Pacific Theater during World War II.* Washington, D.C.: Office of the Surgeon General, USAF, n.d.

Link, Mae M., and Hubert A. Coleman. *Medical Support of the Army Air Forces in World War II.* Washington, D.C.: GPO, 1955.

Litoff, Judy Barrett, and David C. Smith. *We're in This War, Too: World War II Letters from American Women in Uniform.* New York: Oxford University Press, 1994.

Mangerich, Agnes Jensen. *Albanian Escape: The True Story of U.S. Army Nurses behind Enemy Lines.* As told to Evelyn M. Monahan and Rosemary L. Neidel. Lexington: University Press of Kentucky, 1999.

May, Charles P. *Women in Aeronautics.* New York: Nelson, 1962.

Monahan, Evelyn, and Rosemary Neidel-Greenlee. *All This Hell: U.S. Nurses Imprisoned by the Japanese.* Lexington: University Press of Kentucky, 2000.

———. *And If I Perish: Frontline U.S. Army Nurses in World War II.* New York: Knopf, 2003.

Moseley, Esther Baer. *Lady Don't Stop Here.* Peachtree, Georgia: N.p., 1988.

Murray, Mary F. *Skygirl: A Career Handbook for the Airline Stewardess.* New York: Duell, Sloan, Pearce, 1951.

Nielsen, Georgia P. *From Sky Girl to Flight Attendant: Women and the Making of a Union.* Ithaca, New York: Industrial and Labor Relations Press, 1982.

Norman, Elizabeth M. *We Band of Angels: The Untold Story of American Nurses Trapped on Bataan by the Japanese.* New York: Random House, 1999.

Official Guide to the Army Air Forces. New York: Simon and Schuster, 1944.

Parks, Robert J., ed. *Medical Training in World War II.* Washington, D.C.: Office of the Surgeon General, Department of the Army, 1974.

Peckham, Betty. *Women in Aviation.* New York: Nelson, 1945.

Pettifer, James. *Albania and Kosovo.* 3rd ed. New York: Norton, 2001.

Poulos, Paula, ed. *A Woman's War Too: U.S. Women in the Military in World War II.* Washington, D.C.: National Archives and Records Administration, 1996.

Pullman, Sally H. *Letters Home: Memoirs of One Army Nurse in the Southwest Pacific in World War II.* N.p.: AuthorHouse, 2004.

Redmond, Juanita. *I Served on Bataan.* New York: Lippincott, 1943.

Rushton, Patricia, Lynn Clark Callister, and Maile K. Wilson, compilers. *Latter-Day Saint Nurses at War: A Story of Caring and Sacrifice.* Provo, Utah: Religious Studies Center, Brigham Young University, 2005.

Sarnecky, Mary T. *A History of the U.S. Army Nurse Corps.* Philadelphia: University of Pennsylvania Press, 1999.

Sterner, Doris M. *In and Out of Harm's Way: A History of the Navy Nurse Corps.* Seattle: Peanut Butter Press, 1997.

Straubel, James D., ed. *Air Force Diary: 111 Stories from the Official Service Journal of the USAAF* New York: Simon and Schuster, 1947.

Tomblin, Barbara Brooks. *G.I. Nightingales: The Army Nurse Corps in World War II.* Lexington: University Press of Kentucky, 1996.

———. *With Utmost Spirit: Allied Amphibious Operations in the Mediterranean 1942–1945.* Lexington: University Press of Kentucky, 2004.

Wandrey, June. *Bedpan Commando: The Story of a Combat Nurse during World War II.* Second ed. Elmore, Ohio: Elmore Publishing, 1991.

Wheeler, Keith. *We Are the Wounded.* New York: Dutton, 1945.

Williams, Denny. *To the Angels.* San Francisco: Denson Press, 1985.

Wolfe, Martin. *Green Light: A Troop Carrier Squadron's War from Normandy to the Rhine.* Washington, D.C.: Center for Air Force History, 1993.

World War II Flight Nurses Association. *The Story of Air Evacuation 1942–1989.* Dallas: Taylor, 1989.

Young, Charles H. *Into the Valley: The Untold Story of USAAF Troop Carrier in World War II, from North Africa through Europe.* Dallas: PrintComm, 1995.

Periodical and Newspaper Articles

"Aerial Nurse Corps." *Trained Nurse and Hospital Review* 107 (October 1941): 281.

"Air Evacuation . . . Returning Wounded Fly under Care of Army Flight Nurses." *Army Nurse* 2 (March 1945): 9.

"Air Evacuation School Awards Diplomas to 39." *Bowman Bomber,* 1 March 1943.

"The Air Medal." *Army Nurse* 1 (May 1944): 8–9.

"Airline Nurse Stewardesses Released." *American Journal of Nursing* 42 (May 1942): 557–58.

"American Nurses—We Are at War!" *American Journal of Nursing* 42 (April 1942): 354–58.

"The American Nurses Aviation Service, Inc." *Journal of Aviation Medicine* 2 (1931): 262–63.

"The American Nurses Aviation Service, Inc." *Journal of Aviation Medicine* 3 (September 1932): 176.

"The American Nurses Aviation Service, Inc." *Journal of Aviation Medicine* 4 (March 1933): 19.

"The Army Air Forces Needs Nurses." *American Journal of Nursing* 43 (June 1943): 599.

"Army Nurse Wins Air Medal." *American Journal of Nursing* 43 (May 1943): 443–44.

"Army Nurses in the Air." *American Journal of Nursing* 42 (August 1942): 954–55.

Baran, Anne M. "Nursing Care of Casualties in Long Distance Air Evacuation." *American Journal of Nursing* 46 (February 1946): 104–6.

Barger, Judith. "Coping Behaviors of U.S. Army Flight Nurses in World War II: An Oral History." *Aviation, Space, and Environmental Medicine* 62 (February 1991): 153–57.

———. "Flight Nurse Firsts: The First Flight Nurse Killed in Action." *Aviation, Space, and Environmental Medicine* 56 (April 1985): 376–77.

———. "Flight Nurse Firsts: The First Formal Flight Nurse Graduation." *Aviation, Space, and Environmental Medicine* 56 (March 1985): 275–76.

———. "Flight Nurse Firsts: The First Use of the Flight Nurse Creed." *Aviation, Space, and Environmental Medicine* 56 (February 1985): 171–72.

———. "Origin of Flight Nursing in the United States Army Air Forces." *Aviation, Space, and Environmental Medicine* 50 (November 1979): 1176–78.

———. "Preparing for War: Lessons Learned from U.S. Army Flight Nurses of World War II." *Aviation, Space, and Environmental Medicine* 62 (August 1991): 772–75.

———. "Rivalry for the Sky: A Prelude to the Development of the Flight Nurse Program in the US Army Air Forces." *Aviation, Space, and Environmental Medicine* 56 (January 1985): 73–78.

———. "Strategic Aeromedical Evacuation: The Inaugural Flight." *Aviation, Space, and Environmental Medicine* 57 (June 1986): 613–16.

———. "U.S. Army Air Forces Flight Nurses: Training and Pioneer Flight." *Aviation, Space, and Environmental Medicine* 51 (April 1980): 414–16.

Bernard, Suella, and Marijean Brown. "Nurses Pick Poppies While Awaiting First Wounded." *Newark Call,* 12 June 1944.

Berquist [Bergquist], Erling [Ehrling]. "Discussion." In "Air Evacuation Activities," by David N. W. Grant. *Journal of Aviation Medicine* 18 (February–December 1947): 177–83, 191.

"Biggest Army Hospital Ship to Date Named in Honor of Army Nurse Killed on Duty." *Army Nurse* 2 (June 1945): 3.

Bintliff, Douglas J. "Aerial Nurse Corps." *Air Trails,* November 1940, 25, 53–54.

"Bowman Field Nurses Appear on Army Hour." *Louisville Times,* 28 December 1942.

"Bowman Nurses on Army Hour." *Louisville Times,* 28 December 1942.

"Bowman Trainee First Woman Decorated in South Pacific." *Lousville Courier-Journal,* 22 June 1943.

Byrd, Lois. "Nurse Here Is First Woman to Win Air Medal." *Louisville Courier-Journal,* 27 March 1943.

———. "39 Air Evacuation Graduates Face Quick Action." *Louisville Courier-Journal,* 19 February 1943.

"Call to Service." *Trained Nurse and Hospital Review* 107 (October 1941): 281–82.

Church, Ellen E. "Nursing Up in the Air." *Public Health Nurse* 23 (February 1931): 73–74.

Clarke, Alice R. "Thirty-seven Months as Prisoners of War." *American Journal of Nursing* 45 (May 1945): 342–45.

Coble, Donald W. "Our Silver-Winged Angels Turn Twenty." *Airman* 7 (July 1963): 34–36.

"Constitution and By-Laws of American Nurses Aviation Service, Incorporated." *Journal of Aviation Medicine* 3 (March 1932): 43–52.

Crowe, Alberta E. "Miss Nightingale II." *Woman Bowler,* February 1945, 5–8, 14.

"Denver Plans to Have Its Own Unit of Aerial Nursing Corps." *Denver Post,* 31 January 1941.

De Witt, Jean. "Angles [*sic*] Are Well Groomed." *R.N.* 8 (January 1945): 34–36, 78, 80.

———. "Flight Nurse." *R.N.* 6 (March 1943): 32–34, 72, 74, 76.

"Discontinued for the Duration." *Trained Nurse and Hospital Review* 108 (April 1942): 268.

Edstrom, Ed, and Joe Creason. "These Angels Fly on Man-Made Wings." *Louisville Courier-Journal Roto-Magazine,* 28 February 1943, 6–8.

Farrer, James. "Flying Nurses Do without Glamor." *Dayton Sunday Mirror,* 20 April 1941.

"The First Flying Nurse." *Public Health Nurse* 22 (September 1930): 471.

"First Reserve Quotas!" *American Journal of Nursing* 42 (June 1942): 613.

"Flight Nurse Tells of Life in German Prison." *New York Herald Tribune,* 4 March 1945.

Floyd, Hugh R. "Birds of Mercy: Flying Hospital Ships Evacuate Wounded from Flying Fronts." *7th AAF Brief* 1 (March 1944): 10–11.

"Fly Again!" *R.N.* 9 (December 1945): 40–42, 90, 92, 94.

"Flying Life Savers." *Click: The National Picture Monthly* 7 (July 1943): 4–6.

"'Flying Nurses' Train Here for Defense." *Detroit Evening Times,* 2 February 1939.

Geister, Janet M. "Nurses Stood By to the End." *Trained Nurse and Hospital Review* 108 (May 1942): 343–46.

———. "She Came Back from Bataan." *Trained Nurse and Hospital Review* 109 (October 1942): 252–54.

Gimble, Rosalie. "Air Passenger Travel from the Standpoint of the Nurse." *Journal of Aviation Medicine* 4 (December 1933): 130–35.

"Giving Wings to Nursing." Reprint from *National Aeronautics,* June 1938, 11, 29.

Grant, David N. W. "Air Evacuation Activities." *Journal of Aviation Medicine* 18 (February–December 1947): 177–83, 91.

———. "Air Evacuation of One Million Patients: Review of Operations to VE-Day." *Air Surgeon's Bulletin* 2 (October 1945): 334–36.

———. "The Air Surgeon's Letter." *Air Surgeon's Bulletin* 2 (February 1945): 49.

———. "The Army Air Forces Medical Services: A Two Year Review." *Air Surgeon's Bulletin* 1 (January 1944): 1–4.

———. "A Review of Air Evacuation Operations in 1943." *Air Surgeon's Bulletin* 1 (April 1944): 1–4.

Greenberg, Milton. "Training of Flight Nurses and Air Evacuation Medical Technicians." *Air Surgeon's Bulletin* 2 (October 1945): 328–29.

Guest, Edgar A. "The Nurse." *Trained Nurse and Hospital Review* 112 (June 1944): 436.

———. "The Nurse." *Army Nurse* 1 (July 1944): 11.

Guilford, Frederick R., and Burton J. Soboroff. "Air Evacuation: An Historical Review." *Journal of Aviation Medicine* 18 (December 1947): 601–16.

Hager, Alice Rogers. "Mercy Takes Wings." *Skyways,* September 1943, 18–19, 58, 60, 62.

Halbouty, M. Robert, Attilio D. Puppel, and Charles E. Bybee. "Air Evacuation in the Combat Zone." *Air Surgeon's Bulletin* 2 (October 1945): 337.

Howard, Clive. "Hell's Angels." *Family Circle,* 13 October 1944, 10–11, 27, 30–31.

"Invasion Heroine: The Flying Nurse." *Look,* 11 July 1944, 30, 32, 34.

J.M.G. [Janet M. Geister]. "Nurses Stood By to the End." *Trained Nurse and Hospital Review* 114 (March 1945): 182–83.

Jose, Mary. "Night Shift in an Army Hospital." *American Journal of Nursing* 45 (June 1945): 430–33.

Kalisch, Philip A., and Beatrice J. Kalisch. "Nurses under Fire: The World War II Experience of Nurses on Bataan and Corregidor." *Nursing Research* 25 (November–December 1976): 409–29.

———. "When Nurses Were National Heroines: Images of Nursing in American Film, 1942–1945." *Nursing Forum* 20 (January 1981): 14–61.

Kernodle, Margaret. "Army Nurses Sprout Wings." *Cincinnati Enquirer,* 23 March 1943.

"Kicks from Air Nurses: Fliers Learn How to Beat Davey Jones." *Louisville Times,* 29 July 1943.

Knight, Charlotte. "Flight Nurse." *Air Force* 27 (October 1944): 28–30, 62.

La Vriha, Jack. "Heads Training of Aviation Nurses." *Cleveland Plain Dealer,* 5 April 1943.

"The Last Word—Flying Nurses." *Trained Nurse and Hospital Review* 111 (November 1943): 360–61.

Lee, Genell. "History of Flight Nursing." *Journal of Emergency Nursing* 13 (July–August 1987): 212–18.

Lent, Wm. [William] T. "AAF Medics." *Air Force* 27 (July 1944): 51.

"Lieutenant Audrey Rogers." *American Journal of Nursing* 44 (February 1944): 180.

Lochridge, Patricia. "Flight for Life." *Woman's Home Companion,* January 1945, n.p.

MacDonald, Florence. "Nursing the Sick and Wounded at Bataan and Corregidor." *Hospitals* 16 (December 1942): 31–33.

"A Makeshift Windpipe." *Trained Nurse and Hospital Review* 114 (March 1945): 197.

"Man with Throat Cut Saved by Army Nurse." *New York Times,* 23 December 1944.

McCallum, Walter. "Our Wounded Come Home on Wings." *Washington, D.C., Star,* 3 December 1944.

"Meeting of the American Nurses Aviation Service." *Journal of Aviation Medicine* 4 (June 1933): 68–69.

Meiling, Richard L. "Wings for the Wounded." *Air Force* 26 (December 1943): 21–23, 53.

"Men Nurses and the Armed Services." *American Journal of Nursing* 43 (December 1943): 1066–69.

Mydans, Shelley. "Flight Nurse." *Life* 18 (12 February 1945): 51–52, 58.

"No 'Glamor Girl' Life, Hero Nurse Avers." *Louisville Courier-Journal,* 3 August 1944.

Nolan, Elsie G. "Angel Footprints." *Cosmopolitan* 117 (December 1944): 60–61, 167.

"The Nurse in Aviation." *Journal of Aviation Medicine* 3 (March 1932): 5.

"The Nurse in Aviation." *Journal of Aviation Medicine* 3 (June 1932): 116–18.

"Nurse Wins Air Medal." *Louisville Times,* 26 March 1943.

"Nurses Mobilize for Duties in New Home Defense Service." *Los Angeles Times,* 23 March 1941.

"Nurses Released from Airline Positions." *Trained Nurse and Hospital Review* 108 (March 1942): 207–8.

"Nurses, to the Colors!" *American Journal of Nursing* 42 (August 1942): 851–52.

Pace, John W. "Air Evacuation in the European Theater of Operations." *Air Surgeon's Bulletin* 2 (October 1945): 323–27.

Palmer, Catherine. "Flying Our Wounded Veterans Home." *National Geographic* 88 (December 1945): 363–84.

"'Parachute Nurse' Timely; 'Halfway to Shanghai' Fair." *Hollywood Reporter* 8 (September 1942): 4.

"Parachute Nurses?" *R.N.* 5 (February 1942): 17, 56, 58.

Pearson, Jean. "Detroiter Receives Ideal Job." *Detroit Free Press,* 6 October 1942.

"Policy Governing the Duty Assignment of Flight Nurses." Taken from AAF Letter 35–164, 6 December 1944. *Army Nurse* 2 (January 1945): 7.

Porter, Amy. "Balkan Escape." *Collier's* 113 (1 April 1944): 15, 64, 66.

Porter, Marion. "Nurses with Wings." *Collier's* 113 (22 April 1944): 22–25, 69.

"Relief Wings, Inc." *Journal of Aviation Medicine* 12 (September 1941): 259–61.

Rice, Dorothy M. "Flight to Kirawagi." *American Journal of Nursing* 45 (January 1945): 10–11.

Richardson, Henrietta. "Flight Nurse." *Air Force* 26 (December 1943): 8.

———. "Skyway Nursing." *American Journal of Nursing* 44 (February 1944): 102–3.

Rosen, Fred. "Flight Nurse." *Trained Nurse and Hospital Review* 115 (July 1945): 21–22.

Sanders, Virginia. "From Chickens to Flying." *Cleveland Plain Dealer,* 16 December 1932.

Sinks, Katherine. "Aviatrix Joins Air Wacs." *Glendale (California) News-Press,* 27 July 1944.

Skinner, Robert E. "The Making of the Air Surgeon: The Early Life and Career of David N. W. Grant." *Aviation, Space, and Environmental Medicine* 54 (January 1983): 75–82.

———. "The Roots of Flight Nursing: Lauretta M. Schimmoler and the Aerial Nurse Corps of America." *Aviation, Space, and Environmental Medicine* 55 (January 1984): 72–77.

Smith, Esther. "Ex-Bucyrus Airport Manager Turns to Movies." *Mansfield News-Journal,* 16 August 1942.

Stakeman, Grace. "Medical Care of Casualties in Long Distance Air Evacuation." *Aviation Medicine* 18 (April 1947): 192–98.

Stevens, Susan V. "Aviation Pioneers: World War II Air Evacuation Nurses." *Image: Journal of Nursing Scholarship* 26 (Summer 1994): 95–99.

———. "Sale of the Century: Images of Nursing in the Movietonews during World War II." *Advances in Nursing Science* 12 (July 1990): 44–52.

Stevenson. Ralph T. "Air Ambulance Brings Them Back Alive." *Modern Hospital* 2 (August 1943): 53–54.

Stroup, Leora B. "A New Service in an Old Cause." *Trained Nurse and Hospital Review* 105 (September 1940): 186–87.

Stuart, John. "Air Evacuation." *Flying,* September 1943, 21–23, 126, 128.

"Swim to Live Program In Full Swing." *Louisville Carrier,* 5 August 1943.

"Three Aerial Nurse Pioneers Reunited at Bowman Field." *Louisville Courier-Journal,* 2 March 1943.

"30 Pairs of Eyes Follow Nurse across Ocean." *New York Telegram,* 11 May 1945.

"The Time Is Now!" *American Journal of Nursing* 42 (August 1942): 924–25.

Toombs, Alfred. "Flight Nurse." *Woman's Home Companion,* December 1943, 36, 117–18.

"Trumbull Woman Heads Nurses Doing Air Evacuation of Pacific Wounded." *Ohio Nurses Review* 2 (October 1945): 167–68.

"Urgent Need for Nurses." *American Journal of Nursing* 44 (November 1944): 1017.

"War-Time Needs Come First." *American Journal of Nursing* 42 (April 1942): 449–50.

Whelton, Alfred D. "A Heroine Comes Home." *Boston Advertiser,* 9 September 1945.

White, Ruth Y. "Army Nurses—in the Air." *American Journal of Nursing* 43 (April 1943): 342–44.

Whitley, Joe. "Flight Nurses." *Brief* 1 (14 November 1944): 10–11, 14.

Yeagle, Alice M., and Alice E. G. Jones. "Flight Nurses near the Front Lines." *Public Health Nursing* 37 (December 1945): 605–6, 611.

INDEX